Food Culture in
Japan

Food Culture in
Japan

MICHAEL ASHKENAZI AND JEANNE JACOB

Food Culture around the World

Ken Albala, Series Editor

GREENWOOD PRESS

Westport, Connecticut · London

Library of Congress Cataloging-in-Publication Data

Ashkenazi, Michael.
    Food culture in Japan / Michael Ashkenazi and Jeanne Jacob.
        p. cm. — (Food culture around the world, 1545–2638)
    Includes bibliographical references and index.
    ISBN 0–313–32438–7 (alk. paper)
    1. Cookery, Japanese. 2. Food habits—Japan. I. Jacob, Jeanne. II. Title. III. Series.
TX724.5.J3A88   2003
394.1′0952—dc22   2003049317

British Library Cataloguing in Publication Data is available.

Library of Congress Catalog Card Number: 2003049317
ISBN: 0–313–32438–7
ISSN: 1545–2638

First published in 2003

Greenwood Press, 88 Post Road West, Westport, CT 06881
An imprint of Greenwood Publishing Group, Inc.
www.greenwood.com

Printed in the United States of America

The paper used in this book complies with the
Permanent Paper Standard issued by the National
Information Standards Organization (Z39.48–1984).

10 9 8 7 6 5 4 3 2 1

Illustrations by J. Susan Cole Stone.

The publisher has done its best to make sure the instructions and/or recipes in this book
are correct. However, users should apply judgment and experience when preparing
recipes, especially parents and teachers working with young people. The publisher ac-
cepts no responsibility for the outcome of any recipe included in this volume.

In memory of Okuyama Shunzô, friend, mentor, philosopher, and gourmet.

Contents

Preface

For the average American diner, knowledge about and interest in Japanese food seemed to be confined to a few popular dishes until fairly recently. American exposure to Japanese food was largely limited to Japanese steakhouse chain offerings and deep-fried *tempura*. One primary ingredient epitomized for the non-Japanese person Japanese food at its pinnacle—raw fish. However, authentically prepared Japanese cuisine using raw fish as its centerpiece was for many years unavailable outside Japan. The ingredient itself was also a major barrier to undiluted worldwide acclaim of Japanese cuisine. To the uninitiated diner decades ago, *sushi* (raw fish and vinegared rice balls) or *sashimi* (raw fish slices) were breathtakingly aesthetic in concept and very visually tempting, but all interest stopped there. Those who did not wish to offend their hosts surreptitiously deposited *sashimi* into a convenient paper napkin, or else swallowed it unchewed and washed it down with copious gulps of beer or *saké*.

It does seem an injustice that for a very long time Japanese food did not receive the widespread recognition that it deserves. Many first-time eaters, though bowled over by its aesthetic presentation, describe Japanese food as insipid, because the subtlety of Japanese haute cuisine, as demonstrated in the *kaiseki*, or tea-ceremony, style of cooking, is lost on palates expecting elaborate blends of seasoning. Highly seasoned Chinese or intricately sauced French dishes are more likely to win over experimenting palates. Palates have to be educated to fully appreciate Japanese food beyond the familiar stews, *tempura* (deep fried), and the lavishly seasoned grilled dishes. Tongues have to learn to become sensitive to the slight nuances of taste, to discern the intrinsic and undisguised natural flavors in each ingredient.

The aesthetic presentation of Japanese food naturally encourages this focused attention. In classical Japanese cuisine, before each diner is an array of small individual servings, each a work of art framed in its own exquisite receptacle. "Feed the eye first," is the first injunction to the Japanese cook. Artistry is not limited to the table arrangements, outdoor gardens, or exterior and interior architecture of the venue and main rooms. In the washrooms you may be fortunate to see an exquisite seasonal floral arrangement in a bamboo receptacle, to match the bamboo paneling on the walls, or perhaps a rustic stone sink.

The visual appeal of a feast can be bewildering to the uninitiated. Plates of all possible geometric shapes—square, rectangular, crescent- or fan-shaped—in many colors, sizes, and textures decorate the table. Not all are porcelain—slabs of wood, baskets, even chestnut husks can hold food. Garnishes can be greens, similar to parsley, to which most non-Japanese people can relate; but what does one do with red maple leaves, pale pink ginger shoots, and stalks with flower buds? Is one expected to eat these as well? (Yes, but not the maple leaves.)

And, to complicate matters particularly during a banquet, where is the rice? Having been told that rice is the foundation of all east Asian meals, the uninitiated diner at a celebratory meal is perplexed. There is no rice to be glimpsed among the vast array of artful tidbits arranged at the table. Endless rounds of *saké* (rice wine) are offered, awkwardness disappears, everyone else starts eating, and no one seems to mind that there is no rice. Finally when everyone is bursting to repletion and *saké*-muddled, the rice appears with pickles and *miso* (soybean paste) soup. The neophyte eater cannot imagine room for another morsel, but everyone digs in, all miraculously sobered up, relishing the salty pickles and commenting on them with nostalgia, particularly if the ingredients and flavoring are an unusual combination.

What does this say about food in Japan? That at its best, it is an overwhelming sensory aesthetic experience. And it is that meticulous attention to every phase—from selecting the freshest ingredients, choosing the serving receptacles, and most of all, the graciousness of service and attention to guests—that characterizes the fine art of Japanese *omotenashi* (hosting a meal).

Compared to 20 or even 10 years ago, in most cosmopolitan cities, it is no longer difficult to find places that serve Japanese food. Noodle bars specializing in variably flavored *udon* or *râmen* have sprung up, joining the proliferating *kaiten zushi* (budget-priced restaurants featuring ready-made *sushi*) as the east Asian competitors to Western fast foods. Even *miso* (soybean paste) soup has found favor with Western chefs dabbling in East-West fusion cooking.

On a personal note, because of the initial scarcity of Japanese restaurants where we lived, and later because the Japanese dishes that we wanted to eat were not available, we began to cook our own. As amateur cooks, we could not hope to attain the virtuoso expertise of Japanese chefs with years of traditional training behind them. Although we had cooked our own meals while living in Japan, there were certain dishes that we had only sampled at restaurants that specialized in one type of food. These specialist restaurants were favorites because we could watch the cooking process as *tempura* was fried to unmatchable light crispness or chat with the sushi chef to ask which fish was in season as we sat at the counter slowly savoring our tea.

In those days, unlike today, laver (edible seaweeds), Japanese soy sauce, *miso*, and buckwheat noodles were impossible to get at our local supermarket in England and so we resorted to having them sent from Japan and keeping them deep frozen, rationing our supplies so that we could cook them throughout the year. We had acquired a few traditional kitchen knives and miscellaneous tools, including variously shaped tableware, and set about teaching ourselves to cook the Japanese way. As a result, our two younger children, who had never been to Japan, have come to prefer Japanese food to all other food. Their childhood favorites, in common with most Japanese children, were *furikake* (a powdered mixed seasoning for cooked rice) and *nori*, and remain so, even in their teens.

More than the elaborate multicourse *kaiseki* banquets, it was the simple everyday dishes, such as blanched vegetables, grilled fish, and plain fresh tofu, cold or hot, or, in Michael's case, hand-cut *soba* noodles, that we longed for most when we craved Japanese food. Except for freshly made silken tofu (*kinugoshi*), unobtainable locally, very fresh green vegetables and freshwater and air-shipped sea fish are now readily available. The ultimate objective in serving Japanese food is to use local and fresh ingredients in season as much as possible.

In practical terms, a mix of ingredients sourced locally and elsewhere is usual for all but the most exacting Japanese chef. Even classical Kyoto cooking, which is considered the acme of refinement, has always used dried foodstuff such as marine fish and seafood brought in salted and preserved from elsewhere, because landlocked Kyoto was self-sufficient only in freshwater supplies.

The key to good food is fresh quality ingredients; this is the recurring message of professional cooks and literature the world over. The Japanese have taken this message to an extreme, and the vegetables and fruit in supermarkets, department stores, and greengrocers in Japan are not only fresh, but also of perfect appearance, shape, and size. Fish and seafood are bright-eyed and glisten attractively: there is none of the dense and incriminating fishy smell that from a distance unmistakably identifies fishmongers elsewhere. Twenty years ago, most Japanese shopped for food every day to ensure freshness, something that would be difficult to do now even in Japan. The realities of working life force even the authors to stock up on food items so that we shop as rarely as possible. However, when we do, and we find superb ingredients, we cook these immediately in the Japanese style. And these days, even nonlocal foodstuffs can be of impeccable quality and freshness. Modern freezing and transportation methods have made exotic marine foodstuffs and fresh Asian vegetables and fungi available to all. Organic crop production and local farmers' markets are also making it easier to find chemical-free produce nearby.

Aside from its gustatory and aesthetic appeal, there is one more compelling reason to cook and eat Japanese food. It is good for you. Not only is it a balanced diet in its combination of rice, vegetables, and emphasis on fish and seafood, with a modicum intake of animal protein and fat, but many of its components have disease-preventing qualities.

This book attempts to relate Japanese food to its cultural surroundings in a way that makes sense to non-Japanese readers. Chapter 1 supplies context: the historical and geographical factors that have shaped Japanese food. Chapter 2 shifts to a closer examination if the various major components of this cuisine. We discuss the primary foods: the rice, soybean paste, and stock that appear at virtually every meal, and the other major food items used. Chapter 3 covers *who* prepares food and *how* it is prepared: the various cooking methods that make up the repertoire of the Japanese cook. Chapter 4 presents the different types of Japanese meals. Japanese eat out a great deal, and chapter 5 concentrates on the various types of restaurants, some of which serve food that is difficult or complex to make even for a Japanese housewife and is, therefore, rarely encountered, even in the Japanese home. Chapter 6 examines foods served for festive occasions and on special days and continues to explore the dynamic area of aesthetics in Japanese food. Finally, chapter 7 looks at the modern Japanese diet and nutrition.

Throughout the book, the reader will find recipes that complement the narrative. These are not intended to compete with the many fine cookbooks on Japanese food available today: more than 100 in English alone (a selected list is found in the Resource Guide at the back of this book). However, as any good cookbook writer should, we have experimented with all these recipes. The recipes range from the simplest home foods to elaborate fare more commonly available in restaurants. Students and other readers should be able to readily find the special ingredients in Asian grocery stores and some in the Asian section in the supermarket. The Resource Guide also includes a brief annotated list of suggested readings, films/videos, and Web sites.

Acknowledgments

It's always a pleasure to work on a subject that one is passionate about. Besides our own love of Japanese food and cooking, preparing this book has taught us a great deal. The book, however, would not have been possible without the help of many people. Ken Albala, the series editor, first proposed that we tackle this subject during a meeting of the annual Oxford Food Symposium, and we are grateful to him for the opportunity. Thanks are also due Wendi Schnaufer at Greenwood Press for encouragement and reading the manuscript before its completion. We are also grateful to the members of the Oxford Food Symposium for informal advice and criticism (often otherwise unacknowledged) during the writing of the book. We are grateful to the many members of the H-Japan and H-Asia Internet discussion lists, who came through with suggestions and obscure bits of data we were unable to track down.

Oren Ashkenazi deserves thanks for helping translate and select items for inclusion, as do Erez and Maayan Ashkenazi for judgmental and informed tasting of the recipes and dishes mentioned here. Chef Rob Shipman, who afforded us a glimpse behind the scenes of a modern Japanese kitchen and who proves every day that Japanese food has become international, gave encouragement to the idea that we can all learn from Japanese cuisine.

The Japan Foundation provided money, over a period of some years, for research in Japan, and we are, as always, in their debt. The Ajinomoto Food Institute in Tokyo gave us free run of their wonderful library, for which we thank them again. We are also grateful to the libraries and librarians of the School of Oriental Studies in London, and Gyosei College in Reading, UK, who were as helpful as always.

A great deal of thanks is owed to the many chefs, researchers, and friends in Japan who, over many years of research, have offered us guidance and encouragement as we explored the world of Japanese food. Many of these are anonymous, some we only met fleetingly. We are obliged to all.

Our greatest debt, inevitably, is owed Okuyama Shunzô. For more than 25 years, he was a close friend and mentor. He loved good food and good company and had a fine discernment of the aesthetic and sensory dimensions of Japanese food and art. A wonderful human being, we have been privileged to know him. Sadly, he passed away during the writing of this book.

Timeline

7000 B.C.E.–710 C.E.	Prearistocratic period (for historians, the Jômon, Yayoi, Yamato, and Kofun eras). Japanese culture gradually moves from a farming/hunting-gathering economy to an agriculture-based state. Pottery and metallurgy are learned, possibly from Korean origins. Staple foods are bulbs, roots, and various types of millet. Rituals related to purity and food offerings to the deities are established and practiced.
531–580	Buddhism is introduced from Korea, along with Korean artisans in ceramics. The King of Paekche in Korea sends an image of the Buddha to Emperor Kimmei. In consequence, the path is set for a cuisine that uses little meat. Buddhist monasteries, in particular, develop their own meatless cuisine, and their cooks exert a great deal of influence on Japanese cooking.
607	First Japanese embassy is sent to China to learn Chinese ways. New forms of food and luxuries are imported from China.
710 onward	Start of the aristocratic period with the establishment of a permanent capital at Nara. Rice cultivation based on mainland models commences, and rice meals become a feature of court life.
774–835	Life of Kôbô Daishi, founder of the Shingon Buddhist sect, which helped codify Japanese aesthetic ideas, and who is credited with many miracles, including reviving a dried fish at the site of Mackerel Temple on the island of Shikoku.

794–1185   Historical Heian era. The imperial capital is established at Heian-kyô (modern Kyoto). A rich court life develops as the aristocracy in Heian-kyô refines its tastes. Lavish ritual feasts are performed at temples and recorded in novels, diaries, and paintings.

838   Twelfth and last embassy to China.

1180–85   The Gempei War between the Minamoto and the Taira clans of warriors brings about the end of the aristocratic period; warriors establish a political capital at Kamakura, near modern Tokyo. The start of the *samurai* period brings with it a more austere aesthetic in art as well as in food.

1480–1568   The Sengoku (Civil War) era.

1542 or 1543   Portuguese arrive at Tanegashima and introduce Western firearms. Subsequently, as more Europeans arrive, the *namban* (sweets using lots of egg yolks and sugar, such as *kasutera*; meat cookery; and *tempura* deep frying) cooking styles are popularized; these styles gradually spread to the capital. New vegetables such as sweet potatoes and peppers are introduced to the Japanese, probably by Spanish visitors from the Americas.

1585?   The tea ceremony rules are codified by Sen-no-Rikkyu (1522–91). Sen also lays the foundation for *kaiseki*-style cuisine, based partly on Buddhist temple cooking styles.

1600–1868   Historical Tokugawa (or Edo) era. Power is assumed by the Tokugawa clan. The political capital is moved to Edo. During this period, Japan is secluded and no foreigners are allowed to live in the country, nor are Japanese allowed to leave it. As a consequence, Japanese food customs develop and mature with minimal influence from other cuisines.

1868–1912   Historical Meiji era. The emperor returns as ruler, and the imperial capital is moved to Edo, which is renamed Tokyo. Start of the modern period as Japanese society introduces industrial and other forms of technology. First beef stew restaurant is opened in Tokyo. A brewery is established in Yokohama by Americans, which becomes the forerunner of the Kirin beer company. Bread becomes common and is even requisitioned by a rebel army in the first years of the era.

1870   Bread is publicly sold by the many bakeshops that now open in Yokohama and Tokyo. Ice cream is first sold in Yokohama, and the first Western food restaurant opened in Yokohama.

1873   The first railway in Japan between Shimbashi and Yokohama opens, and Emperor Meiji tries beef, giving a boost to meat consumption and the opening of the first Western-cooking restaurant in Tokyo.

1878   The first Japanese winery opens and Western wine is sold to the public.

1886   The first "station box lunch" (*ekiben*) is sold at Utsunomiya Station, starting a culinary tradition that continues today.

1889   A coffee specialist shop opens in Tokyo, influenced in part by the popularity of coffee as a hot drink among Japanese soldiers stationed in northern Hokkaido.

1904–05   Russo-Japanese War. First defeat of a European power by a non-European one as the Japanese fleet sinks the Russian Far-East Fleet in Tsushima Straits.

1905   Women's magazines start publication and introduce to the public menus, recipes, and new ways of cooking.

1915   Calpis fermented milk drink manufacturing and sale creates serious popular interest in milk products.

1932   The ministry of education starts a school lunch program to combat child malnutrition.

1937   Outbreak of war with China. Hinomaru (Rising Sun) lunch box becomes a fad to display patriotism and support the war effort.

1941   Japanese attack on Pearl Harbor starts the Pacific theater of World War II. During the war, rice shortages and rationing become common. Potatoes are introduced as a substitute for rice for many people.

1945   Kamikaze attacks. Japan surrenders to the Allied Powers after the U.S. atomic bombing of Hiroshima and Nagasaki.

1970   American fast food companies start making inroads into Japan and establish branches throughout the country. Both hamburgers and fried chicken become popular foods, in both American and Japanese versions.

1975   Cheesecake becomes popular in Japan as a major Western confectionery, and demand for cheese and other milk products soars.

1979   Calorie-free devil's foot root jelly (*konnyaku*) rises in popularity as a diet food as the Japanese public becomes more weight-conscious; increased health-consciousness inspires the development of reduced-salt soy sauce and sports drinks, in addition to other health drinks, become available.

1983   Post Office begins a delivery service shipping packages of "home-town foods"—delicacies from small farming communities around Japan—to city residents.

1991–   Heisei era. Death of Shôwa Emperor (Hirohito). Succession by his son, the current Emperor Heisei. Organic, locally sourced food is in demand, and homemakers' cooperatives are formed to source food directly from farmers. There is a boom in highly spiced food, and heightened interest in ethnic cuisines, health food, and vege-tarian food *(shôjin)*.

1

Historical Overview

To understand Japanese food, it is necessary to have geographical and historical context. The history of Japan is strongly dictated by its geography: the society that developed on this chain of volcanic islands was strongly influenced by the Asian continent. Japan is close enough to the Asian mainland to be influenced by Asian culture, yet far enough off the coast not to be affected directly by continental events. The types of foodstuffs the Japanese people ate, though often derived from Asiatic continental sources, were modified by Japan's relative isolation, by the environment of fertile volcanic valleys watered by monsoon rains and artificial irrigation, and by reliance on the sea. The nonmaterial component of food will also be discussed: the ideas and sentiments that the Japanese have about their surroundings powerfully influenced their foodways.

GEOGRAPHY AND CLIMATE

The geography and climate of Japan have not changed materially throughout Japanese history, with the exception of the arable areas (only about 15 percent of the land is arable), which were gradually brought under the plow.

Geography

Japan is a group of more than 3,600 islands stretching 3,500 km long, roughly the area of California, but without its expanse of habitable terrain. Steep mountains make up over 80 percent of the four main islands, in the order north to south, Hokkaido, Honshu, Shikoku, and Kyushu. The major cities of Tokyo, Kyoto, Osaka, and Kobe are on Honshu island. Sapporo and Nagasaki are two major cities on Hokkaido and Kyushu, respectively.

Surrounded on all sides by the sea or the mountains, the Japanese naturally look to these sources for their food and lyrically refer to food as the delights or treasures of the seas and the mountains (*umi no sachi, yama no sachi*). Japan straddles four climate zones, with most of its landmass enjoying distinct temperate seasons. Hokkaido as well as northern and eastern Honshu have a cold temperate climate with heavy snowfall for over half of the year, beginning as early as October and only melting in April. The rest of Honshu and Shikoku have a cool temperate climate, while southern Kyushu and the Okinawan islands have a subtropical climate. The four seasons are regular and clearly defined; the one oddity, from a North American perspective, are the monsoon rains between May and July. The food culture of the Japanese is much constrained by three geographical features: river valleys, mountains, and the sea.

River Valleys

Wide valleys where arable agriculture was practicable determined much of Japanese history. The region west of the fortified barrier that controlled passage to and from the imperial court in Kyoto (the *Kansai*) encompasses what is now the Kyoto-Osaka area. At its center is the Yamato plain, the cradle of Japanese civilization. This is where both the refined cuisine of the Kyoto imperial court and the sumptuous cuisine of the Osaka merchants developed. Kyoto taste exemplifies the most refined of all Japanese regional cuisines. Landlocked Kyoto, without easy access to marine produce, focuses on the excellence of its vegetables and freshwater fish. Osaka's cuisine is noted for its brash showiness. A conspicuous wealth of luxurious and rare items as well as an appreciation for hearty eating characterize the bourgeois cooking favored by moneyed businessmen.

East of the ancient barrier is the *Kantô* area. Life was rougher here, but in many ways easier since the well-irrigated, reasonably flat plain was ideal for agriculture and a large landlocked bay allowed easy fishing. One fishing village, Edo by name, became in the seventeenth century the political capital of Japan. By the eighteenth century, and for some time after, Edo (now known as Tokyo) was the largest city in the world. This is where the retainer-warriors (*samurai*) of feudal lords came to stay at the order of the effective political ruler, the *shogun*. And this is where a robust cuisine evolved, based on bounty from the fields and the sea, becoming the dominant Japanese cuisine today. Some of its representative dishes, such as *sushi*, otherwise known as Edo *sushi* to distinguish it from Osaka *sushi*, have become synonymous with Japanese cuisine world-wide.

About midway between these two dominant valleys and their cuisines lies another fertile coastal plain. Centering more or less around the modern city of Nagoya and backed up against the mountains, the southern plain (*Nanzan*) provides another culinary center, from which many marine foods come, since it is one of the centers of pelagic and seaweed farming.

The Japan Sea side of Honshu, from the cities of Kanazawa to Niigata, is an area of lush, well-irrigated valleys and good access to the sea. Kanazawa cuisine is as lush and luxurious as the area it comes from and its barons in the Japanese Middle Ages were among the wealthiest in Japan. Other areas in Japan, such as the plains around Sapporo in the north and the cities of Nagasaki and Kagoshima in the south, also evolved their own cuisines based on the wealth of the countryside.

Mountains

The mountains of Japan have been formidable barriers throughout its history. Covered with forests, they were also the source of much desired foodstuff—mushrooms, wild greens, wild fruit, and roots—called collectively *sansai*, which the Japanese still adore to this day. The mountains were also the domicile of the gods, and therefore, any food with that provenance was considered something of a blessing. Significantly, too, the mountains served as barriers between various political entities and regional cuisines and preferences, each of which has contributed, in modern times, to the entity we know as "Japanese cuisine."

The Sea

Developed by dwellers on an archipelago with many fine bays and a large inland sea, Japanese cuisine, no less than its history, is affected by the ocean. Fish and marine products have always been major food items. Marine cultivation started in Japan in early history. The sea not only provided a bounty, it also provided this bounty according to a regular routine, so that feelings of dependency, expectation, and even anxiety were bound up with feelings about the sea. Because, regular as the sea was in the long-term, there were no guarantees of short-term success, and the lives of those working the sea are always perilous. The *Seto-nai kai* (Inland Sea) is connected to the Sea of Japan on one side and the Pacific Ocean by three narrow straits; its many bays and rocky islets are the setting for the earliest of Japanese legends, as well as for numerous local cuisines based on the sea. Crabs with the faces of heroic warriors prowl the depths. Whales swim past. Shoals of fish such as bonito, tuna, and mackerel flash by. This is also a sea of miracles and legends: dried salted mackerel brought back to life and allowed to swim away by a Buddhist saint; bream that provide heroes with fishing magic, seaweed-girt monsters. The Seto Inland Sea is important not only because of the food it provided (and still does) but also because it served as a highway along which ideas and foods traveled constantly from one area to another.

Climate

Japan's climate ranges from cool in Hokkaido to semitropical in the Ryukyu Islands of Okinawa Prefecture to the south. Summers tend to be hot and humid. Winters in the mountains and in the lowlands of Hokkaido and Honshu can be snowy, with the Northeast receiving up to six feet of snow in some areas.

The seasons are well defined. Spring (around March/April) is marked by the emergence of blossoms and of green buds that were, historically, an important food source for the poor. Spring ends with the monsoon season in May, when torrential downpours last until July. The monsoon is essential for the growth of Japan's most important staple crop, rice. Summer ends around October, when the weather gradually cools and settles down in a lengthy, often dry season that lasts until January, when winter rains and snow start.

Seasons not only affect growth on land and the crops available. There is also a clear set of seasons in the seas around Japan. Certain species of fish appear at regular intervals and are best eaten at particular times.

HISTORY

Japanese history can be divided into three broad periods. The aristocratic period, running roughly from the dawn of Japanese history in the third or fourth century C.E. to the twelfth century, was an age of noblemen—officials who were dependent on the emperor for their position and income. The Japanese Middle Ages started with the rise of warriors—

samurai—who ruled Japan until the ranks were abolished in 1868. The cuisine of the *samurai* period was strongly influenced by the *samurai* ethic and ideals of frugality and restraint. From 1868, Japan entered into a modern period which persists to this day.

Aristocratic Period

The Japanese state emerged from a welter of smaller kingdoms around the fifth century C.E. Centered near modern Kyoto, it managed to control the Japanese islands by about the tenth century C.E. During most of this time, it was ruled by an emperor, who managed the country through a small group of courtier-officials, a system based upon Chinese models. Older sons inherited their fathers' office, younger sons were sent to manage estates in the countryside. The capital, called variously Miyako and Heian-kyô at different times, was the center of culture and learning. Refined living was the major goal of life for most people, but only the aristocratic few could manage it in practice, and men and women of the aristocracy were expected to excel in the arts. The mass of the population was rural, poor, and spent their lives toiling in the fields. A small urban class emerged, mainly people serving the aristocracy.

The food of this period was marked by a substantive change. In the period before the start of urban living in Japan (before about the fifth century C.E.), the dominant crops were tubers (yams, lily bulbs, taro) and various forms of millet. The introduction of rice cultivation after the fifth century C.E. revolutionized Japanese food—rice is far more nutritious than the other staples—and Japanese society as well: the surpluses from the cultivation of rice allowed the emergence of a court and imperial system. Nonetheless, the food was relatively simple, and records we have of feasts from the early Heian period (794–1185) show large mounds of multicolored rice decorated with millet and a few simple dishes. Gradually, as wealth was accumulated, the food became more elaborate. This process accelerated when the Japanese started sending embassies to China to learn from the Chinese. Preservation methods such as fermented soybean paste (*miso*), ceramic technology to improve cooking, chopsticks and rice bowls, and the making of confectionery were all introduced and adapted based on Chinese models. By the end of the aristocratic age, the Japanese had inducted all these new ideas into their own cuisine, making modifications along the way.

Miso is to Japanese cooking what tomatoes and olive oil are to southern Italian cooking and it exemplifies one such introduced food. It is made by fermenting soybeans for a period of between six months and two years. *Miso* is an original Chinese flavoring that entered Japan via Korea sometime in the early aristocratic period. By the middle of the *samurai* period, *miso* was being made in Buddhist monasteries and by the fifteenth century it had become commonly available to all. By the 1620s, *miso*-making was widespread throughout the country.

The importance of chefs was recognized very early in traditional Japan. Entire clans (groups of related families) would struggle for the right to cook the emperor's food. The position was so important that in the eighth century an interclan dispute over the right to be the emperor's chef almost broke out into open warfare. The processes of preparing foods for the emperor's table, particularly fresh fish and the mounds of multicolored rice that were an integral part of ancient banquets, are still preserved in the rituals and offerings of some shrines in modern Kyoto.

Liquor has been associated with the Japanese way of life since prehistory, and there are many pottery pieces from the prehistorical Jōmon period that were apparently intended for the brewing and consumption of liquor. Liquor plays a central part in Japanese myth, considered the medicine par excellence. In one often-told story, a certain deity, Susano-wo, was banished from the realm of the deities. In his wanderings, he came upon a weeping couple who had sacrificed each of their daughters except the last to a nine-headed dragon. Susano-wo bid the couple brew triple-strength liquor, which he divided into nine barrels, placing each barrel before a gate in a palisade. The nine-headed dragon stuck a head through each opening, consumed a barrel of liquor per head, and fell into a drunken stupor, whereupon the hero killed the beast and won the girl's hand.

Brewing and drinking alcohol were so much a part of life in ancient Japan, that it remains today a major part of the offerings made at Shintô shrines. Early Chinese reports felt consumption of liquor was so excessive among Japanese that it merited special mention and was recorded in the earliest outsider observations we have of Japanese society.

One of the greatest introductions from the mainland was religion. In 545 C.E., a Korean king sent the Japanese emperor an image of the Buddha and some sacred Buddhist books. The Japanese, after a period of hesitation and struggle, adopted the new religion. Buddhism dovetailed neatly with the existing Japanese religion, Shintô. Shintô emphasized purity, naturalness, and kinship with the gods, but spoke little of the afterlife or transcendent things. Buddhism is largely flexible in the matter of gods, and concentrates largely on the afterlife, so the two religions reached a very satisfactory accommodation which is still in evidence today. Besides reinforcing Japanese preferences for vegetables and the abhorrence of meat, Buddhism brought a series of refinements to Japanese cuisine such as strict aesthetic canons and the uses of color symbolism. It also brought and popularized the drinking of tea. The tea bush (*Camellia sinensis*, a relative of the ornamental camellia plant, well known for its roselike flowers) has a long history of use in China. The young leaves are cut from the bush, dried, sometimes smoked, and sometimes powdered. The resulting infusion tends to be green in various shades from pale yellow-tinged to bright jade green color. The same leaves, fermented and roasted to ensure preservation, make the black tea leaves that yield the reddish brew more common in the West.

Tea, unlike rice wine (*saké*), which all Japanese who could consumed in large quantities, was the province of the refined and the aristocratic. A special ceremonial way of drinking tea evolved based on a Chinese model and was used for meditative and medicinal purposes, particularly in the many Buddhist temples and monasteries that were sprouting up throughout the empire.

Middle Ages/*Samurai* Period

By the twelfth century, the aristocratic system was collapsing. Rioting by rival Buddhist groups and claimants to the throne destroyed the elegance of the capital. Rural aristocrats, the descendants of younger brothers sent to the provinces, intervened. Leading their soldier-retainers (*samurai*), they swept away the old power system. The emperor was retained, as were the aristocrats who served him, but power was reserved for the *samurai* clans, who moved the seat of government away from the imperial capital of Kyoto to Kamakura in eastern Japan, where an official dictator (*shogun*) ran the affairs of the land. The *samurai* practiced and preached restraint and frugality. In the fifteenth century, the country fell into a never-ending series of civil wars. Armies of warlords repeatedly tried and failed to unify the country and to control the person of the emperor. European visitors first came to Japan in the early sixteenth century, bringing with them Christianity, firearms, and new ways with food such as baking.

Notwithstanding the constant warfare in the earlier part of the *samurai* period (between the thirteenth and the seventeenth centuries there was a war somewhere in Japan every year), this was also a period of cultural inflorescence in many ways, as the warlords competed in displaying their power and refinement in art and luxury. Any warlord worthy of his name was compelled to appreciate the finer things, and poetry competitions, fine ceramic ware, and tea tasting competitions were a feature of every warlord's court. The pinnacle of refinement in this period is owed in part to a certain Sen-no-Rikkyu (1522–91). He formalized the aesthetic and behavioral rules for properly drinking and appreciating tea. These became a formal ritual—the tea ceremony—which is still practiced today by millions of Japanese (and many non-Japanese as well). The tea ceremony founded by Sen-no-Rikkyu (his twenty-fourth-generation descendant still heads the school he founded) was based on a Chinese model but far surpassed the original in its refinement and elaboration. It is a form of aesthetic appreciation not only of the drink, but of an entire way of life and thinking, and of specific goods—ceramics, fine iron and bamboo work, fabrics, painting, flowers—that were and are an essential part of the ceremony. The institution as a whole has contributed immeasurably to Japanese culture and to its food as well: a full tea ceremony, which can encompass an entire day, includes a multicourse meal called *kaiseki*, which is the province of the most refined of Japanese cuisine.

In 1600, one warlord, Tokugawa Ieyasu, defeated his major rivals and a few years later was declared *shogun* (general), which made him the effective ruler of Japan. Some years later *samurai* from the Satsuma domain in southern Kyushu subjugated Okinawa, until then an independent kingdom, and made it part of Japan. Okinawa to this day retains a distinctive Okinawan cuisine. In 1637, Christians were expelled from Japan and Christianity suppressed, but the two other contributions—firearms and food—continued to be adapted by the Japanese. At the same time, Japan was closed to all foreigners except a small Dutch trading post in Nagasaki. The Tokugawa capital at Edo grew over the following two-and-a-half centuries of peace in Japan to become the world's largest city. The sixteenth century onward, especially during the Edo period (1600–1868), saw the rise of the merchant classes. The merchants, barred by law from politics, poured their energy and wealth into the refinements of city living. Restaurants and drinking places became places of assignation, and every large city had its pleasure quarters, where food, drink, theater, sex, and other forms of entertainment were refined and fashioned. Food dishes that had been local specialties before became widely known. Both tea and *saké* consumption became widespread. Many merchants, particularly in the areas of Osaka and Sakai, made their fortunes brewing and selling *saké*. Since *saké* is brewed from rice, this often led to riots during periods of food shortages, which were blamed on the brewers.

Since the dawn of history, Japanese people have been great travelers. Pilgrims have crisscrossed the islands on their way to holy places. Poets have done the same, in search of inspiration. And even the common people could travel in groups to visit famous beauty spots. Travel writing—in the various forms of poetry, plays, and travel guides—has been a popular type of literature since the ninth century. By the eighteenth century, Japan had a flourishing internal tourism industry, with all the features of a modern one. There were a multitude of inns, and brochures and travel books enlightened stay-at-homes about conditions in other places. There were even organized tours for those who wanted to travel with people they knew. Many common people saved up for several years for an opportunity to visit one or more of the three most beautiful sights in Japan: Matsushima Bay near Sendai, Itsukushima "Floating" Shrine near Hiroshima on the Seto Inland Sea, and Ama-no-Hashidate on the Sea of Japan, to climb Mt. Fuji, or to visit one or another of the great temples or shrines.

Of course, all of this traveling required food. Two wonderful food practices that are still maintained today emerged from this period. First, every traveler was expected to bring back a gift—*omiyage*—to those who had stayed at home. Accordingly, travel destinations competed with one another to produce the local food specialty, which had to survive the long trip. Thus a lengthy tradition of preserving, wrapping, and boxing was born. Second, the travelers required food for the day's journey. Thus the invention of box lunches (*obentô*). This was the period that also saw the emergence of a food that, in Western eyes, exemplifies Japanese food more than any other and that was influenced by the humble lunch box.

Sushi, perhaps the most evocative and "Japanese" of foods, was created by the frugality and business acumen of Osaka merchants during the late *samurai* period. This large city, the powerhouse of Japanese mercantile activity, has been a merchant city since its founding: no effete aristocrats or swaggering *samurai* here, please. The Osaka merchants traded in everything, including fish. Fresh sea fish were in high demand in the hinterland, and the merchants looked for ways to supply this demand. Of course, in the Japanese Middle Ages refrigeration was unknown. Fish could be salted and dried, then transported inland, but dried fish, however good it might be, has a flavor that is unlike its fresh counterpart. This meant, in effect, that fish could be transported for at most a few hours from the coast.

Some thrifty merchant noticed that if he packed fresh fish slices in vinegared rice, the product kept better. And when the rice was slightly fermented, the fish kept even longer. A new practice started: selling fish wrapped in cooked, slightly fermented rice. The (more or less) fresh fish was consumed happily by the inland dwellers (maybe they were not getting *really* fresh fish, reasoned the Osaka merchant, but if they could not tell the difference....) and the rice was thrown away. Still later, some merchant, no doubt pained to the bottom of his soul by the wasted rice, learned to control the fermentation by use of vinegar. A new product was born: *sushi*. In the Osaka original, the fish acquired some of the flavor of the vinegared rice. It was vinegared and pressed into block shapes by a wooden form (to make it easier to pack and transport), and Osaka developed a taste for this new convenience food: rice and fish in one.

Enter the *samurai* of Edo, the capital (now Tokyo). They lived by the seaside and knew what fresh fish tasted like. And to ensure that the fish was indeed fresh (none of the nonsense from the Osaka merchants please!), they demanded an adaptation of the Osaka dish that was starting to become popular. So instead of pickled fish pressed in a form, they insisted on little rice balls decorated with the freshest fish available. The vinegared rice, however, was kept. And so a famous dish—*Edozushi*, known throughout the world as *sushi*—was born.

In 1853, the British, Russian, and U.S. navies raced one another to Japan in an attempt to expand their respective colonialist enterprises. An American, Commodore Matthew Perry (1794–1858), entered Edo Bay with a flotilla of steamships, which the Japanese had never seen before, and forced the *shogun* (the seventeenth-generation descendant of Tokugawa Ieyasu) to open the country to European trade, embassies, and missionaries. This ushered in the modern period of Japanese history and also created wide-ranging changes in the Japanese diet.

In late medieval Japan, meat recipes started to become common, and with the arrival of the Spaniards, Portuguese, and Dutch in the sixteenth century, became more elaborate. A style of cooking—southern barbarian (*namban*) in which slices of meat are stir fried with leeks—came into being, though it was never very popular, nor was meat commonly available until the start of the modern period. When Japan opened its doors to the West after 1856, when Commodore Perry forced the Japanese military government to accept foreign envoys, meat-eating became popular. In fact eating beef, in particular, was used as a euphemism for "modernity," and Japanese intellectuals vied to be seen eating beef. Meat restaurants serving steaks sprang up, and meat cuisine and production developed apace. The earliest meat dishes served at these avant garde restaurants were beef hash with rice (*hayashi raisu*) and meat curry with rice *(kare raisu)*. Nationalist feeling just prior to Japan's entering World War II and subsequent wartime austerity struck all foreign dishes (in common with all things foreign) from the Japanese table. However, with improved economic conditions, in the 1960s American fast-food chains such as McDonald's and KFC started making inroads into Japan. Today, Japanese fast-food conglomerates that serve similar menus, but with a Japanese twist, compete neck and neck with the giant American food companies.

Modern Period

The humiliation of the *shogun*'s policies of seclusion by the Western powers after 1856 brought about a change of government. The emperor was brought from his seclusion in Heian-kyô in 1868 and reinstated as ruler in Tokyo (the newly renamed Edo), taking the name Meiji. The country was thrown open and a swift process of modernization began. Western cultural and technical items, including foods, were adopted hungrily by the Japanese. In 1905, the Japanese navy destroyed the Russian fleet at Tsushima: the first victory of a non-Western power over a Western power in modern times. The Japanese started a massive two-pronged program of colonialism on the one hand and industrialization and modernization on the other. In 1890, the northern island of Hokkaido underwent a process of settlement by Japanese immigrants who displaced the forest-dwelling Ainu aborigines. The island's original residents—the Ainu—subsisted like the Native Americans of the northeast boreal forests, on hunting and gathering. Hokkaido's cold seas yield a plenitude of fish. Salmon and whale were eagerly sought after, and laver *(konbu)* was raised in sheltered bays. In 1910, Japan occupied Korea. In 1936, the Japanese army embarked on a futile war in China, bringing misery to millions, and in 1941, the Japanese navy attacked Pearl Harbor, which culminated in Japan's defeat and withdrawal from its conquests in Asia by 1945.

This period marked the beginning of a change in the Japanese diet. Meat restaurants opened in Yokohama (a port city near Tokyo where most foreign merchants and consulates were located). Curried rice was introduced to the Japanese by expatriate British businessmen who had come to Japan from India. A few Japanese took to the new-fangled foods (after puzzling out the use of Western utensils: no simple task). Overall, however, it wasn't until after World War II that the Japanese populace as a whole took to the new foods, and for a period they remained the domain of the adventurous and the intellectual and political elite.

Until the middle of the twentieth century, the Japanese rarely ate much fruit, even though the name for confectionery—*okashi*—originally meant fruit. A few fruit varieties were cultivated commercially. Others were eaten only by a few people who raised them in their gardens as curiosities or picked them from the wild. About 150 varieties of native apples were known by the eighteenth century, as were oriental pears *(nashi)*, persimmons, melons, grapes, and mandarin oranges. Virtually all of these had been imported from China. Dried fruits were more commonly consumed than fresh, and dried persimmons are still a major cottage industry product. With the arrival of Europeans, and with the opportunity to travel abroad and sample European and North American fruit, the Japanese started growing and demanding their own.

With the influx of foreign-style food when Japan opened up to the West, new types of drink became available. Coffee, the most common drink in Japan today, began to be imported. It has now become so popular that few Japanese do not drink a cup or two a day, and, during the height of Japan's economic prosperity, Japanese companies bought up almost the entire crops of luxury varieties such as Jamaican Blue Mountain.

The winds of change in choice of alcohol consumption began to blow in the modern period. Grape wine was introduced from Europe, and Yamanashi Prefecture in central Japan started developing varieties of wine in the nineteenth century, leading to a flourishing wine industry today. Beer was introduced to the Japanese during the nineteenth century as well. Japanese study missions abroad soon found that their studies, particularly in Germany and Holland, were lubricated by this new drink, and they brought the beer thirst back with them to Japan. Beer brewing was started by European brewers in the nineteenth century, and world famous breweries such as Kirin and Asahi, which are now exported, were started by American, Swiss, and German brewers.

The late nineteenth century familiarized the Japanese with yet another type of beverage: what we would call today soft drinks or soda pop. The British had introduced fizzy lemonade to India in the middle of the nineteenth century, and they did the same for the Japanese. Lemonade bottles, made with a glass marble held in place by gas pressure from the liquid, can still be found today in Japan, and the sweet fizzy drink with a slight lime flavor is still called *ramuné* (lemonade). Similar bottles can still be seen in most exhibits of Victorian daily life in Western countries, but the only place they are still manufactured and used, to our knowledge, are Japan and India: last vestiges of a colonial past. Another soft drink, Mitsuya saidâ, has been manufactured in the Japanese town of Kawanishi in Hyogo Prefecture since 1884.

Notwithstanding foreign incursions into food and food preferences, Japanese cuisine still retained its vigor. Its vitality was ensured by people such as the artist and aesthetic theorist, Rôsanjin. Born to a poor family in Meiji-era (1868–1912) Kyoto, he made his way to Tokyo, working as a potter and artist. While living in Tokyo, he became interested in cuisine, and decided that he had something unique to contribute to the field. Rôsanjin set out to preserve the best in traditional cooking while adapting it to contemporary times. Together with a friend, he opened a famous restaurant, designing not only the dishes, but also the utensils and the interior of his establishment. His motto can roughly be translated as "it has to fit." Food, utensils, location, and company had to come together in a complementary harmony to enhance the dining experience. His pottery, sometimes in imitation of famous pieces of the past, was designed to please with touch, look, and utility and to enhance the food he served.

Many of Rôsanjin's spiritual descendants can still be found throughout Japan: cooks without formal training, but with flair and desire to please the palates and eyes of their customers. Many small bars owe their existence to the desire of the owner-operator to provide a particular kind of cuisine, an array of drinks, or a particular atmosphere for a small and select clientele.

Subsequent to 1945, the Japanese concentrated on development and modernization. Domestic demand rose. Electronic goods became commonplace. The specter of famine, which had been a feature of the lives of Japanese commoners since the aristocratic period, was vanquished. Japanese trade abroad brought new ideas, new foods, and new methods to Japanese lives. Perhaps the two most remarkable changes in Japanese food, which started in the nineteenth century, but accelerated after the war, were the growth in meat and milk-product consumption. At the end of the twentieth century, Japanese meat consumption per capita was approaching that of Western Europe. Milk products, particularly in the form of various flavored yogurts and other fermented products, took off in the 1950s and are now exported overseas. One consequence of this dietary change has been an increase in average height in Japan, by about eight inches (20 cm) for males born after World War II. The wider spaces of Hokkaido, less populated than the other main Japanese islands, have allowed for farms specializing in meat and dairy production: Hokkaido today has the greatest concentration of gourmet cheese makers in Japan (more than 50 handmade cheese manufacturers in 2001).

Part of the changes in the Japanese diet are the result of government policy. Aware of the poor state of nutrition (malnutrition was rife among children in post-war Japan, and many elderly Japanese today still show signs of beriberi and other malnutrition diseases), the Japanese government made stringent efforts to ensure that children had a proper nutritive base for the day. Though upper-level schools no longer supply a standard school lunch to all their students, school is one of the places where Japanese children learn (and adults have learned) about food. The spread and consumption of two foods is an almost direct consequence of government involvement: rice and milk, both of which were supplied to schools. As a consequence, virtually every person in Japan in the latter half of the twentieth century has come to recognize rice as the staff of life (in the past, poor people ate millet and tubers more often than rice, which went to paying taxes). And this practice also benefits rice farmers (and the government that is strongly reliant on them because of the Japanese election system). The provision of low-cost milk at schools, similarly, has stimulated the milk industry. Until this practice became common in schools, weaned Japanese children rarely had access to milk, and therefore quickly developed lactose intolerance after weaning. With this program, milk consumption in Japan continued into adulthood, and far fewer adult Japanese in the twenty-first century have lactose intolerance: the Japanese milk market is booming, and demand for milk, yogurts, milk-fermented drinks, and cheese approaches Western levels. The provision of school lunches has also had another, perhaps unintended effect. Since food policies for schools are set at a national level, most children for the past half-century have been exposed to the same diet, in effect creating a sort of "national" cuisine: a lowest common denominator of familiar and preferred foods.

Scotch whiskey became extremely popular in Japan after the war, and besides importing large quantities, the Japanese make several types of their own. Japan imports large quantities of lagers and American beers. Beer gardens open in the summer in most urban concentrations, allowing people a respite from the muggy climate. And, perhaps most importantly, beer is the beverage of choice for toasts and friendly meetings.

Fruit and vegetable juices, in a diversity of combinations with exotic fruit such as guarana, as well as incorporating vitamins and various stamina-boosters, are plentiful. Yogurt drinks with live bacilli or health-giving aloe vera are also popular.

Regional Cuisines

The geography of Japan influenced its political makeup, as is true in any country. For centuries, the central government was more of an idea than a reality. Some areas, less certain of themselves, or simply because of isolation, secluded themselves by formidable customs and immigration barriers, and in the process brought about unique local cuisines. In the far west, overlooking the Tsushima Strait leading to Korea, the people of the Choshu clan, one of the few clans to survive the tremors of civil war that engulfed Japan from time to time, developed a xenophobic attitude to foreigners but also forced themselves to rely heavily on the seas that surrounded them. The center of blowfish (*fugu*) and other specialist fisheries in Japan to this day, the area abounds with rocky coves and with crabs that are the magically transformed Taira warriors who, together with the emperor, were drowned in those waters in the twelfth century.

Two other famous "political cuisines" can be tried in Japan, sprouting from two rather polar sources. Of the reclusive and secretive feudal clans, few were as reclusive as the Tosa, who dominated a fourth of Shikoku island. Visitors, tax-gatherers, pilgrims, tourists, or foreigners were barely tolerated, if at all, during the premodern eras. The Sanuki area, as it is called, is known for its curious customs ranging from bullfights and female sumo wrestlers to its dances and festivals. It is also the home of thin, specially cut noodles (*sanukiudon*) eaten with one of the many species of fish that inhabit the Seto Inland Sea on which Sanuki sits. Today, Kagawa Prefecture (the modern name for the Sanuki area) is a lot more open to visitors, and these renowned noodles can be found outside the borders. Still, it is interesting to speculate what the secretive former rulers of this state would think of the plethora of visitors slurping their noodles.

The southern part of Kyushu island, a land of deep bays and rocky inlets, subtropical and given to typhoons and volcanoes, is interesting in its own right. But it is also the place of contact where Japanese and European civilizations interacted for several centuries before Japan opened itself to exposure to the rest of the world. Portuguese explorer-traders first arrived on the island of Tanegashima in the early sixteenth century. They introduced the locals to firearms (the word *tanegashima* meant a firearm in Japanese until the nineteenth century). Today the island is, appropriately, the site of the Japanese National Space Agency, and, more importantly, new forms of cooking. Meat stews with leeks and grilling—a style that became known as southern barbarian (namban) cooking entered Japanese cuisine. Pastry baking was introduced, and sponge cakes called kasutera (perhaps derived from the Spanish castillo, castle) are now a local specialty in many southern cities such as Kagoshima. Notwithstanding the sequestration of foreigners for more than 200 years in a small trading post in Deshima, near Nagasaki, traces of European tastes filtered through. Thus the cooking of Kagoshima and Nagasaki in western Kyushu are characterized by, among other things, influences from Europe and from China (the Chinese and the Dutch were the only foreigners allowed to operate in Japan between 1637 and 1856), albeit adapted to Japanese sensibilities.

Agriculture in Japanese History

Agriculture—mainly millet and root crops—entered Japan with the prehistorical Jōmon period (approximately 1000–250 B.C.E.). The population mixed gathering wild crops with small-scale cultivation and hunting. In the Yayoi period (250 B.C.E.–250 C.E.) that succeeded the Jōmon, intensive rice cultivation was introduced from the Asian mainland and rice became the staple grain for those who could afford it. Since then, paddy-rice farming has been a main branch of agriculture and so important that even a famous swordsman such as Miyamoto Musashi, the "sword saint," so named because of his skill, was just as proud of his reclamation of rice fields as of his swordsmanship. Subsequent to World War II, the Japanese made an effort to become as self-sufficient as possible in basic foodstuff production, even though it has become cheaper to import many foods.

For most of history, farming was done by households living on their land. The household (called ie) was the basic building block of society, both urban and rural. It was (and to some degree still is) a paramount cultural imperative that the household's survival be assured at all costs. The limited amount of arable land available means that ie never split up their land, and only one child, normally a male, carried on the business of farming. The other children left, often for life in the city, but they maintained ties with their farming relatives. As a consequence, many Japanese urban households have ties to their rural origins, and acquire at least some of their food, and many of their food preferences, from their rural relatives.

Until the land reform after World War II, many of these farmers were tenants. The landholdings to this day are relatively small. Farming households, whether they live amidst their own fields or in a cluster, are part of

Rice Fields

a hamlet, a small group of households of up to about 20 households. Several such hamlets form a village, which is an administrative unit. In traditional times, each hamlet had shared-use areas: a bamboo grove, a grass field (for construction; the grass field also was used for grazing livestock used for the plow), mountain groves of chestnuts, stands of vines for weaving baskets, or riverfront. Some of these traditional shared areas still produce food to this day.

One of the first (and arguably the most beneficial) things the American occupiers of Japan did after 1945 was to initiate a rapid program of land reform. Large landowners were deprived of their lands, which were sold at reasonable prices to the tenants who had farmed them for generations. This ensured both employment and civil equity. There was a significant cost initially, in terms of efficiency, because mechanized agriculture favors larger plots, but greater returns in terms of access to food.

POPULATION AND DEMOGRAPHICS

Japan's population today is around 127 million (as of 2001), of whom 99 percent are ethnically Japanese. In the north, some 40,000 people claim descent from the Ainu, the forest-dwelling hunter-gatherers of Hokkaido. To the far south, in the warm tropical seas, lies the Ryukyu archipelago. The population of this group of tiny islands is linguistically and culturally distinct from the mainland Japanese and had an independent kingdom of

its own until occupied by Japanese forces in the seventeenth century.
Close to a million people in Japan today are descendants of people who
migrated there willingly or as forced labor from Korea before and during
World War II. By and large, the food of all these people is dominated
today by Japanese food culture. More than 90 percent of the population is
urban (until the start of the twentieth century, some 80 percent was
rural), and only about 5 percent of the population engages in full-time
farming.

The modern Japanese family is a small one. The fertility rate is about
1.5, which means that Japanese families usually have at most one or two
children. Most families live in what, by U.S. standards, are very cramped
quarters. An average house or apartment usually has about three rooms,
one or two serving for living, studying, and sleeping, and one "combination dining-kitchen" area. The living zone is usually floored in fine woven
straw mats (tatami) and converted to a sleeping zone at night by folding
any furniture away and bringing out sleeping quilts (futon) from built-in
storage closets. The dining-kitchen area often has a Western-style dining
table and chairs. More and more the traditional style of living "on the
floor" is being superseded by Western-type (though still Japanese-sized)
accommodations and furnishings.

ATTITUDES TOWARD FOOD

The sources of Japanese attitudes to food emerge from a combination of
historical experience and religious ideology. These attitudes were codified
in a number of ways. Literature and art provided a source of allusions and
references. The daily ritual and festive practices of people reflect and reinforce attitudes concerning food. Foreign food elements imported from
China and Europe are fitted into this mosaic as well.

Scarcity, Frugality, and Religion

Notwithstanding the fertility of the land, the small area, periods of civil
unrest, and other factors have meant that Japan has frequently been
threatened by famine. Crops failed, typhoons blighted growth, fires rav-
aged people's domiciles and destroyed crops. Though the threat of famine
has been eradicated in modern Japan, Japanese children are still exhorted
to finish the last scrap of rice. And elderly Japanese will still wash out the
remains of rice in their rice bowl with the dregs of the tea they have
drunk, then drink the mix. In fact, a type of rice dish has been created
from this custom of scarcity: boiled rice in tea with garnishes (ochazuke).

The attitude toward food has also been affected by the two great religions that the Japanese follow. The majority of Japanese participate in two religions: Shintô and Buddhism. Shintô was the sole religion of the Japanese until the sixth century. It is a religion that relies heavily on ideas of purity, as well as on the presentation of food offerings to the deities. Buddhism, which complements Shintô and deals largely with the afterlife, has two ideas that affect food choice: simplicity and a reluctance to take life. These two religious orientations, which all Japanese share to a certain degree, reinforce one another in the realm of food.

Shintô presents the origins of food in the following myth.

The moon god went to visit the food goddess. She entertained him graciously. Then she vomited up all kinds of good foods, extracting other foods from her genitals and anus. When she offered them to him, he was insulted that she had offered him polluted food, and drawing his sword, he killed her. He went back to heaven and told his sister, the sun goddess, who is chief of the gods, what he had done. His sister was furious at his behavior and banished him to the night sky. Then sending another messenger, she had the food goddess's body collected. From the corpse's eyes, ears, eyebrows, genitals, and rectum grew rice, silkworms, cattle, beans, and other crops useful to humans and necessary for their survival.

Food is part of a natural cycle of death and decay, says this myth, and one would do well to remember and follow this. Food grows on land. To be able to produce food for humans, the land needs its own sustenance from what humans excrete or no longer need.

Shintô rituals always involve offering food to the gods. At a Shintô shrine where these rituals take place, the altar will be laden with immaculate piles of vegetables, rice, seaweed, fruit, and other delicacies arrayed on ritual trays made of the fragrant, unadorned and unpainted pale wood of Japanese cypress.

Both Shintô and Buddhism share an ideal of simplicity. For Shintô, it is important that human activities be in harmony with nature, and that cleanliness and purity are at the heart of every action. In Buddhism, renunciation of wealth and the embrace of poverty and restraint were important basic principles. Thus the ideas of restraint and elegance, and of simplicity and frugality of both these religions dovetailed neatly in Japanese food attitudes.

Buddhism's attitude toward food also arises from the Buddhist proscription against taking life (*ahimsa* in Sanskrit). Buddhist clergy traditionally did not eat any foods of animal origin (though this proscription has been relaxed in many Japanese Buddhist sects). The influence of Buddhism gave rise to two distinctive forms of Japanese cooking: the multicourse

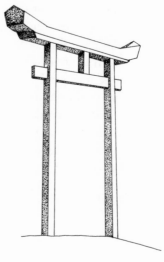

Torii–Shintô Arch

banquet *(kaiseki)* that accompanies the tea ceremony and vegetarian cuisine *(shôjin)*, which uses the versatile soybean in place of fish or meat.
Food is a very important aspect of the Buddhist monastic tradition. So
much so that Dogen Zenji (1200–1253), founder of the Soto Zen Buddhist sect, was moved to write religious treatises on the treatment, preparation, and consumption of food that are still read today in Buddhist
monasteries, where the guardian god of the meal and of dining (Ida-ten)
presides in effigy over the proceedings.

Nature and Seasons

The well-defined climatic environment has given the Japanese a profound sensitivity to the seasons, and this sentiment is an essential element
of Japanese culture. In traditional Japan, during the Heian era
(794–1185), the year was divided into 24 short seasons. Each of these had
its own special atmosphere, a period at which particular sights, flowers,
and acts were at their peak. In contemporary Japan, the peak of perfection—*shun*—of foods is rarely observed fully. The concept still exists in
Japan today, and it is a rare Japanese person who cannot point to the *shun*
of his favorite food, fruit, or fish.

Partaking of the first foods of the season *(hatsumono)*—whether fruit,
herb, vegetable, or cereal—is an event eagerly awaited by gourmets and
tea ceremony practitioners. The "first" of anything is important in all

aspects of Japanese culture, most markedly during the New Year when the first session of calligraphy or other visual and martial arts is assiduously observed by practitioners. Partaking of the first foods of a season is believed to add 75 days to one's life. Due attention to the season during which food ingredients are at their peak is reinforced constantly by cookery journals, television shows, and various media. Moreover those, such as modern Japanese youth, who have only a slight acquaintance with traditional culture, will nevertheless have come across the significance of the seasons in classical poetry or literature, for example, included in compulsory school subjects.

Presentation

The presentation of Japanese food is strongly oriented toward the visual. A diner expects the food not only to *taste* good, but also to be visually appealing. Between the eighth and the eleventh centuries, the imperial court and aristocracy—about 20,000 individuals at most—developed an aesthetic sensibility that influenced Japanese culture until today. Extreme preference was given to understated elegance (perhaps largely because there were simply not that many material goods to go around). This preference was found in plays on words and punning, in the creation of short *waka* poems of 31 syllables, and in the use of physical allusions—flowers, fruit, particular knots, fabrics, color combinations, and other manufactured and natural items—to classical poetry, painting, and literature. If you did not have style, and if you could not express the style properly, you were nobody. This affected the world of food as well. For example, a certain Empress Jingû in seventh-century Japan fished for sweetfish (*ayu*, a delicately flavored river fish) with a single grain of rice as bait when she returned from Korea. Thus, in June and only in June, *ayu* can be referred to as "rice-caught." Not only that, but *ayu* are considered delicious *only* when caught by a woman using the traditional bait (although at other times other means are used by men, which are considered perfectly satisfactory).

Since the Heian period, the Japanese have regarded subtlety as the height of civilized behavior and culture. Literary and poetic convention required indirect allusions to the seasons, and this was satisfied by citing birds, flowers in bloom, or natural events within the text of a letter or Chinese-type poem (*tanka*). In the course of time, these spontaneous seasonal allusions became codified into symbols that are still used to this day, whether as patterns painted on a silk kimono or a ceramic bowl, or as garnishes accompanying food.

Flower Arrangement

A related intricate etiquette prescribed which colors and fabrics to wear, depending on the season, the circumstances, and the social rank of the person. The importance of appropriateness—the right color, the right robe, fitting the proper flower to its own season—cannot be overestimated. As late as the seventeenth century, a lord (*daimyô*) lost his life and lands because of wearing the wrong trousers. During the Heian period, not being able to recognize an allusion to a particular flower could lead to suicide.

Many of these meanings and allusions refer to Chinese classical literature, to poetic fancies, and to specific sights in Japan. Some of these have survived to the present day in the form of allusions and plays on words about food.

Food Arrangement

Visual clues are implicit in the arrangement of food on a plate; the shape of the plate and its material, glaze, and decoration; and garnishes (some edible, some not) that might accompany a dish in Japanese food culture. Foods and garnishes are often shaped and colored to indicate the season or event. One amusing feature is the little green fringe-cut plastic film often found in box lunches. Box lunches are, of course, perishable. In olden days there was no requirement for printing "Consume by" labels. To indicate freshness, box lunch (*obento*) makers would place the food on green bamboo leaves, which desiccate at a fairly predictable rate. If you opened the box and the leaves were green, good and well. If they were turning brown, the food was clearly not as fresh as it should be. However, the tradition of using freshly cut bamboo leaves is hard to keep up in modern Japan, and so the evergreen plastic strip has been substituted

Food can be arranged on a plate in any of a number of formally recognized patterns, usually in ones, threes, or fives of the same kind. One general rule is that not all items must be visible from a single vantage point: there should always be something hidden from the eye. Another rule is that if at all possible, food should reflect the season, for example, reds and golds (autumn), whites (winter), and pinks (spring).

Colors

Colors have important meanings in Japanese life, and this is reflected in food. Preserving or stabilizing the natural color of ingredients is an important consideration in Japanese cooking. So much so that the process has been given a specific term: *iroage* (literally, "raise color"). It is a frequent instruction in cookbooks, particularly for green vegetables, as well as those that tend to discolor or oxidize. To ensure that green vegetables such as leaves, pea pods, and string beans keep their bright green color, they are plunged in cold or ice water immediately after cooking. Another trick is to add a pinch of salt into the cooking water to ensure that a vegetable's color does not change. To keep vegetables such as eggplant from oxidizing (changing color when exposed to air) before cooking, they are soaked in brine or water acidified with one to two tablespoons of vinegar.

Colors representing seasons and seasonality are very obvious: white for winter, pink and green for spring, red and green, or purple, for summer, orange and yellow for fall are fairly obvious. But other colors are used to represent symbolic meanings anchored in Japanese culture. Red and gold represent felicitous occasions such as weddings, silver and black represent mourning (and therefore, are a combination to be avoided). Some foods may be added to a dish, therefore, because of the symbolic referent, rather than because of their flavor.

Textures

An important aspect of all Japanese foods is their texture. So important is food texture in Japan, that there are over 20 words used to describe different kinds of crispness alone. Thus, one says *karikari* of vegetables that are chewy and yield reluctantly to the pressure of teeth, whereas *shakishaki* is used to indicate fruit or vegetables that have a crispness throughout, like water-chestnuts or fresh young carrots.

The best Matsuzaka beef is described as "soft enough to cut with a fork." Some foods are prized solely for their texture: flavor can be added at will. Such foods include soybean curd (tofu), which in its natural state is bland, and, most prominently, devil's foot root jelly (konnyaku), whose stiff, jelly-like texture is highly prized. On its own, the jelly adds texture to the varied tidbits, each its own texture, of oden stew. Flavored with perilla leaves, the jelly becomes a chewy counterfoil to the taste and texture of rich tuna belly sashimi.

Life-Cycle Rituals in History

Soon after birth, a Japanese infant was introduced ritually to its family and the world around it. Since this is a precarious time of life, there were many ritual activities associated with this period, some of which are still practiced. The child was also introduced to the local deity, who is, in the Japanese way of thinking, a distant and respected relative, and parents with newborn children still make a special visit with the newborn to their local shrine. Until the late nineteenth century, the transition to adult status was marked in Japan by changing the hair style. Men shaved off their side locks and started wearing a topknot whose style (depending on the historical period) differed for different classes. Women bound their hair up and received a red sash or petticoat signifying sexual maturity. In the early teenage years, boys were inducted into the local young men's association, which assumed jobs such as fire-fighting and community policing. Marriage followed soon after, but a young man was considered a youngster until the age of 42. Marking the transit from youth to maturity, 42 was a particularly dangerous age for men (for women it was 33), so this period was observed ritually as well. At 60, men and women, having lived through an entire cycle (12 zodiacal years times the 5 elements), retired formally, and this was again marked by ritual. After death, a series of rituals lasting for several years allowed the living to say farewell to the departed. Many of these rituals, as noted, remain in Japan in very local or abbreviated form today.

Foreign and New

Food was, and indeed still is, considered a precious resource: one is not supposed to leave behind food on one's plate, and gift exchanges of food are always welcome. Younger Japanese have grown up in a society that is very affluent: they can eat, literally, anything they desire. Many do. Metropolitan Japan is full of restaurants serving exotic delicacies from all corners of the world. Fast food abounds, and children are more sophisticated and daring in their tastes than are adults.

Japanese cooks have been welcoming new and foreign dishes since the first Korean and Chinese ambassadors and immigrants started arriving in the sixth century. Many foods that are considered typically Japanese today are originally from elsewhere. These new foods do undergo a period of assimilation and enculturation, during which they are modified to Japanese tastes, but eventually they are accepted into the fold. As a general rule, Japanese have been culturally open to new foods, *provided* a niche can be found for them within the canons of Japanese aesthetics and taste preferences.

Since early in its history, Japan has demonstrated a canny ability to accept, adopt, and modify foreign cultural practices to its own ends. Buddhism was introduced into Japan in the sixth century and very quickly assumed the unique Japanese characteristics that make it today a distinctive belief in contrast to other forms of Buddhism. The Japanese learned to write from the Chinese and rapidly adapted Chinese writing to their own needs, modifying it as they went. The Japanese court, modeled as it was on the Chinese governmental system, was soon radically altered. The same process of japanization occurred in food. For all the superficial similarities between the food of Japan and its east Asian neighbors, Japanese food is unique in its coherence and its underlying approach to what food is for, how it is to be prepared, and how enjoyed.

In the contemporary era, Japan has continued to adopt foods from abroad. In the past thirty years, a large number of new products have entered Japanese cuisine and been turned from curious foreign items to parts of local dishes. Milk and other animal products were adapted to Japanese taste, and the uses to which they are put—the dishes the Japanese produce—are often unique to Japan. Foods such as aloe vera and coconut jelly were adopted from the United States and from Southeast Asia and were quickly melded with Japanese foods to produce uniquely Japanese flavors. Young jute leaves (*Corchorus olitorius*, in Japanese, *moroheya*), a favorite green in the Middle East, have been adopted into Japanese cooking and prepared in Japanese ways because the cooked leaves' slippery, silky texture echoes that of other favored native vegetables with similar sensory characteristics. American hamburgers are now a part of the Japanese diet as are butter and various types of cheese.

Prepared Foods: The Gourmet Boom

The 1980s were economic boom years in Japan, and the accompanying consumers' rush to spend affected food consumption patterns as well. It was at this period that the term *gourmet (gurume)* became a prominent feature of social discourse. Courses in proper table etiquette and the pursuit and appreciation of fine food, drink, and dining became accessible to a wider audience than before, becoming a fashionable hobby. Luxury domestic and imported food items became commonplace in many households. The gourmet boom lasted several decades, and its echoes are still apparent. Even small backwater towns are assured of delivery of any gourmet food item within 24 hours, so popular and accessible have these items become.

Gourmet items from all over the world are supplied by various trading companies having a long history of procuring foreign goods. Imports range from single-malt whiskey from Scotland, Beaujolais nouveau and other French or Italian wines, Jamaican Blue Mountain coffee beans, French cheeses, Chinese mountain delicacies from Sijuan, and of course fish from all the seas of the earth. Hundreds of slick, illustrated journals periodically feature the 100 best restaurants in major cosmopolitan areas, maps of directions, and these restaurants' specialties and articles on how to prepare classical international and Japanese dishes, or the best time and place to collect wild greens. Japanese tour organizers offer gourmet tours of France, China, Italy, and other culinary capitals. The difficulties with a sudden thirst for the gourmet experience are obvious. The benefits, however, must not be overlooked: the Japanese populace as a whole has become more culturally and culinarily sophisticated, and Japanese culture, as it has done from time immemorial, is now engaged in the lengthy process of absorbing and japanizing the new food finds.

Natural Foods

In recent years a "natural food movement" has emerged in Japan in reaction to the effects of industrialization. Industrialization has distanced consumer from the producer. Long supply chains of intermediaries provided food for retail stores and supermarkets. This meant higher prices for the consumers, as well as decreased quality: food suppliers were more concerned with shelf-life and regular sizes than with flavor. Colorants and preservatives have been so unrestrainedly used, even when unnecessary, that widespread concern and dismay arose at the execrable quality of foods offered by the large supermarket chains and stores.

In the mid-1980s, many homemakers, under the aegis of the powerful Housewives Federation, began to rebel against the domination of large industrial firms in their food supply. Many have started food cooperatives that source food directly from farmers to their tables. Natural food stores have also proliferated widely in urban areas, both owner-operated and chain stores. The movement has also brought about greater consumer choice in wholesome bread and baked goods, fruit and vegetable juices, low-salt and low-fat content, functional foods (foods that have additional medicinal or disease-preventing qualities), and foods such as tofu, *miso*, and soy sauce made in the traditional manner without chemical additives.

THE TRADITIONAL KITCHEN AND ITS UTENSILS

The traditional Japanese kitchen centered around the stove *(kamado)*. A charcoal or wood-burning affair, it was made of clay with a fire hole at the side and one or two potholes on top. Traditional Japanese pots were made of iron or pottery, with a protruding rim a third of the way down. This rim kept the pots from slipping down into the fire. A wooden lid was laid over the top of the pot. This form of rice pot has become an icon in modern Japan, representing rice cooking and good food, though few modern Japanese have seen, let alone used, one.

A traditional kitchen would also include a wooden cutting board, metal and wooden chopsticks for handling food, a number of knives, containers for various foodstuffs, and as many dishes as the family's circumstances would permit. A stone sink with cold water served for washing food and utensils. Kitchens were definitely the women's domain: most traditional Japanese men had never set foot in the kitchen in their lives, even as late as the second half of the twentieth century. Some cooking was also carried out in a fire pit *(irori)*. This was usually of a standard dimension (one-half *tatami* mat, or three square feet). The fire pit was edged with a border of hardwood set flush with the floor and filled with sand. A small charcoal fire was laid in the sand to heat the room, but which could also serve for cooking such dishes as meat, fish, and rice paste grilled on skewers thrust into the sand. Above the fire pit was suspended a toggled rope-and-beam contraption *(jizaikagi)*, which allowed the raising and lowering of a hook. An iron pot *(tetsu-nabe)* was suspended from the hook for cold-weather stews or heating water. In some areas, a wooden frame was set around the shaft of the *jizaikagi* and used either to dry wet-weather gear, or to smoke dry fish and radishes and other vegetables for pickling.

2

Major Foods and Ingredients

Japanese food ingredients differ from familiar ones in the West both in the emphases and in some ingredients that are almost unique to Japanese food culture. This chapter looks at the foods and ingredients that make up Japanese cuisine from the Japanese perspective, as discussed in chapter 1. Japanese food thinking revolves around two fundamental concepts. First is the concept of a "staple," which, for most modern Japanese is rice, but to which we shall add two other ingredients, both manufactured rather than naturally occurring: a fermented soybean paste *(miso)* and a processed fish product, the basis for stocks, called *katsuobushi*. The second concept is the idea discussed in chapter 1 that food is described as the bounty of a particular domain: paddy and dry fields (rice and other grains), truck fields (vegetables and roots), orchards (fruit), mountains (wild vegetables), rivers and ponds (freshwater fish and some vegetables), and the sea. This chapter presents the food ingredients as the Japanese order them but in modified form, rather than by botanical or Western meal ordering. This chapter then discusses two related topics: Japanese food sources and consumer preferences.

THE THREE MAJOR INGREDIENTS

The three major ingredients that define Japanese cooking, emotionally, culturally, and in terms of prevalence, are rice, soybean paste, and fish stock. These are therefore covered first.

Rice

In Japanese cooking, rice is mostly served cooked on its own, without any flavoring, not even salt. It is neither wholly boiled nor wholly steamed but a bit of both, and emerges a glistening white. Each grain is separate and whole, yet it sticks to its neighbors with a tenacity that is instantly dissolved by a liquid, yet is strong enough to allow a diner to move a large ball of rice using only two chopsticks.

Rice like that—*gohan*—is always served, oddly enough, in a tea bowl. Korean potters had been making such bowls for drinking tea, and the name stuck even though the use differed. Until then, rice was cooked into large mounds, placed on flat trays, and eaten with a spoon. Even today, the significance of rice as a ritual staple is critically important. A full meal is defined as a meal with rice. Anything without rice, is, by definition, not a meal.

Most rice eaten is simply steam boiled. This is the staple that comes with meals. A smaller proportion is eaten in the form of fried rice (that is, after cooking, small pieces of vegetables, fish, or meat are added and the whole dish is then stir-fried), as *sushi* rice (slightly vinegared, either formed into a ball with a topping, or tossed with bits of fish and vegetables into a sort of salad), or cooked with beans, taro, or some other vegetable. Special varieties of rice with a very high starch content are steamed and pounded into a gluey, doughy consistency called *mochi*, which is a requirement for many kinds of ritual. *Mochi* rice, which is stickier and richer than normal rice, is mixed with mushrooms, fish, or meat, then steamed in a bamboo-leaf wrapping to make a highly nutritious hand-meal.

The proportion of rice in the modern meal has declined throughout Japan as foreign foods have proliferated. Households with older people probably still eat rice three times a day. Younger people tend to have rice once, perhaps twice a day.

Plain White Rice
- 4 cups round grain good-quality rice (Koshihikari or Sasanishiki varieties are very popular)
- 6 cups water

For best effect, wash rice in several changes of fresh water (you can reserve the water for cooking daikon radish), then allow to drain for half an hour. Place in heavy pot with a well fitted lid. Add 1 1/2 the amount of water to the amount of rice (quantity of water may vary depending on age of rice: the older, the more water). Cover pot. Heat on medium flame until boiling furiously. Lower heat to lowest setting. Allow 10 minutes. Check rice. Once all water has been absorbed, switch off heat and allow to stand a further 10 minutes.

Soybeans

The second major food base in Japanese cooking is fermented soybean paste (*miso*). *Miso* is a versatile seasoning. It adds flavor, aroma, and body as well as a distinctive character. It is a major ingredient in the soup that is a central component in Japanese meals. It is used as a pickling medium, flavor agent, and dip.

There is an almost infinite variety in *miso*. In color it ranges from creamy pale yellow, through tan, orange, red, and brown to black. Flavors vary as well. The darker varieties, preferred in western and southern Japan, tend to have stronger flavors. The lighter varieties, fancied in eastern and northern Japan, tend to be milder and sweeter (though there are exceptions to all these characteristics). The color, consistency, and, most important, flavor, depend upon many factors: the variety of rice used, the grain used for fermentation starter (*kôji*) and the way it was treated, the length of fermentation, even the water, the size of the barrel, and the time of year will affect the final product.

Some well-known rice-based *miso* are Edo *miso* (from Tokyo), which is red and mildly sweetish, and Shinshu *miso* (from the central Honshu highlands), which is yellow and salty. Sendai *miso* (from northeastern Honshu) is red and fairly strong; it also contains barley. Wheat-based *miso*

Miso Barrel and Bean Pods

is also called country-style *miso*. *Hatcho miso*, which is extremely dark and dense, its flavor strong and robust, does not use any cereal at all in its manufacture and takes about two years to mature. It is also much more expensive than other types and not as widely available. Whatever its color, origin, or strength, *miso* has a very savory aroma and imparts an almost meaty taste to any dish it is added to. In Japan, a store will offer several varieties of *miso*, the choice depending on which area of the country the store is located.

Most commonly made from late spring to early summer, soybeans are soaked, steamed until soft, mashed, then mixed with salt and a fermentation starter *(kôji)*. *Kôji* is made commercially (the process is too delicate and difficult to accomplish at home) by infecting freshly cooked warm rice, barley, or wheat with a mold, *Aspergillus oryzae*. The starter is matured for at least 48 hours, then mixed with the soybeans, water, and salt in proportions that differ from one maker to the next (and are often a trade secret). The soybean-grain-*kôji* mixture is left to ferment in wooden barrels (the barrels are made of perfectly fitted Japanese cedar wood staves bound with bamboo rings; metal, say the purists, would ruin the flavor) usually for one summer, sometimes for a year or more. The greater the proportion of *kôji* to soybean, the sweeter the finished *miso*. The amount of *kôji* also affects the length of maturation of the *miso*. *Miso* with a high proportion of *kôji* can be made in as few as 20 days; the result is a sweet *miso*. *Miso* emerges, fragrant as a mushroom, from its wooden vat. It is then divided into smaller portions and sold to wholesalers, who might divide it into the small 1 kg (just over 2 lb.) packages found in neighborhood stores or supermarkets. Making *miso* used to be an annual household activity but is now done by large companies. Few cooks would bother nowadays (except in counter-reaction to the uniformity of big brands, and to produce an organic product).

The most frequent use for *miso* is in the *miso* soup that accompanies a bowl of rice at every traditional Japanese meal. The *miso* forms a dense cloud within the translucent broth, which must be stirred to be thoroughly savored. Depending on the region, miso soups vary in color from dark to very light. Japanese in western Honshu (Osaka, Kyoto, Kobe westward) favor pale, almost whitish miso soups, while from Tokyo northward, dark miso soups are preferred. Northwest of Kyoto, the preferred variety is red.

One of the finest uses for *miso* is in pickling. In most pickle factories great tubs of vegetables soak in a thick paste of *miso*. The vegetables, which have usually been slightly dried first, become wizened caricatures of their fresh selves. Gradually the flavor of the *miso* penetrates. When they are finally ready, usually after about half a year of patient soaking, the vegetables have their original flavor enhanced by the thick smoky flavor of the *miso*. Vegetables commonly pickled in *miso* are eggplant, cucumber, gourd, radish, burdock, ginger, and carrot.

A subtle way of imparting *miso*'s distinctive flavor while pickling is through cheesecloth or muslin. Slices of very fresh fish—such as grouper, bream, mackerel—as well as fish roe, shellfish, pork, chicken, and beef are wrapped in clean cheesecloth, covered all over with an even layer of *miso*, and stored in a well-sealed container in the refrigerator from one to four days, after which the pieces can be grilled or quickly seared with no additional seasoning. *Miso* can also be enjoyed by itself, as a dip or spread. Long slices of crisp cucumber, carrot, celery, or lettuce leaves can be dipped into a sauce of *miso* thinned with rice wine and a bit of cooking wine (*mirin*) to taste. *Miso* can also be used as a salad dressing, again thinned with rice and cooking wine, or with rice vinegar. An excellent topping for grilled eggplant is also made with a mixture of *miso* and rice and cooking wine. Grilling gives a smoky, caramelized aroma to the *miso* topping that is readily absorbed by the tender flesh of the eggplant.

Shallots with Miso-Walnut Dressing
This is a very simple salad (*aemono*).

- 8 oz. very small shallots, peeled
- 2 cups water
- 1 Tbs. *miso*
- 2 Tbs. walnuts
- 1 Tbs. *saké*
- 1 tsp. *mirin*

Boil water in a pan. Add peeled shallots, lower heat and simmer for three minutes. The shallots should be tender but still retain their shape. Drain and plunge at once into cold water to arrest cooking, drain again.

Blend *miso*, walnuts, rice wine, and *mirin* in a blender. If using a traditional grinding bowl (*suribachi*), chop walnuts as small as possible beforehand. Crush a little at a time in the bowl, adding more walnuts until all have been added to the bowl. Keep crushing until oil is released from the nuts. Add the *miso*, stir into the bowl and add rice wine and *mirin*. Serve in small servings in small bowls with deep sides, sauce ladeled over the vegetables but leaving the ends exposed, garnished with a sprig of trefoil or flat-leaf parsley.

Katsuobushi

Katsuobushi, for which there is no good English translation, is absolutely essential to Japanese cuisine. Without *katsuobushi*, Japanese cuisine would be radically different than it is, since it is the main flavoring ingredient of the universal stock *(dashi)* that in turn flavors so many Japanese dishes. The starting point for this flavorful dried product is the bonito, a small variety of tuna *(Katsuwonus pelamis)* about two feet in length, which schools off northern Japan in the spring, and off southern Japan in the autumn. Bonito fillets are boiled gently, air dried, then smoked over cedar chips. This causes the fillets to shrink, losing 50 percent of their volume and moisture. The dried fillet is then treated with a bacillus, *Aspergillus glaucus*, and stored for several months in cedar chests under sand. The end result is a brown woody lump about eight to ten inches long and about two inches at its widest. The *katsuobushi* "log" will keep for a long time in a dry airy place. In traditional Japanese kitchens, *katsuobushi* is stored in its own cedar box which incorporates a blade in the lid. When stock is needed, the dried fillet is planed and the fresh shavings (which must be used immediately, since they lose aroma and flavor rapidly) fall conveniently into the box's storage drawer. The shavings can now be bought in labor-saving ready-made packets. A further time-saving innovation is dried stock granules.

Another use of the shavings is as a garnish. They may be scattered onto parboiled spinach as a wonderful seasoning, or over cold or hot tofu together with finely minced spring onions, for a refreshing summer meal or winter appetizer.

Besides its obvious intrinsic culinary and dietary value, *katsuobushi* allows the Japanese to indulge in the pleasures of punning. Written using

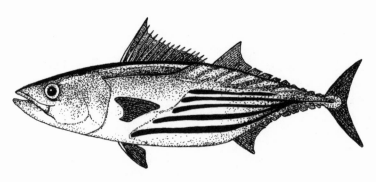

Bonito Fish

different characters, but pronounced the same, *katsuobushi* can also mean "victorious warrior." It is therefore an appropriate gift for wishing a man success in some endeavor, or congratulating him on success.

Fish Stock

A fish stock *(dashi)*, made largely of *katsuobushi*, is for many Japanese dishes the basic and most important flavoring ingredient. "Fish stock" is a bit of a misnomer. The stock has two basic ingredients, each of which has a complex process behind it: dried bonito *(katsuobushi)* and kelp *(konbu)*. The full process of producing the stock, however little time it takes in the kitchen, is a lengthy one.

In late autumn, the Kuroshio current that passes east of Japan brings an annual visitor. The *katsuo* (bonito) arrives in great schools off the coast of Japan. For centuries, the Japanese have harvested this bounty from small boats. The fresh fish are filleted, the fillets intended for one of two uses: as *katsuo-tataki* (seared rare fish steaks) and for *katsuobushi*. The first use, albeit delicious, is short-lived. The latter lasts for years with care. The second ingredient of the stock comes from a complex origin as well.

Off the coast of Hokkaido and the northern coasts of Honshu, giant kelp *(konbu)* ribbons grow in the sea. In those cold clear waters, they can grow to great size. The kelp strands are harvested, then dried into long leathery sheets, which are folded over and over again into smaller packets for sale. The end result is a dry leathery bundle, too tough to tear apart, almost too hard to cut. The cook snips off a small length of the dried *konbu*, allowing it to soak for a while in a dish of cold water. The dried greeny-gray papery object turns into thick shining green sheets of kelp once more. The kelp is then allowed to simmer briefly in the stock, imparting an enhanced iodine-like flavor (and, so it is reported, excellent antioxidant properties) to the stock.

The cooking process of stock in the kitchen is surprisingly simple. Shave off as much *katsuobushi* as needed, boil some water, and simmer the kelp briefly. Take off the fire, steep the *katsuobushi* shavings for a minute or two. Remove shavings (and kelp if desired). The resulting pale liquid is a slightly salty-meaty transparent liquid that barely acknowledges its fishy origins. This so-called "first stock" *(ichibandashi)* will be used for the very best stocks, for sauces, and for clear soups that are served with the most delicate foods. Steeping the shavings once more will yield an inferior stock, or "second stock" *(nibandashi)*, used to flavor more robust dishes, and usually enhanced with other flavor-giving ingredients such as dried sardines or soy sauce.

Dashi

- 1 oz. *katsuobushi* shavings
- 1 oz. kelp *(konbu)*
- 5 cups water

Be careful not to wash the kelp (the white powder-like covering has most of the flavor).

Place the kelp in the water and bring to boil. Remove the kelp just as the water starts bubbling. Immediately add about 1/2 cup cold water. Add *katsuobushi* shavings. Remove the *katsuobushi* shavings just as the water starts bubbling (For best effect, run liquid through fine sieve). Remove from heat.

The kelp can be cut into smaller pieces and returned to the soup. The kelp and *katsuobushi* shavings can be used again for a secondary stock to which dried sardines *(niboshi)* are added for stronger flavor, after which they are discarded.

FOOD FROM DRY FIELDS (NOODLES AND BREAD)

Though rice is the normative staple in Japanese culture, products of other grains—the "products of fields"—are important as well, both as an element in daily meals and as snacks.

Noodles

Noodles have been a feature of all Asian cuisines for centuries. Japan has several varieties, some of them foreign imports, others ancient native favorites. Japanese-style noodles, made of wheat or buckwheat, are eaten in soup or with dipping sauces, hot or cold. The choice of meat, seafood, or vegetable toppings is vast. As in the United States and other countries, Italian-style pasta and pizza are widely eaten. These food items are most often dressed with familiar Italian-style tomato or cream sauces with meat or seafood and cheese, or innovatively adapted to traditional taste with Japanese-style sauces featuring native perilla *(shisô)*, chili-preserved cod roe and pickled plum puree. The pride of place goes, however, to various "native" and Chinese noodle dishes.

Buckwheat and Wheat Noodles

Buckwheat (*soba*) and wheat noodles (*udon*) are perennial favorites. The chewy, pale brownish-gray, thin *soba* noodles and the thick, cream-colored *udon* can substitute for one another in many dishes. They are considered a native dish in contrast to other forms of noodles. *Soba* is made of a mixture of 30 to 60 percent buckwheat, the rest being wheat flour. The buckwheat (not a grain at all, but the seed of a plant related to flax) makes the noodles chewy and adds a pleasant, slightly bitter flavor to the mix. Most *udon* noodles are fairly thick, though some, like the famous *sanuki udon* from Shikoku island are thin. The standard serving method is a large bowl filled with noodles and broth and garnished with the diner's choice of items.

Specialist shops make their own hand-rolled noodles. Unlike some Chinese noodles that are made by pulling and swinging dough, *soba* and *udon* are made by rolling out even, thin sheets of dough, folding them over, then cutting them with a large sharp cleaver. This takes great skill, and in some specialist restaurants, the noodle master works at a shop window giving passers-by a glimpse at his craft.

The cook takes a handful (usually 40 to 42 noodles per serving), and puts them into a briskly boiling pot of water. Once the water reboils, cold water is added, and when this reboils too, the noodles are ready. *Soba* noodles need to be chewy, al dente. *Udon* can be softer, yet still "offering resistance to the teeth." The hot noodles are slipped into a warmed bowl and garnishes added.

The bowls vary in shape, color, and decoration depending on the garnishes, of which there is a plethora, most with allusive names from folk mythology. The garnishes (and their mythical names) apply equally, whichever noodles are ordered: buckwheat or wheat. Thus, fox-style buckwheat noodles (*kitsune soba*) and fox-style wheat noodles (*kitsune udon*) will both come with the same broth and garnish, but different noodles.

Fox-style (*kitsune*) includes a cake of fried tofu, which foxes are reputedly fond of. Raccoon-dog-style (*tanuki*) will have bits of tempura batter: that sly creature, often called a badger in translated literature, has stolen the vegetables and fish from the tempura, leaving behind only the batter crumbs. Moonview-style (*tsukimi*) is the poetic name for a raw egg, which, as it cooks gently in the hot liquid, refers the diner to a classical theme of the moon peeping through clouds. *Namban* (southern barbarian) refers to slices of pork, chicken, or duck sautéed with slices of Japanese leek. Other garnishes have more prosaic names. In addition to these nationally known staples, regional specialties using local produce abound.

In the cold of winter, or the heat of summer, *soba* and *udon* can appear in other dishes. One such is the classic winter stewpot wheat noodles or *nabe udon*. A whole meal in a dish, it is a simmering concoction of vegetables, egg, meat, soup and wheat noodles (*udon*) in a stoneware pot that has been placed directly over the fire. It comes to the table furiously bubbling, so that it is hot enough to cook both the egg and the other ingredients. With the egg broken and stirred slowly into the soup, the soup becomes tinged yellow, with whitish streaks as in egg-drop soup. In summer, in contrast, cold drained *soba* are placed on a flat bamboo basket, garnished with strips of crisp, flavored laver sheets, and served with a cold dipping sauce based on stock, sweet rice liquor (*mirin*), and soy sauce. The only garnish necessary is finely chopped chives or green onions and some grated horseradish. Other local variants offer dipping sauces based on sesame paste with a light rice-vinegar sauce. Garnishes may include wild vegetables or chilled mandarin segments or even slices of raw fish, depending on the season.

Chinese-Style Noodles

Chinese-style noodles tend to be wheat-based, and as with the serving styles for the native Japanese varieties, a multitude of garnishes comes into play. They are served at a softer consistency than Japanese noodles, however, and the flavoring stock is different. For Chinese-style noodles, the stock is similar to that with which most American and European cooks are familiar, that is, made of pork bones, chicken, and vegetables. Because of the importance of well-flavored stock in both Chinese-style and Japanese-style noodles, the exact proportions of the basic ingredients and flavorings are kept secret by professional cooks.

Chinese-style noodles (*râmen*) are most commonly eaten in a bowl of soup. The noodles are pale yellow because of the potassium or sodium carbonate in the dough that gives *râmen* its distinctive texture and flavor. Unlike Japanese noodles, which are straight when dry, *râmen* are wavy. Popular garnishes are slices of flavored bamboo shoot, fresh bean sprouts, and thin slices of roast pork. Variations include fermented soybean paste (*miso*) flavoring and seafood garnish.

A popular variant of Chinese-style noodles is stir-fried noodles (*yakisoba*). The name of this dish is slightly confusing, because the *soba* in this instance does not refer to buckwheat noodles, but is a generic term for noodles. Wheat noodles are stir-fried in flavored oil and garnishes are added for extra flavor. The most common garnishes are fresh bean sprouts, red pickled ginger strips (a different and stronger, red-dyed ginger pickle than that used for *sushi*), sesame oil, garlic, soy sauce, and Worcestershire-type sauce. This is a very inexpensive dish, most commonly encountered on the streets sold from barrow stalls, and evokes for many Japanese memories of their student days. The unmistakable combination of Chinese, Japanese, and English flavorings is one that also wafts around food stalls set up during religious and secular festivals and fairs, at which these fried noodles are among the first to get sold out.

In summer, fine wheat or barley thread-noodles, or even transparent bean noodles, are lightly cooked then plunged into ice water. Usually served in chilled glass bowls with pieces of fresh, equally chilled garnishes such as peeled mandarin segments, hard-boiled egg slices, tomatoes and cucumbers, these summer noodles come with a light sweetish-savory sauce pepped up with hot Japanese mustard. Another chilled noodle variant is cold drained Chinese-style wavy noodles mounded with very thinly sliced strips of cucumber, fruit (sometimes canned cherries), and ham or Chinese-style roast pork, called "chilled Chinese" (*hiyashi chûka*).

Bread

Bread is commonly eaten at breakfast instead of rice or as a snack. There are several large commercial bakeries producing American-style white bread. Specialty bakeries make high-quality handmade breads of wheat or rye to European standards. Bakeries also make a variety of rolls and buns, both plain and with fancy fillings ranging from cheese and curry, to melon- and green-tea flavored.

MORE FROM THE FIELDS: THE SOYBEAN IN ITS MULTIPLE GUISES

The second most important source of food to the Japanese is the soybean. This versatile vegetable is prepared and consumed in manifold ways, and is one of the major foundations of Japanese cooking. The bean grows in a small hairy pod on a low (about two to three feet, or 60 to 80 cm, tall) annual bush. Each pod contains from one to five small fingernail-sized seeds. The pods and beans are green until harvest, but are then dried. Once dried the pod splits open easily to reveal the beige seeds. Soybeans also come in green and black.

There is one delicious alternative to be tried even before the pods have dried. In the summer, grocers display large bunches of green soy pods (*edamame*) in bunches. The pods are stripped from the branches and dropped into boiling salted water to very briefly blanch, no more than two to three minutes, depending on the beans' maturity. Their green color intensifies and, after draining, the pods are plunged into cold water to stop cooking and retain the lovely color. They are good served either slightly warm or chilled, with perhaps a scattering of more salt, with a frosty glass of beer or *saké*. To eat, the pod is brought to the lips, squeezed, and out pops one or more of the beans with a wondrous nutty sweetness and aroma, accentuated by the salty pod: like eating peanuts or popcorn, it is impossible to stop eating the beans. *Eda-mame* are also available frozen and ready to cook.

Eda-mame aside, most soybeans are allowed to ripen and dry in the pod and are then stripped, destined for one of three main uses: *miso* (discussed previously), soy sauce *(shoyu)*, and tofu, which we have all become accustomed to associate with most Asian cooking.

Soy Sauce

The best known of the soybean's products, soy sauce comes in many flavors and varieties. The two most common ones are plain soy sauce, which is brewed in enormous vats by specialist manufacturers, and *tamari*. Soy sauce brewing is, paradoxically, of relatively recent advent in Japan. Until the middle of the Edo period (1600–1868), the Japanese rarely used soy sauce. At this time, *miso* was the usual flavoring or a sauce made by skimming off the liquid from salt-fermented fish *(uoshoyu)*. Soy sauce has taken over *uoshoyu's* role since about 1750.

Kikkoman Bottle

In addition to flavoring during cooking, soy sauce is also a table condiment, used to add a deeper salty flavor to fish or pickles (but it is not considered proper to pour it over white rice in a bowl!). In *sushi* bars, a small dish of soy sauce (usually pre-mixed with stock to the owner's taste) is provided for flavoring the fish. One requires a certain adeptness to turn the *sushi* over, so that only the fish is moistened, leaving the rice white and intact. Once the rice touches the soy sauce, it would then crumble into individual grains. From this it is evident why *sushi* aficionados prefer their fingers to chopsticks.

In addition to soy sauce, which is used commonly for both cooking and the table, there is another related product called *tamari*, a specialty of Mie and Aichi prefectures. Unlike soy sauce, which is brewed with rice or other grain, *tamari* is brewed only with soybeans, a mold, and salt water. After a year's fermentation, the liquor is carefully collected by sinking a bucket into the fermenting vat, assiduously avoiding bringing up any of the soy solids. This collected liquid is *tamari*, a darker, thicker, and heavier sauce than regular soy sauce. Containing more complex and richer nuances of sweetness, flavor, and aroma than regular soy sauce, it is regarded as the forerunner of modern soy sauce. Its name comes from the way it is collected (*tamaru* means "to collect liquid"). Its use is exclusive to *sushi*, *sashimi*, and special dishes.

Japanese soy sauce is different in taste, aroma, flavor, and thickness from Chinese or other types of soy sauce. Japanese natural brewed soy sauce, which is readily available outside Japan, is lighter in color and flavor than the Chinese equivalent. It comes in light and dark varieties, the light being saltier than the dark variety. Non-Japanese soy sauces do not substitute well for the Japanese variety in cooking and flavoring.

Tofu

After soy sauce, tofu is probably the best known of all the soybean's children outside Japan. In appearance it resembles a block of soft white cheese, and tastes, on first impression, like bland cottage cheese. Tofu is in fact made very much like cheese. The bean is ground and its liquid extracted. The liquid, which is like milk (and is in fact often sold as soymilk), is coagulated with a souring agent. Gypsum (which makes up plaster of paris) is most common, but one can use vinegar equally well. The liquid soymilk soon begins to thicken. It is gently ladled into a wooden mold lined with cheesecloth. The watery whey runs out, and the remainder is pressed lightly into a cubic cake, again, very much like a cheese. Unlike cheeses, however, tofu must be eaten fresh. Tofu delivery bicycles still rush hither

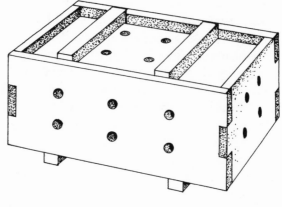

Tofu Press

and yon about Japanese neighborhoods. Purchasing handmade tofu straight from the maker, often a neighborhood workshop, is preferable to the standard homogeneity one finds in supermarket chains.

Despite the initial blandness, tofu has a naturally sweetish and wholesome aftertaste. Its silkiness (especially the silk-drained type) leaves a sensuous trail on the tongue, which allows it to be eaten almost as-is.

Plain Garnished Cold Tofu (Hiyayakko)
For each serving:

- 1/2 standard "brick" of tofu, preferably the silken (fine) variety
- 1 Tbs. *katsuobushi* shavings
- 1/2 tsp. finely minced shallots or spring onions
- 1/2 tsp. grated ginger

Drain blocks of tofu gently. Place each on dish with the garnishes mounded on top. Season with soy sauce.

Plain tofu is an element in a variety of dishes. Small cubes garnish *miso-shiru* soup. It is used as part of many other dishes as well. And tofu is so plastic, so willing to accept any flavor and to change its texture that a great many dishes incorporate some form of tofu that can fool the eye, and even the tongue, into believing it is eating meat or some kind of vegetable.

Tofu also comes in the form of deep-fried cakes called *abura age*. The brown deep-fried tofu cakes are hollow inside and form a convenient container for various fillings, the most common being *sushi*-flavored rice. The frying process in oil also transforms the tofu's flavor into something approaching roast meat. Blanched to remove excess oil and stewed in an aromatic mushroom broth, deep-fried tofu becomes "mock" duck.

Another soybean product comes in the form of sheets. When soybean milk is gently simmered, a film forms on its surface. The film, carefully lifted and drained, is a creamy-white sheet, *yuba*. Fresh, it is used to wrap around various fillings and the resulting roll simmered in flavored broth. *Yuba* sheets also store well when dried. Besides sheets, they are formed into various fanciful shapes, such as bows and small rolls. To use in cooking, the dried *yuba* sheets are simply soaked in water to rehydrate them and then added to stews, whose flavoring is readily absorbed. In this manner, *yuba* can be made to taste of almost anything, making it one of the most protean forms of protein. One popular food made from *yuba* is a sweet kind of *sushi*, called *inarizushi*, which Japanese people believe is a favorite food of foxes.

Inari, god of rice and of prosperity, is one of the most popular Japanese gods. The red-painted shrines to Inari, signified by red asymmetrical arches, can be found throughout the countryside and the towns as well. Before each such shrine are one or more fox statues. The fox is Inari's messenger. Foxes wander around throughout the night and report back to their master on human doings. Indeed, at the back of an Inari shrine is almost always found a small round hole, so that the fox might freely come and go.

Foxes, according to legend, are immensely fond of fried tofu, particularly in the form of *inarizushi*: simple balls of rice soaked in a light syrup and rolled in fried *yuba* sheets. Indeed, just around the fox hole, there is likely to be the remains of some *inarizushi* that someone has offered to bribe the fox to overlook an indiscretion or two.

Other Soybean Uses: *Natto*

One of the ways in which Kanto (the area around and north of Tokyo) natives tease their guests is by offering them fermented soybeans wrapped in straw (*natto*). A popular soybean product in the Tokyo metropolitan area and farther north, *natto* is relished for breakfast, mixed with freshly beaten raw egg and soy sauce, over steaming hot rice. Adding the de rigeur condiments of grated slippery yam (*tororo imo*) and crisp flavored seaweed strips would truly make an Edokko's (a Tokyo-born Japanese) day. For most non-Japanese and even many Japanese however, *natto* is an acquired taste. To make *natto*, steamed soybeans are treated with a kind of hay bacillus, wrapped in little straw packets, and left to ferment under a controlled temperature for several days. The resulting fermentation, which breaks down the complex soy bean proteins and makes them easier to digest, also generates sticky threads among the beans. The beans taste slightly meaty, and their smell is akin to a rather overpowering cheese. *Natto* is also sometimes added to *miso* soups and can be requested as a filling for rolled *sushi* in some Tokyo *sushi* bars.

Soybeans are consumed in a number of other ways as well. Fresh soybean sprouts are available from any greengrocer. Soybean oil is one of the major cooking oils used in Japan. Soybean flour *(kinako)* is used to coat or flavor some rice cakes.

Other Beans

Besides their edibility and usefulness as manufactured foodstuffs, beans have two other qualities that attract the Japanese cook: color and texture. A range of beans—purplish red *azuki*, yellowish mung beans, green fava beans—are widely used. With colors ranging from bright grass green to deep black, beans are used to decorate or add a necessary seasonal color to rice or other dishes. Mounded and piled on a *shisô* leaf, a mound of red and yellow beans add a hint of late autumn, white beans, a hint of snow. Black beans can represent river pebbles. Moreover, as beans have different textures, they can be used to punctuate softer or harder foods to provide an accent. Quite often, one or two fava beans, or three or four soy beans might appear on their own as a separate side dish. These are invariably sweetened with cooking wine or sugar. The syrupy coating does facilitate picking the slippery little objects up with a pair of chopsticks.

A major (and delightful) use for the purple *azuki* bean is dark sweet bean paste *(an)*. Cooked and sweetened with sugar syrup (the traditional sweetener was made from malted millet), the beans achieve a dark purple color and a flavor that in some ways resembles rich chocolate. The most popular way of consuming *an* is with glutinous rice cake *(mochi)*. Glutinous rice cakes are either rolled in *an* or stuffed with it, rather like a jelly doughnut. In either case, accompanied by a cup of green tea, it makes an excellent snack. *An* comes in two versions: as a smooth, silky puree achieved by passing the soft beans through a fine sieve, thus leaving out the bean coats; or chunky style, with the occasional whole bean adding a surprising element of texture. *An* can also be made from white beans, and is then called *shiro* (white) *an* to distinguish it from regular dark purple *an*.

OTHER FIELD VEGETABLES

Japanese cuisine relies heavily on vegetables. Partly as a result of the adoption of Buddhism by the Japanese people in the sixth century C.E.,

the Japanese have evolved a complex and rich repertoire of purely vegetarian dishes in which a wide array of roots, fruit, seeds, leaves, bulbs, and
other parts of plants are used in imaginative and exquisite ways. Japan's
culinary way with vegetables is quite distinct from that of China, from
which Buddhism was borrowed, as well as that of Korea, the stepping
stone by which Buddhism came into Japan. Unsurprisingly, there is a vast
array of ways to prepare, cook, pickle, and serve them. The brassica family—cabbages, radishes, and turnips—are probably the most commonly
used. Other familiar vegetables are bean sprouts, carrots, tomatoes, potatoes, onions, and Japanese leeks. More exotic and relatively less well
known are chrysanthemum flowers and leaves (all chrysanthemums are
edible provided they have not been chemically sprayed), devil's foot root
(*konnyaku*), taro, burdock, and Japanese angelica. Over the centuries, native vegetables have been augmented by imports that have become natu-
ralized to become intrinsic parts of Japanese cuisine. Small purple
eggplants, tomatoes, and sweet and hot peppers have been adopted, as
well as young flax plants, potatoes, and European cabbage.

Chinese Cabbage

Chinese cabbage (*hakusai*), sometimes called Napa or celery cabbage in
the United States, arrived in Japan presumably with visitors from the
mainland. Its manifold uses are in one-pot dishes, soups, pickles, and
blanched salads (*hiyashi*). One delicious way of preparing this vegetable is
to quarter it lengthwise, cutting off the stem, and stew it briefly in stock
with pieces of fried bean curd (*agedofu*). It is raised in large commercial
hothouses and hydroponically, but almost every gardener will keep a small
patch of this useful vegetable. It is eaten raw, usually as a finely shredded
garnish, pickled in many ways, and cooked in stews and soup.

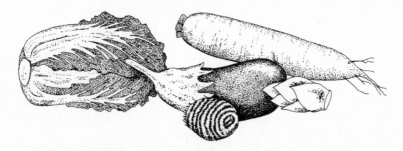

Chinese Cabbage, *Daikon*, Eggplant, Bamboo Shoot, Taro

Giant Radish

Giant radish (*daikon*) is a large white tubular root vegetable that appears in many forms. Grated and shaped into snow-white cones, *daikon* not only serves as a garnish for many dishes, particularly *tempura* and grilled mackerel, but as a condiment, its refreshing astringency and natural sweetness serving to neutralize any lingering oil or greasiness. Very fine, thread-thin white strips will accompany a *sashimi* platter. The young green first leaves of just-sprouted giant radish seeds add a delicious sharpness to hand-rolled *sushi* or to *sashimi*, particularly of fatty fish. A mound of julienne-cut *daikon* and dried persimmons cooked in *dashi* and vinegar makes a pleasantly astringent vegetarian dish.

Giant radish is also a regular component of slowly simmered stews and one-pot dishes, its crisp flesh readily absorbing and harmonizing flavors with other vegetables, seafood, or meat without losing its shape during long periods of cooking. Simmered and flavored with mushroom stock, the pale brown cubes, decorated with sesame sauce, are a common dish in Buddhist monastery cooking.

Dried (sometimes smoked) and then pickled in brine, bran, or *saké* lees, giant radish becomes crunchy *takuan*, undoubtedly the most common pickle served at home and at restaurants. Unfortunately, these days the deep natural yellow-brown color of true *takuan* is achieved with food dyes, and the subtle sweet smoky flavor of the natural product has been perverted by the addition of sugar. Undyed *takuan* (and other pickles) are available but take some persistence to track down.

Daikon's versatility reaches its height during festive food for the New Year. Its flesh is easily carved into bells, arrows, and other fortuitous symbols, and its color makes it the perfect partner with carrots for making the auspicious white-and-red salad.

Bamboo

In between the wild and the domestic, and sharing the qualities of both, is the bamboo. So important is bamboo to the lives and work of east Asia in general, and Japan in particular, that every Japanese hamlet had a common bamboo patch from which the villagers could cut bamboo in prescribed amounts at prescribed times of the year. Without bamboo, life would have been infinitely harder. And it is in the kitchen, no less than elsewhere, that bamboo shows its versatility.

As the source of utensils, bamboo is beyond compare. Chopsticks cut from a fresh bamboo stalk, one side still a bright green, add immeasurably to the experience of dining during the tea ceremony, where the feel of nature and the natural is so important. The texture of the walls of this giant grass, as well as the sweet grassy aroma that rises from the chopsticks, add to the pleasure of the food. Large columns of bamboo, easily cut, become trenchers for a variety of summer foods. Woven baskets of the outer covering of green or semigreen bamboo make baskets for the consumption of drained *soba* noodles just waiting to be flavored by a dipping sauce. And shaped bamboo becomes the whisk and the tea spoon used in the tea ceremony.

In spring, when giant bamboo (usually the variety *Phyllostachys heterocycla*) sprouts have barely broken from the ground, they are dug up and cut from the caulm, or underground bamboo matrix. The outer husk is carefully cut away, exposing the soft woody interior. The texture is somewhat like that of a carrot or turnip. Cut lengthwise, one can see a series of chambers that would evolve into the compartments of the hollow stem. Properly prepared by precooking in several changes of water to remove its bitterness, then simmered in stock, either whole or in strips, bamboo shoot becomes a versatile and delicious cooked vegetable. It is often served on its own, simmered gently in *dashi* and soy sauce, drained, then garnished with finely minced spring onions. Or else it might be part of a more elaborate dish of bamboo strips cooked with sweet potatoes and devil's foot root jelly *(konnyaku)* in a sesame seed sauce. Tiny bamboo shoots from a different variety of bamboo, quickly simmered with green soy beans, make an excellent side dish too, the colors, textures, and shapes contrasting pleasantly.

Eggplant/Aubergine

The Japanese eggplant is slightly different from the variety used in the West. Sweeter and (unlike its cottony Western relatives) firm-fleshed, it does not need presalting and draining to leach out any bitterness. Simmered in a little stock, it soon becomes meltingly soft and requires little more than a sprinkling of ginger, thick soy sauce *(tamari)*, and dried *katsuobushi* flakes to make a delicious dish. Another way of serving this vegetable is to grill round slices with a *miso* topping flavored with grated Japanese lime *(yuzu)* zest. Perhaps one of the most important elements in eggplant is not just its delicious taste and sensuous texture, but also the brilliant inimitable purple color of the smooth skin. This alone justifies this fruit an honored place at the Japanese table.

Tubers and Starchy Roots

Tubers and starchy roots have also found their way into the Japanese kitchen. Before the introduction of reliable high-yield grains such as millet and rice, soon after 200 C.E. or so, tubers such as true yams *(yamaimo)*, taro, and lily bulbs were the staple of the proto-Japanese peoples' diet. Modern Japanese people prize these tubers not only for their taste but also for their textures.

Taro (*Colocasi esculenta*) can be served on its own in many ways. Plain boiled and salted they become a snack elegantly called "silk robes" (*kinukatsugi*) for the ease with which their skins slips off the flesh. Or they can be served as part of "Southern barbarian duck": thin slices of duck or chicken, sautéed with leeks and soy sauce, mounded on plain boiled taro.

Yams (*Dioscorea japonica*) are a large (some are over six feet long) root that grows throughout the eastern Pacific. Pieces are used in soup and stews. A highly prized way of preparing mountain yams (*yamaimo*) is to grate the peeled raw root into a glutinous foamy astringent sauce (*tororo*) that is often added to complement breakfast offerings or soup. *Tororo* is almost flavorless, but its texture and astringency cleanses the palate after a large meal.

While taro and yams were native to the Japanese islands, or were introduced prehistorically, white potatoes and sweet potatoes (called, confusingly, yams in the southern United States, but bearing no botanical relation to the true yam of the genus *Dioscorea*) were introduced from the New World after the arrival of the Spanish and Portuguese in the sixteenth century. Both are widely cultivated in Japan today, and in the eighteenth and nineteenth centuries, sweet potatoes were the staple food of many poor farmers in central and southern Japan. Sweet potatoes were also the mainstay during periods of austerity, such as during and immediately after World War II.

FOOD FROM THE ORCHARDS: FRUIT

The Japanese love fruit, and, in fact, the word used today for cakes and candy was, in the Heian period (794–1185), used for fruit. Perhaps the most beloved fruit is the mandarin orange (*mikan*), and large orchards cover many of the temperate areas in Japan. There are also several unique varieties of grape developed from American species, from the tiny-berried, intensely sweet Delaware to choice plum-sized seedless Kyôho. Apples, persimmons, Asian pears, watermelon, melons, strawberries, and exotic fruit such as loquats are common and have been eaten by the Japanese for centuries. Continuous agricultural improvement has resulted in new varieties such as Mutsu and Fuji apples, crisp Twentieth Century Asian pears, the super-sized seedless Pione grape, and, a gift-giving novelty, conveniently square watermelons.

Most fruit is eaten as snacks, and in the summer, most homemakers will quickly quarter, seed, and peel a fruit to offer to guests. Fruits are sold in small mounds or baskets by greengrocers, and it is as small mounds of four or more fruits that they are offered to the deities at temples and shrines. Imported fruits are highly prized, ranging from bananas, mangoes, and pineapples from central America and Southeast Asia, through exotic fruit such as mangosteens and lychee.

FOOD FROM THE MOUNTAINS: FUNGI AND MOUNTAIN GREENS

Mountains have traditionally been places of mystery in Japanese thought. They were the abode of goblins and witches, who, though dangerous and unpredictable, could also provide tenacious and bold people with gifts and power. They were also the abode of the gods, and therefore a source of health and prosperity. Wild, or "mountain" vegetables therefore have an important place in Japanese cuisine. They are sought after and have been a traditionally important foodstuff because they are associated with well-being and health, and no less, because of their unique flavors and textures.

Precedence in the wild foods stakes must be given to mushrooms. Japanese farmers have domesticated many varieties for generations. Fungi constitute a major agricultural crop. Of about 180 known edible Japanese fungi, about 10 are widely cultivated commercially, and some are known outside Japan. Perhaps the most well-known is the brown, thick-fleshed *shiitake*, widely available all year round, fresh or dried. It is a component of soups and stews, is grilled and eaten on its own, and serves as a garnish for other food. *Shimeji*, *enokitake*, *hiratake*, tree ears, *nameko*, *maitake*, and champignon mushrooms are also common. Supplementing the cultivated fungi are those collected from the wild.

The most notable of all Japanese fungi is the pine mushroom (*Armillaria edodes*, in Japanese, *matsutake*) avowedly the most delicious and aromatic of all. This fungus has only recently been successfully raised commercially. The choice *matsutake* is the Japanese counterpart of the European truffle. Intensely flavored, these small, long-stemmed mushrooms grow only on certain species of pines in the hilly areas of central Japan. Cut from the ground, they are quickly grilled with a scattering of salt or sprinkled with *tamari* and Japanese lime (*yuzu*) and promptly eaten. Fortunate owners of tracts of wild land where pine mushrooms are known to grow will go out hunting for them in the fall equipped with little more than a bottle of *saké* and a net-topped brazier. Although the earthy aroma of the fungus per-

Matsutake

meates the cool air, it takes an experienced eye to spot the brown caps of
the pine mushrooms well camouflaged under piles of leaves. The locations
of these prized fungi are guarded zealously by collectors, in much the same
way as truffles are in France and Italy, and as with truffles, the price of *matsutake* is exorbitant, and a small specimen with its cap still unopened can
easily fetch $30 for an ounce. In Kyoto, mountains on which *matsutake*
flourish are often briefly leased by exclusive restaurants as venues for autumn gastronomic parties. Course after course of dishes featuring the
revered fungus are served al fresco to clients prepared to pay steeply for
the privilege of enjoying the *matsutake* as soon as it is picked. Korean- and
Chinese-grown *matsutake* at reasonable prices are now available, but their
flavor and texture do not compare.

In rural town markets, farm women set up stalls to sell assorted wild
mushrooms they have just collected. Coral red staghorn mushrooms vie
with coal-black fungi that look like tangles of black string. There are giant
white plates similar to the European chicken-of-the-woods and numerous
others. These wild fungi benefit from the simplest treatment: a quick
grilling or cooking in simple stock. This preference illustrates a major
principle in Japanese food. Most natural foods, particularly those that
come directly and unmeditated from nature, benefit from the least possible handling.

Mountain vegetables (*sansai*) are the other treasures brought back by
(mostly women) plant hunters. The list of available foodstuffs from the
forests and wild places of Japan is enormous, the subject of numerous
books. The stems of giant coltsfoot (*fuki*) are gathered, peeled, and parboiled to make pickles or preserves by slow cooking with soy sauce and
sweet rice liquor (*mirin*). Fiddlehead ferns are treasured for their silky-
crisp texture, and after soaking in lye water to leach out bitterness, are

fried in a light *tempura*-style batter or quickly blanched in broth. Wild lily roots are much sought-after in salads dressed with rice vinegar (*sunomono*); the crisp bulbs have been a staple of hunter-gatherers in Japan for at least 50,000 years. Table 2.1 summarizes the most common of the mountain vegetables.

Although some of these wild vegetables have now been domesticated and grown commercially to make them more widely available, it is the un-domesticated strong taste of these greens—whether astringent, sour, bitter—and their texture, form, and color that are prized. Most contain alkaloids and other plant chemicals that are beneficial to health, but there are a few that contain mild poisons or skin irritants. Pretreatment of these slightly toxic vegetables by soaking in lye and several changes of water is necessary. Despite some wild vegetables' year-round availability, *sansai* are still regarded as harbingers of spring. The greatest variety and quantity of mountain vegetables are found in Akita and Yamagata in Northeast Honshu's snow country, as well as other snow-bound regions in Gifu, Nagano, Toyama, Niigata, Gunma, and Fukui prefectures.

Two important vegetables that originated in the wild, and whose wild varieties are in much greater demand than their domestic counterparts, are burdock root and devil's foot root (*konnyaku*). Burdock is a thin root, slightly woody and crunchy like a carrot. Peeled, it is cut "pencil-wise," that is, into julienne-like sections, and lightly poached into a chewy vegetable with an earthy flavor. Devil's foot root requires lengthy preparation. It must be soaked in lye water (or, in the traditional method, ashes) to ex-

Table 2.1
Wild ("Mountain") Vegetables

	Latin Name	Part Eaten	Common English Name
fuki	Petasites japonicus	bud	coltsfoot or butterbur
itadori	Polygonum cuspidatum	bulb	Japanese knotweed
junsai	Brasenia schreberi	shoot	water shield
katakuri	Erythronium japonicum	young leaves	dogtooth violet
kogomi	Matteuccia pennsylvanica	fiddlehead	ostrich fern
nanohana	Brassica napus	bloom	rape and related plants
ôbagibôshi	Hosta sieboldiana	buds	plantain lily
okahijiki	Salsola komarovii	leaves, stems	saltwort
seri	Oenanthe javanica	young leaves	Japanese parsley
tampopo	Taraxacum platycarpum	young leaves	dandelion
taranome	Aralia elata	shoots	angelica tree shoot
tsukushi	Equisetum arvense	young shoots	field horsetail, mare's tail
udo	Aralia cordata	stems	Japanese angelica
warabi	Pteridium aquilinum var latiusculum	crozier	bracken
yomogi	Artemisia indica, Artemisia princeps	young leaves	mugwort, wormwood
zenmai	Osmunda regalis	young shoots	royal fern

tract a jelly from the root. The resulting gray speckled hard jelly is almost completely flavorless. It will readily adopt any flavor and is completely lacking in calories: it is desirable solely because of its texture and ability to absorb and retain other flavors and colors.

FOOD FROM THE SEA

The sea is and has been critical for the Japanese diet. The sea is the source of most protein in the Japanese diet and it provides fish, seafood, and even vegetables. Freshness is prized, though over the centuries, the Japanese people have also developed many innovative ways of processing seafood.

Seasons and Freshness

Fish and seafood, perhaps more than other food, must be eaten in the proper season. Most people are aware that one can only eat oysters in months with an 'r' in the name. This ensures that during the breeding season (May through August) when the oyster's flesh is inedible, and sometimes dangerous, it will not be consumed. But a variety of factors, including breeding season, temperature, and the activities of the fish or other seafood in question affect the flavor. Over the centuries, Japanese cooks have devised very accurate tables that indicate the time (*shun*) during which the fish (or other food) is at its peak and should be consumed. Modern freezing methods have made many fish available outside their season. Even if frozen immediately following being caught in *shun*, a fish can lose many of its special characteristics. Table 2.2 provides a guide to the *shun* of some popular fish and other foods from the sea. A full list would cover an entire chapter. It is well worth remembering, however, that this table applies to the seas around Japan: the same fish or other seafood is likely to have a different *shun* off the coast of North America.

Even though freshness is the ideal, before the modern era of refrigeration, Japanese in inland places rarely had access to fish. Japanese merchants and fishermen developed a number of ways—pickling (the origin of *sushi*), drying, fermenting—to keep fish edible for long periods and to transport it inland. Larger fish—salmon, cod—are salt-dried in steaks. Medium-sized fish—mackerel, herring, saury, and smaller salmon—are split, salted, and dried whole. Sardines, sole, and herring are dried whole. Small fish such as whitebait and small sardines are often threaded on straw ropes and dried in rows. Tinier fish might be dried for use in flavoring

Table 2.2
Selected Fish Seasons in Japan

English Name	Japanese Name	Shun
Angler Fish	ankô	November–February
Ark shell	akagai	December–March
Bonito	katsuo	April–June
Cod	tara	November–February
Conger eel	hamo	June–October
Halibut	hirame	November–February
Herring	nishin	April–May
Mackerel	saba	May–June, September–October
Oyster	kaki	November–February
Pomfret	managatsuo	October–January
Salmon	sake	November–December
Saury	sanma	September–October
Sea bream	tai	October–April
Sea urchin	uni	November–August
Squid	sumi-ika	October–February
Sweetfish	ayu	June–August
Trout	masu	March–April
Tuna	maguro	November–February
Yellowtail/amberjack (mature)	buri	December–February
Yellowtail/amberjack (young)	hamachi/inada	May-July

stocks or as garnish for *misoshiru*. Some small sardines are dried in a compressed mat called *tatami iwashi*, their shapes calling to mind the blocks of *tatami* mats that floor traditional homes. Seafood such as scallops, squid, and abalone, and most seaweeds are dried, or sometimes dried and smoked.

Fish

Japan has been extremely fortunate in the matter of fish and seafood. Stretching from cold subarctic to warm tropical seas, the coastline is full of large and small bays, many of them shallow. The Inland Sea (*Seto-nai kai*) provides a calm haven for fishing fleets in its many bays. A major current, the Kuroshio, swings past Japan's coastline, bringing annual migrations of bonito, herring, salmon, and whales.

For all of these foods, there are numerous ways of preparation. Whether eaten raw, broiled, pickled, fermented, or stewed, the same principle applies: freshness and appropriateness to the season wherever possible. Simplicity is always best. Japanese cuisine has a niche for all fish caught in Japanese waters. Over the years, the list of most desired fish has changed, particularly as certain fish species have become rarer, or more common.

For example, tuna today commands enormous prices (a large bluefin tuna, the most desirable fish for *sashimi*, will net a fisherman anywhere in the world around $20,000). In the Edo period, however, it was considered a low-class fish, and the upper class *samurai* would rarely eat it. Salmon too, which is considered a staple by many Japanese today, and which is eaten salt-grilled for breakfast by millions, was considered a fish not worth catching except for its roe until after World War II.

The demand for freshly caught fish, it has to be noted, has had a disastrous effect on marine ecology. Some desirable species have almost been wiped out, and much of the demand (and the predation) has come from the insatiable Japanese market. Cod, tuna, and even some species of squid are now rarely found off Japanese shores. Japanese fishing boats have ventured into the oceans of the rest of the world, often denuding them as well. Particularly injurious (and, in many ways, self-defeating) is the consumption of roe. The ruby glow of salmon roe, the citrus yellow of herring roe are as attractive to the eye as they are to the taste buds, but each bite represents fewer breeding fish.

The list of fish that the Japanese eat is too long to reproduce here. Some of the most desirable pelagic species are familiar outside Japan as food fish. Tuna, of course, is most often eaten as *sashimi* or *sushi*, or, more rarely, broiled. Tuna meat can come as regular "red" meat, or as the more highly desired *tôrô* (fat belly), which is softer and more flavorful due to the surrounding flavor-carrying fat cells. Salmon, in contrast, in the past was rarely eaten as *sashimi*, but now has become popular, largely as a result of the widespread desirability of smoked salmon. One fish that is rarely eaten by anyone but the Japanese is puffer fish (*fugu*), which is very highly prized, particularly the tiger puffer fish (*torafugu*). The attraction of the puffer is not solely its wonderful taste. Its translucent flesh is sliced very thinly and served as a wonderful *sashimi*. Its fins and head, when cooked in a *saké*-laced stock, are eagerly awaited. But it is also much desired because of the frisson of danger associated with its preparation and consumption. It contains tetrodotoxin, a deadly poison produced by a bacterium that has colonized the fish's tissues. The poison is concentrated in the liver, which cannot be sold in Japan. Specialist cooks, who undergo an arduous training period of several years on top of their regular training as cooks and who require a government license, are the only ones allowed to prepare this delicacy. Specialist restaurants, advertising with dried puffer fish outside the premises, their licenses prominently displayed, make sure the food is safe. Part of the thrill, particularly for male diners, is the danger of dining with death.

Obviously, different preparation methods are used for different fish, depending on the quality of the flesh and the size. The same principles that apply to all other foods apply to preparing fish as well. Preference is given to absolutely fresh fish, in the form of *sashimi* and *sushi*. Light-grilling over charcoal or on a griddle also helps preserve the fresh flavors. A variety of simmered dishes, usually in stock, help show off certain fish such as *tai* to advantage. Finally there are many preservation methods that have moved from regional specialties to common delicacies.

Japan's rivers and lakes offer a plenitude of freshwater fish. The four most popular are trout (*masu*) introduced from North America in the twentieth century and eaten grilled or sometimes in the form of lightly pickled *sushi*; sweetfish (*ayu*) tasting somewhat like a very delicate trout and prepared best as salt grill (*shioyaki*); carp (*koi*), which besides being admired for its strength and bravery, is considered very good eating when raised in running water, and is eaten often as *sashimi* or a simmered dish (*nimono*); and eel, which are raised in fishponds and are a great favorite during the hot midsummer days, most often served as grilled eel (*kabayaki*). Other freshwater fish abound, including loach (*dôjô*), which is sold live in pails by many fishmongers. These tiny fish are popularly cooked in a pot while still live. A large cake of tofu placed in the cookpot

Ayu ponds. Courtesy of the authors.

allows the loach some protection from the heat, and they burrow into the tofu, which, when cooked, is sliced and served, making an interesting textural contrast between the blandness of the tofu and the flavor and texture of the fish.

Seafood and Seaweeds

The Japanese eat a great variety of foods from the sea other than fish. Some of the more familiar favorites are various forms of crustaceans, seaweed, shellfish, squid, and octopus. Less familiar are sea urchins (*uni*, from the genus *Echinoidea*), sea cucumber (*namako*, *Cucumaria japonicus*), and sea squirt (*hoya*, from the genus *Ascidiacea*): acquired tastes, but once acquired, they can become a passion. Crustaceans of various sorts are in great demand for *sushi*, *tempura*, and other dishes. Perhaps the one in greatest demand is a Japanese crayfish (*Ise-ebi*) that has the flavor of a very delicate lobster. This is often served split and grilled, brushed lightly with *mirin* and soy-sauce, or simply salt grilled.

Octopus is in high demand as well. Not often sold raw, since the flesh can be rubbery unless treated properly, it is usually pickled in brine and light vinegar, and the tentacles sliced into rounds that make a wonderful *sushi* but that may also be found in simmered dishes (*nimono*). Squid of many species takes precedence, however. Freshly caught young squid make a wonderful *sashimi* or *sushi*, though unless it is absolutely fresh, the flesh can be somewhat astringent. Bits of squid can be batter fried in *tempura* and made into a variety of stews (*nimono*) and vinegared dishes (*sunomono*) or simply grilled in a soy marinade.

Two delightful ways of eating squid are from one of the stalls at a street festival or as *surume*. Cleaned squid, well dipped in a sweet sauce of soy, *mirin*, and sugar, are stuck on a stick and grilled over a charcoal fire, while being dipped repeatedly in the marinade. They are eaten like corndogs or candied apples, straight from the stick, and the smell of the grilling squid is almost as good as the sound of *mochi*-pounding and firecrackers for announcing a street festival. Much squid, however, is split and dried into *surume*. The whole animal, dried and flattened and cut into strips or fine shreds, is a wonderful accompaniment to beer and can often be found sold at railway stations as a snack for travelers. The best *surume* comes from bays in Hokkaido and Tohoku (northeastern Japan), but much today is imported from Korea and China where it is produced commercially for the Japanese market.

In a famous myth, Ôkuninushi, the deity who completed the creation of the land and who is worshipped as the deity of wizardry, was killed by his stepbrothers. Kamimusubi (one of the first deities to come into being) sent her handmaidens, Umugi-hime (Clam princess) and Kisagai-hime (Ark-shell princess) to revive him, which they did with shavings from their shells. This legend may well be a remnant of the lengthy time in Japanese prehistory in which shellfish, including the clam and *akagai* (the modern Japanese name for the blood clam, or ark-shell), were the staple of much of the population. Shellfish have always been viewed with particular relish among Japanese gourmets, and the best way to eat most of them, clams and ark-shells included, is as *sushi* or *sashimi* so that the full fresh flavor of the shellfish comes to the fore. Tiny cherrystone clams are also served as a common garnish in *misoshiru* soup.

Perhaps the most romantic shellfish of all is the abalone (*awabi*). This deepwater snail with a shell the size of a man's hand has delicious meaty, though muscular flesh. It is caught by diving into deep cold waters in the Inland Sea and the coast of the Japan Sea. Early on in prehistory it was discovered that women have much more stamina for this work than men, and thus were born women deep-sea divers (*ama*). It was not only their almost superhuman lung capacity that enabled them to stay underwater longer than men but the fact that they practiced their craft almost in the nude that contributed to their awesome reputation among the straight-laced Europeans writing about them in the nineteenth century. With little more than a pry-bar and face mask, they dive to extract a controlled number of the shellfish and bring them to the waiting boats on the surface. Though young women used to dive in the past, nowadays the traditional *ama* are restricted to tourist villages and are usually well-covered middle-aged women: educated younger women can find better-paying and less strenuous jobs on land. For the Japanese themselves, the abalone is romantic for another reason. Always in high demand, it was found early in history that it dried well. It became a custom to bring dried abalone as gifts for felicitous occasions such as weddings. Today, traditional giftwrap and related stationery (*noshigami*) are always printed with an icon of dried abalone.

With the exception of fish, the most important marine product is undoubtedly the many kinds of sea vegetables. The minority of these are gathered wild. For centuries, however, Japanese residents of the seashore have been farming various marine vegetables, two of which—kelp (*konbu*) and laver (*nori*)—are crucial for Japanese cuisine. Kelp is cultivated mainly in the cold Japan Sea waters off Hokkaido and northeastern Honshu. The long leathery strands are cut into short lengths, and then dried (for later rehydration) as an essential ingredient in the making of stock or eaten fresh as salad or in pot dishes (*nabemono*), salted as a snack, or even chewed raw. There are three named varieties whose use differs (for *dashi*, for drying, for eating raw), and they are sold under many different names, depending on the cut and use.

Laver (*nori*), a form of colony algae, is dried, compressed into sheets, and sold in bundles or small packs. Its major use is as a wrapping for *sushi*. Cut into thin strips, it is used as a garnish for various dishes such as drained noodles or chicken omelet on rice. Several varieties are eaten fresh in salads, as are other marine vegetables such as sea cabbage. Travelers along the coast of the Seto Inland Sea will pass miles of seaweed farms bathed in the warm waters of the many bays. Further inland, mirroring the racks in the bays, are tall drying racks, draped with seaweed, looking like black tattered rags fluttering in the wind.

Many other more exotic marine products are also eaten. Sea cucumber (*namako*), a kind of slug, is eaten freshly cooked. Sea squirt (*hoya*) is a seasonal delicacy. Looking somewhat like cactus fruit without the prickles, it is peeled, sliced, and served either as *sashimi* or, pickled and fermented in salt, as an accompaniment to drinks.

Processed Marine Products

A significant element of Japanese cuisine is the many varieties of processed marine products. The three major foods in this category are fish roe, fermented products, and fish paste.

Roe

The flavor of fish roe is the concentrated essence of the flavor of the mother fish (unsurprising since all animals invest heavily in their breeding). Roe is a major feature in Japanese festive meals. The glistening orange-red spheres of salmon roe are a delicacy throughout Japan. Where possible, particularly in those areas that border the cold waters that salmon prefer, it is served and eaten fresh. Each little gemlike bead pops against the palate with an almost audible sound, flooding the tongue with the essence of fresh salmon. It's not bad salted either, and areas far from rivers or the sea need to be satisfied with the salted variety, which is sold in glistening, jeweled clusters at the end of the year. A well-known delicacy of Hokkaido is a bowl of freshly cooked rice topped with a layer of fresh salmon roe (*ikuradon*).

Cod and herring roe are still traditional breakfast foods. Pink salted cod roe (*tarako*) with its tiny pinhead eggs is served in the bilobal sac in which it is naturally enclosed, as a breakfast dish, and particularly as part of New Year foods. In the past, cod roe (as with other salted foods such as whale "bacon") was artificially dyed a bright red, but the modern penchant for natural foods has thankfully put a halt to this execrable custom. Bright red cod roe these days is more likely to be colored from the copious dried chili flakes added to cater to traditional Kyushu-style taste. (The fondness for red-hot chili in some Kyushu dishes is unusual in Japanese cuisine and may be derived from either Korean or Iberian influences earlier in history.)

Herring roe ranges from pale to bright yellow and looks somewhat like a peeled citrus segment. Its texture is firmer and crisper than cod roe, being filled with slightly larger eggs that give an audible crunch.

Other types of roe are served too, usually fresh. Two are worth mentioning. Crab coral (*kaniko* or *kanimiso*) is highly prized. It is sometimes served on its own, but, since the quantities are small, is more often considered a prized part of a simple boiled crab, particularly the much sought-after hairy crab (*Erimachrus isenbeckii*, in Japanese, *kegani*) of Hokkaido. Sea urchin (*uni*) is not really roe, but the gonads of the sea urchin. The buttery yellow, smooth-textured mass is best eaten raw, perhaps with a drop of soy. It takes some getting used to when seen for the first time, looking like an uncooked egg-yolk. But the flavor is a concentrated taste of the sea, with pronounced sweetness and a lingering taste on the palate that demands another helping. It is often served as a *sushi* topping. The counterman cleverly molds a strip of *nori* to wrap around a bite-size ball of rice and fills the remaining top space carefully with a spoonful of sea urchin. The glossy, lacquer-black seaweed frames the egg-yolk yellow sea urchin splendidly. Like many other roes, sea urchin might be used to stuff slices of raw cucumber; soft and sweet, it goes well with the vegetable's crisp texture.

Roe has also become a desirable seasoning and flavoring agent in its own right. Thus, salted sea urchin is mixed into salad dressings or salted cod roe flavors a Japanese-style spaghetti sauce.

Fermented Fish Products

Preserved seafoods are usually eaten as drinking snacks, to increase alcohol intake, but are flavorful enough to be eaten on their own. Sea cucumber, small octopus, squid, and other marine life are fermented with salt into *shiokara*. The most delicious (and not for the squeamish) is *konowata*, which is made from the entrails of sea cucumbers. *Shiokara*, often served as an appetizer at bars, has chunks of flesh in a purplish sauce, all tasting strongly of the sea. It has the benefit of increasing both appetite and thirst.

The process of salting and fermenting fish is important to Japanese cuisine in a historical sense as well. Soy sauce was introduced into Japan from China in about the fifteenth century. It only became widely available in the late Edo period (about the eighteenth and nineteenth centuries). The most common dipping and flavoring sauce before that was a fish sauce called *uoshoyu* (literally "fish fermented oil") from small whole fish fermented in salt or a heavy brine for months. The resulting oil is skimmed off and bottled. Many Americans will probably know variations on this theme—Vietnamese *nuoc mam*, Philippine *patis*, Thai *nampla*—and it has even been a feature of the Roman diet as *liquamen* or *garum*. As a sauce it is salty and pungent, with a strong aroma of fish. Today it is a feature of Akita and other regional cuisines in northeastern Japan, much being made from a local fish called *hatahata*.

Processed fish also features in *kusaya*, a highly pungent preparation of fermented dried fish and seaweed. This is a favorite of working class people in Edo (traditional Tokyo). It has a limited appeal, because, as its name implies (*kusai* means "stinky") the smell can very well put off an unwary neophyte. In fact, *kusaya* is sold in small jars, which go a long way, as a garnish for breakfast rice or tea rice (*ochazuke*).

Fish Paste

More complex forms of processing fish for consumption are almost now never made at home. *Kamaboko*—a fish paste that, like tofu, is extremely versatile and malleable—is one of these. The flesh of white fish that are otherwise not in high demand—shark, for example—is ground, washed (to rid the product of excess oils and gluten), steamed, mixed with starch, then shaped. The most common shape is a half cylinder dyed pink on the outside. Fluted spirals, cylinders, and other shapes and colors are traditionally available. *Kamaboko* may be mixed with additional starch, egg white, and flavorings, shaped into cylinders, then grilled on a stick and basted with soy sauce for appetizing color and flavor. The cylinders resemble small bamboo tubes, for which they are named (*chikuwa:* bamboo rings). Many other local forms can be found, including cylinders of large diameter, usually sliced into finger-thick rounds; plain deep fried (*agekamaboko*); mixed with sweet potato and burdock shreds and then deep-fried into colorful patties.

Most varieties of *kamaboko* are rather bland, and only a subtle trace of marine origin remains in the flavor. The texture is like that of a mild hard cheese, but its versatility is such that it can be encountered in many popular dishes as a cheap form of protein. Shredded fish paste (*surimi*) so closely resembles flaked crab meat that it is largely manufactured today in Japan and worldwide, as mock crab legs. *Surimi's* versatility has spawned a number of other commercially significant mock seafood products, such as "giant" or "tiger prawns" or "lobster tails." Japanese technological ingenuity in transforming fish that would otherwise be considered "junk" fish into desirable retail products has been transferred to many countries. Suitably dyed to mimic the reddish tinge of cooked seafood surfaces and appropriately textured, these ersatz shrimp, crab, or lobster now satisfy the seafood cravings of those unable to eat the genuine article for religious or health (allergy, cholesterol) reasons.

In myth, *kamaboko* was invented by the Japanese empress Jingû after she came back from her conquest of Korea. (The story is recounted in a mythical and historical account of the foundation of Japan, the *Nihonshôki*.) Empress Jingû minced fish and starch and, pressing them like a sausage around a reed, grilled them over a fire. The name *kamaboko* might derive from *gamanoho* (cattail reed), which the original resembles. Whatever the origins of the food, there is good evidence that it was made as early as the Heian period (794–1185 C.E.). *Kamaboko* in its various forms is used in a variety of stews and one-pot dishes, as garnishes and additions to soups and noodles, as an essential element in seafood stews called *oden*, in the robust stews called *chanko nabe* that quickly put muscle and fat into budding sumo wrestlers and maintain the girth of established ones, and on its own as a healthy and low-calorie snack or alcoholic drink accompaniment, dipped into soy or miso sauce.

FOOD FROM THE PASTURE: MEAT AND MILK PRODUCTS

The traditional Japanese diet centered on cooked or pickled vegetables or vegetable products, especially those derived from the soy bean, and fish. This is still true to a great degree, but a third food ingredient has become extremely important: meat and dairy products. Among young Japanese in particular, hamburgers and hotdogs are as popular in Japan, some under familiar names, as they are in the United States. And though certain types of meat can be more expensive, they are often preferred to fish by younger Japanese (among other reasons, because of the absence of fish bones which are rather difficult to completely pick out with chopsticks, especially when whole fish are served).

The three most commonly available meats in Japan are chicken, pork, and beef, in the order of their frequency at the average Japanese table. Other types of meat are more rarely available. There are, for example, restaurants which specialize in horse meat, which is often eaten raw in thin slices known as cherry blossom *sashimi* (*sakura sashimi*) from its pink color. Overall, Japanese people eat less meat on average than Americans (and are probably healthier for it). Meat is treated with the same exquisite attention as other foods.

Beef dishes include a variety of stews (*nabemono*), variations on hamburgers, and a number of ways of grilling strips of beef to the diner's choice. Japanese preference is for soft beef, and thus, meat from Japanese cattle (*wagyu*) is considered by most Japanese (and many non-Japanese) to be the most flavorful. Beef variety meat is also popular, particularly among men. Mutton, imported largely from Australia and New Zealand, is often used as a substitute for the more expensive beef cuts. Most Japanese people profess a dislike for the strong smell of mutton, and this is effectively hidden in processed foods as various as hamburgers, sausages, steamed buns, and so on.

Pork has become very popular. So much so, that several dishes such as deep-fried battered pork cutlet (*tonkatsu*) have become national favorites. The influence of Chinese cooking, which uses many preserved meats such as sausages and ham, has helped as well, since in Japan, as in many other countries, Chinese food is often the preferred "second food" (in a similar analogy to English being the preferred second language in non-English-speaking countries). Pork features in a number of cheaper dishes, which are staples of quick food restaurants serving lunches to working people.

Throughout Japanese history, duck was often eaten, and chickens were raised for their eggs and roosters for cockfights. In modern Japan, of course, poultry is raised, as are pigs, on a commercial basis, and much of it is imported from abroad as well. Almost all parts of the chicken are used. The inner strip of tender fillet running under the breast meat, called *sasami*, is in highest demand. But breast and thigh meat, as well as the cleaned intestines, skin, and even testicles, are in demand for grilling on bamboo sticks in *yakitori*, and the minced meat is made into balls and grilled as well. Chicken is served in numerous other forms, as are duck and pheasant. Some smaller birds, such as sparrows, pigeon, and quail are often served in specialist *yakitori* restaurants.

Gender differences in food are common throughout the world. Among some simple hunter-gatherer tribes, women and men are required to eat, or avoid, certain foods at certain times. Some anthropologists have argued that this is an ecological and energetic necessity, ensuring allocation of fats, proteins, and starches to those who need them most (for example, lactating women, or warriors about to go to war). Gender preferences in food are much harder to explain in complex, technologically sophisticated societies, such as that of the Japanese. Women have a near-monopoly on sweet traditional foods (few adult men in Japan will admit to a liking for them). Men have a near-monopoly on certain kinds of meats (few women would do more than peer into the door of an establishment serving them). Of course, these differences are not airtight, but they do tend to persist.

Men in Japanese society are thus often dared by a friend or tempted by curiosity to consume one of the many forms of "exotic" meats. For example, *horumon* restaurants, which serve plain boiled offal/variety meats (liver, kidneys, tripe, lungs, sweetbreads, tongue) are extremely popular as drinking places that are largely unwelcoming to women. So great is the demand, that Japan remains the major customer for variety meats of the U.S. beef industry.

Other "exotic" meats are consumed as well, some of them clandestinely. Tiger meat, bear paws, snake, eagle, and monkey can be found at specialist restaurants in Japan. As many of these meats are illegal (e.g., tiger) they are not advertised, but those who know the right people can always find some. The idea that certain meats enhance masculinity is a common one throughout east Asia. In Japan, such meats are likely to be, at least partially, imports from the mainland, since both the cooking methods and the meats themselves owe much to Chinese influences, and less to the canons of Japanese cuisine. Nonetheless, many men consider it necessary—whether to demonstrate their wealth, to display and enhance their virility, or for belief in their healthy properties—to consume some of these foods. In rural areas many men will catch a viper in early spring, when the reptiles have just come out of winter torpor, and drown it in a bottle of *saké*. The liquor is then drunk throughout the year to enhance health.

Milk was never consumed in premodern Japan. Since World War II, however, milk products have become a staple of Japanese children's diets, and many younger adults retain a liking for these foods as well. The consumption of milk is fostered by the Japanese government, which provided milk for school lunches until some years ago. Another push to the milk market are sweetened milk products, notably milky coffee and tea, ice-cream, and particularly flavored fermented milk products. Many of these are made commercially by the application of one of the many tailored acidophilus bacteria. These produce sweet-sour drinks that are very popular among Japanese children. In recent years, Western cheeses have become popular as well. So much so that Japan has developed an indigenous cheese industry for cheese types such as Camembert that are liked by many Japanese people as a drinking food.

FLAVORINGS—SPICES, HERBS, AND FLAVORINGS

The main flavoring ingredients—stock *(dashi)*, soybean paste *(miso)*, and soy sauce *(shoyu)* have been discussed above. With these, and salt—preferably rough sea salt made the traditional way by evaporation—virtually all Japanese dishes can be made. To uneducated palates, this tends to make Japanese dishes seem bland at first. But these subtle flavor combinations incorporated in foods are punctuated and highlighted by the sharper flavors of a variety of herbs and spices, many of them unfamiliar to non-Japanese. Most of these are added not during the cooking itself, as they would be in non-Japanese cuisines, but as garnishes on the plate, to be added at the diner's discretion: either to the dish, or to a mere mouthful, immediately before eating. Adding herbs to traditional Japanese foods during the cooking process would subvert the essence of this food: the naturalness of the ingredients. The exception is pickled foods, wherein the aroma of certain herbs is allowed to permeate vegetables that, over the duration of the pickling, would lose their characteristic flavor, retaining only their crunchy texture, such as eggplant and cucumber. Most of these flavorings are fresh herbs, a few are dried spices. In the past, the spices were rarely processed beyond drying, grinding, or grating; however modern freeze-drying technology has made available a few of the herbs, such as green perilla *(aojisô)*, Japanese prickly ash *(sanshô)*, and Japanese citron peel *(yuzu)*. The remainder of this section covers the major flavorings.

Cayenne Pepper

Takanotsune (eagle claws), a semihot variety of Cayenne pepper, contradicts the claim that Japanese food is never hot. A favorite on the southern island of Kyushu, it is often mixed with sesame seeds and salt and used as a table condiment for such dishes as *soba* or Chinese noodles. The bright red, pointy peppers (somewhat like jalapeño peppers) whose look (and bite) reminded people of a bird-of-prey's claws, are not to everyone's taste.

Ginger

The ginger family has contributed a great deal to cuisines in east Asia, and Japanese food is no exception. Raw ginger root is grated and used to enhance the tastes of many foods, particularly *tempura*, where it is used to flavor the dipping sauce. *Myôga* (*Zingiber mioga*, a botanical relative of ginger) buds and shoots are used as a garnish to soups and to various other

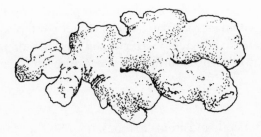

Ginger Root

dishes, where the bright pink bud adds a sharp gingerish flavor. Pickled young ginger shoots (*gari*), whose green-tipped lengths start from a pink base, are often used in summer to add a pungent heat to summery dishes such as grilled fish.

Japanese Horseradish

Japanese horseradish, or *wasabi* (*Wasabia japonica*), is a miniature, green, carunculated version of its Western relative. The flavor is also more delicate. Grated (and consumed immediately since it loses its pungency rapidly: some restaurants bring a piece of root and a grater to the table) it adds heat to *sushi* and *sashimi*. Difficult to cultivate even in Japan, it grows along the banks of swift-rushing, perfectly clear mountain streams. The powdered variety sold in shops and familiar to most people who have had *sushi*, is, alas, rarely made of real *wasabi*. Rather it is a mixture of dried western horseradish and mustard.

Mountain Ash

Yet another flavoring agent is found in the seeds (*sanshô*) and young leaves (*kinome*) of the Japanese mountain ash (*Zanthoxylum piperitum*). The seeds resemble Szechwan peppers in both shape and flavor, and are ground to a powder that is used to garnish fatty foods such as eel. The young leaves can be chopped or served whole. The taste is slightly peppery and very fragrant.

Perilla or Beefsteak Leaf

Perilla (*Perilla frutescens*, in Japanese, *shisô*) is a broad leaf that comes in purple (*akajisô*) and green (*aojisô*) varieties. They taste very much the same; the choice of leaf depends on the color desired. Chopped red *shisô* is used to flavor and help preserve *umeboshi* (salted dried plums). Fresh green *shisô* is often used as a bedding for *sashimi*, particularly for red fish such as *maguro* (tuna). *Shisô* often can be eaten on its own and is a common favorite in the form of *tempura*, where the basil-like flavor cuts through the oil.

Saké

Rice wine adds depth and aroma to foods. It serves the same function in Japanese cooking as wine does in non-Japanese recipes. Most cooks will use a *saké* of their own liking (which allows for the occasional nip), though the quality of the *saké* does not really matter (except, of course, for the cook's pleasure).

Salt-Pickled Plum

The dried salted plum *(umeboshi)* that accompanies many traditional Japanese breakfasts and may appear as well in a box lunch *(bentô)* is also used as a flavoring for dishes. The salty-sour taste of the pickle, in the form of minced flesh with its accompanying *shisô* leaves, can be used in a variety of ways, as a pickle, a garnish, or even a flavoring agent for stocks and simmered dishes.

Sesame: *Goma*

Sesame seeds, oil, and a paste somewhat like Middle Eastern *tahini* are used to flavor and garnish many dishes. The paste is used to make a thick sweetened sauce, as well as a slightly vinegary dressing for seaweed salads.

Seven Pepper Spice

Seven pepper spice (*Shichimitôgarashi*) is a mix of spices including *takan-otsune*, sesame seed, mustard, *nori*, hemp seed, poppy seed, and *sanshô*.

Umeboshi

These mixes vary in different areas. Sometimes called just *shichimi*, *Shichimitôgarashi* is commonly found as a condiment on the tables of noodle and *kabayaki* (grilled eel) restaurants, where the spicy mix helps cut the oily taste.

Sweet Rice Liquor

Sweet rice liquor *(mirin)* is produced by fermenting glutinous rice with potato liquor. It is used to round off many dishes, particularly pot dishes. It imparts a luster when reduced and thickened into a glaze, when it is used to flavor beans and other foods.

Trefoil or Japanese Chervil

A delicate, trilobate leaf (*Cryptotaenia japonica*), trefoil (*mitsuba*), also known as Japanese chervil, is used as a raw garnish in soups and stewed dishes. The herby, chervil-like flavor adds contrast to many foods.

CONFECTIONERY AND SWEETS

Near Shimbashi Station, in the center of Tokyo, is a famous tea-shop. It has been at that location for the past 300 years or so. At the close of the working day, after 5 P.M., there is usually a long line waiting outside for a space at the small tables. The shop itself has a modest, traditional barred-wood front. The wait takes more than an hour. Oddly enough, it consists exclusively of women.

Just as *saké* and organ meat are the province of men, confectionery sweets *(okashi)* are the province of women. In the Heian era (794–1185), the idea of eating fruit as part of a meal entered Japanese cuisine, as many other elements did, from China. Originally, the term *okashi* referred to dried fruit, most notably dried persimmons and jujubes (Chinese dates). Most native fruits were either insipid or sour: oranges *(daidai)*, apricots *(ume)*, and peaches *(momo)* could only be eaten when dried or processed. The varieties of fruit enjoyed today in Japan, including melons and watermelon, grapes, peaches, plums, persimmons, and many others, were Chinese and European imports that took centuries to get established.

In the meantime, the chefs of the Heian imperial court sought for substitutes for those with a sweet tooth. These they found in three main substances: natural sugars that occur in glutinous rice, sugars from malted grains, and *azuki* beans. Brought together, these have become the basis for Japanese confectionery (*wagashi*, in contrast to *yôgashi*, the word for West-

ern confectionery). By and large, women in Japan, and not men, are expected to have a sweet tooth, and few men will admit readily to a liking
for sweet things. *Wagashi*, generally speaking, can be divided into two categories, though the distinction between them is blurred. On the one hand
are the refined sweets invented by the imperial court chefs and since improved upon. On the other are simple sweet foods that comforted towns-
people and villagers. Japanese confectionery comes in three forms. Fresh
namagashi are made from freshly pounded rice and sweet bean paste. Semi-
fresh *hannamagashi* will keep slightly longer and are often made with a
firm gelatin extracted from seaweed *(kanten)* and sweet beans or sweet
bean paste. Dry *higashi* include sweet, sweet-salty, and savory rice crackers
(senbei) and *higashi* proper: a paste of rice flour and sugar, dyed and pressed
into tiny molds in the form of flowers. All of these confections are intended largely for snacks and for consumption during the tea ceremony,
where the sweet confection offsets the slightly bitter taste of tea. They are
rarely served as dessert to close a meal in the European manner.

Using little more than pounded glutinous rice *(mochi)* and bean paste
(an), chefs attempt to recreate the image, and often the flavors, of fruit of
the season. There are specific *okashi* for every season: a replica of a cherry
blossom, in pink-dyed *mochi*, neatly wrapped in a freshly sprouted and edible cherry leaf in the spring; or a sugar and kelp confection cut and dyed
orange-red to simulate convincingly an autumnal maple leaf.

Dry and semidry confections are still characteristic of Kyoto. Small tea
shops with rooms of wood and paper looking out onto a small pocket garden can still be found throughout the city, as they can be found in that
other capital of elegance, Kamakura. Confections are expected to change
with the season, and famous makers can still be found that have been in
business for hundreds of years.

Unsurprisingly, sweets were also attractive to lower-class people in traditional Japan, and an industry rose over the centuries to provide sweets
that were less refined, but no less delicious, for the less elegant people.
Here the word "sweet" is potentially misleading, as many of these confections are savory. The story goes that a poor priest begged a rich man at the
wayside for some of the rice balls the rich traveler was eating. The rich
man refused contemptuously, but after he had eaten his fill, he left some
of the stale ones he had from the previous day to the beggar. The beggar
carefully collected the stale cakes, and, in order to make them palatable,
dabbed them with some soy sauce and toasted them on a small fire. The
resulting crispness and savory taste so delighted him, that he set up a small
business making rice crackers.

Today there are literally thousands of types of cracker. They are sold in packets at supermarkets or from specialty stores that make one or two kinds on the premises. The vast majority are savory, flavored with everything from pedestrian soy sauce or sea salt, through laver sheets or flakes, to gold-leaf. To add to that there are also sweet crackers such as *koroke*, which are sweetened with molasses and malt.

Oshiruko, a soup made of sweet-cooked *azuki* beans, represents a class of sweets that do not occur in Western societies. The liquid is a deep purple, the texture of a *velouté* soup. One or two toasted *mochi* cakes floating in the soup complete it. The country version has beans floating in the liquid, the city version is completely smooth. Either way, this hot confection is a perfect antidote for a snowy day. It is traditionally served to those who have been participating in physical training, particularly in mid-winter when apprentices run naked to their local shrine before dawn during the coldest winter period (mid-January to mid-February).

One important rural confection must be mentioned because it has strong mythical and cultural connotations. Once upon a time, the story goes, an elderly couple prayed for a son. They were pious and poor, so one day the deities sent a giant peach down the river to them. Inside they found a bouncing baby boy they called Peach Boy. He grew in strength and one day asked his parents why they lived in that wild place. They told him that a group of demons had been ravaging the land, and they had come to their hidden hut to live free of depredations. Momotarô, the Peach Boy, promptly made himself a wooden sword. His mother provided him with a banner saying "First in Japan" and with a box of *kibidango*, rice dumplings rolled in millet flour *(kibi)*. Along the way to the demons' castle he fell in with a monkey, a dog, and a bird. To each he gave some of the wonderful dumplings, and each in turn pledged loyalty to him. With their aid he subdued the demons, who, in true Japanese fashion, promised to reform. *Kibidango* remind Japanese children to this day to strive to be the best they can be.

Not all confection in Japan is of Japanese origin. Among the many *hannamagashi* that have become extremely popular is a simple sponge cake known as a *kasutera*. The word, and indeed the confection, is of Spanish or Portuguese extraction. *Kasutera* (from *castillo*, Spanish for "castle") have been made in Kagoshima, Nagasaki, and Hirado where the Iberian influence was strongest since the sixteenth century. It is considered a "famous local product" that tourists are expected to bring home from their travels in that area. *Kasutera* also point to the popularity of Western confections in Japan. Thousands of bakeries produced millions of cakes ranging from cheesecake of the finest consistency to cream cakes whose lusciousness rivals those of Vienna and Venice. In fact, so good are the Japanese at making Western cakes, that several chains have opened branches in Germany.

A great many other sweets produced in Japan are consumed, particularly by children. In many cases, these confections—Japanese versions of common candy bars, bubblegums, toffees, and other candy—have supplemented the less sweet Japanese versions.

DRINKS

The two poles of Japanese drink are the paradigms represented by tea—sober, elegant, refined—on the one hand, and *saké*—intemporate, convivial, and licentious—on the other. Not all tea drinking fulfills all of these qualities, nor does all alcohol consumption. Between these two poles of tea and *saké*, there are many specific drinks and events that characterize specifically Japanese drinking.

Alcoholic Beverages

The most characteristic Japanese drink is of course *saké*, also called *nihon-shu* (Japanese alcohol, as opposed to foreign—grape- or other fruit-

Koji. Courtesy of the authors.

or cereal-based—alcohol). *Saké* is made from rice and comes in two general varieties: dry, which is drunk at blood temperature or even warmer, and sweet, which is generally drunk cold, often with a lick of salt on the cup rim, somewhat like tequila.

A quantity of high-starch rice is steamed, then, when cool, treated with a bacillus (*Aspergillus oryzae*) and a yeast. The resulting "mother of *saké*" is then introduced to a larger mass of cooked rice which has been mixed with pure water. The wort is fermented for three weeks or so, preferably in winter (the best *saké*, like the best beers, is marked by month, and sometimes day, of production). Once the brewmaster decides the wort is ready (at about 22 percent alcohol by volume), the wort is poured into large flax bags. Stacks of these bags are placed in a press and squeezed. The resultant mother liquor has a wonderful aroma and flavor, something like distilled essence of peaches. The liquor is then watered down to legal alcohol percentage levels (16.5 percent for standard, 17 percent for first class, 17.5 percent for premium class *saké*). allowed to rest briefly in cedar barrels, then decanted into traditional-sized 1 *shô* (1.8 liter) bottles. The *saké* should be drunk as soon as possible, as it tends to lose its flavor very quickly.

In the 1980s, *saké* lost ground to other drinks: beer for men, white wine for women. However, it has since made something of a comeback with the introduction of dryer, lighter types of *saké* that attract younger people, and, most importantly, with the introduction of a refined type of *saké* that does not leave the drinker with a foul morning-after breath: the major complaint of young women against *saké*.

Saké *and* Saké *Etiquette*

As in any other culture, alcohol consumption has a ritual of its own. Drinking starts with a full, almost overflowing glass or *saké* cup (*sakazuki*). Drinkers raise the glass or cup, usually with the elbow out to the side, and sip the liquor after a toast that ends with "*Kampai!*" ("Empty cup!").

A major element in group drinking etiquette is that no one fills their own cup: it is the job of one's neighbor, which of course leads to some serious and convivial drinking as neighbors fill one another's cups. Most older and more traditional drinkers will also ensure that they take three sips from a cup of *saké*, as a form of thank-you to the Shintô kami. And, dedicated *saké* drinkers rarely eat rice while drinking. Indeed, no knowledgeable *saké* drinker will have any form of rice with their *saké* (the best *sushi* shops ban *saké* altogether) because they hold that rice and *saké* negate one another's flavors. The majority of people do, however, relish

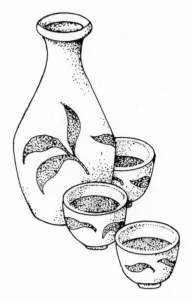

Saké Flask and Cups

their food with *saké*, and vice versa. A distinct category of food, termed *saké no sakana* (*saké* dishes), is meant to be eaten with *saké* or other alcohol.

While some unfussy drinkers drink their *saké* out of water glasses, proper *saké* utensils come in three different forms. Dry *saké*, which is drunk warm, is usually served from a ceramic flask holding between 180 and 300 ml of liquor (*tokkuri*). Though mass-produced ones abound, handmade ones from famous craftsmen, potters, or kilns are easy (and sometimes expensive) to come by. Flasks are often sold in pairs, with matching sets of five *sakazuki* (wine cups), not all of which need be the same size. Glaze, shape, decoration, and size are a function of the buyer's taste and preferences.

Cold *saké*, which is normally sweeter than dry, is usually served directly from an opened cedar barrel into box-shaped cups fashioned of closely planed cedar wood, the rims dipped into rough salt. The liquor is then redolent of the smell of fresh cedar, and the sweetness of the drink is cut by the salt. Festivals are a good time to try this drink. The barrel top is smashed with great hilarity, and a bamboo dipper is used to splash quantities of drink into the cups.

The wedding cups used in the formal toasts during the wedding ritual are of a different sort. They are pedestalled cups made of thinly carved wood (the cup may be paper thin at the edges) and lacquered in red and gold. Such cups are also generally used for the New Year toast.

Beer and Beer Etiquette

Huge quantities of beer are now the norm in most parties, and it is the drink of choice for toasts. Most good drinking places or bars will provide ice-cold beer from a frosted mug in summer. And the native beers—Asahi, Kirin, Sapporo, and Ebisu—have become export items known worldwide. Most Japanese beers are of the lager or pilsner type, made with barley and rice, typically very light and refreshing. Dark beers and English ales have been far less popular. Some breweries, however, stick closely to European traditional methods, making strong European-type traditional ales of barley, hops, and water.

Beer drinking is far more straightforward and less encumbered by ritual than *saké*: any glass will do (happily the nasty and barbaric habit of drinking beer straight out of the bottle is not widespread in Japan), preferably a large glass liter stein. Drinkers pour for their neighbors. Talking, toasting, and changing seats are all encouraged.

Wine, Shôchu, and Umeshû

The Japanese people, like people everywhere, have adjusted to and adopted a wide variety of other alcoholic drinks. Wine has become popular, particularly among young women who dislike the aftertaste (and, so it is said, foul morning-after vapors) engendered by *saké*. The arrival of Beaujolais Nouveau on the third Thursday of November is awaited by many in Japan with as much fervor as in New York, and Japan has often in the past been able to secure a large share of this wine.

Shôchu and *umeshû* are two other alcoholic drinks that many enjoy. The first is a fiery distilled liquor made from sweet potatoes, somewhat like vodka. It is a staple of working-class bars (though its popularity among white-collar drinkers has grown) and of late night snack bars, particularly barrows that sell hodgepodge stews with assorted seafood and vegetables (*oden*). Plum wine or *umeshû* is generally made at home, each family having its own recipe. Large green Japanese *ume* (the same fruit, *Prunus mume*, used for salt pickling, except gathered much earlier) and an equal weight of rock sugar (decreased accordingly for a dryer result) are immersed in a jar filled with white liquor (30-proof grain alcohol) and allowed to rest for a year or more. Particularly if left to mature for several years, the concoction becomes a smooth, plum-flavored liqueur that most

Japanese drink mixed with soda water for a refreshing and not very alcoholic drink in the summer, or neat as a digestive in winter. The remaining soused fruit are also a treat.

Drinking Foods

Drinks, particularly beer and *saké*, are usually accompanied by *otsumami* (snacks). The range is wide and probably infinite. It might be little more than a few pieces of cut cucumber and a dip of country-style, barley-fermented *miso*. It might be strips of dried squid *(surume)* or dry, flavored bite-size seaweed squares. Sometimes it is nothing more than a mix of peanuts and soy sauce and chili-pepper glazed crescents of rice crackers (euphemistically named "persimmon seeds" or *kaki no tane*). Or it can be elaborate snacks of *sashimi*, dried fish, or grilled tidbits. But the crowning drink accompaniment of all are *eda-mame*. These bright green, fresh-picked soybean pods are blanched in boiling salt water, then eaten by hand, the pods discarded like empty wine skins, the rich soft green seeds and salt washed down with beer or *saké*.

SOFT DRINKS

The soft drinks introduced by European traders to Japan in the nineteenth century are still available. Cider *(saidâ)* and lemonade *(ramuné)* are both drinks made from lemon and lime flavorings, sugar, and carbon dioxide–charged water. They have been joined by hundreds, perhaps thousands, of other soft drinks, ranging from natural juices through purely artificial power drinks. *Ramuné*, in its peculiar Victorian era–derived bottle, has become more popular, part of the rural nostalgia boom that has occupied Japan since the nineties. Of course, American brands, notably Coca Cola, are ubiquitous and taste very much like they do anywhere else. But drinks with a specific Japanese touch can be found as well. Perhaps the most interesting is Calpis, a drink derived from the fermentation of milk by lactobacilli. This is sold in oriental shops in the United States as well, albeit under another name, Calpico. Calpis has a sweet, slightly tart flavor and is considered beneficial to health, along with some other milk-derived fermented drinks such as Yakult.

The average Japanese would more often than not drink barley tea *(mugi-cha)* in the summer. This is a bland but refreshing drink made by steeping ground roast barley in hot water, which is then allowed to cool; this beverage continues to be drunk in many households.

Coffee

The drink that has had the most recent impact on recent Japanese drinking habits is coffee. Yet another popular import from the Meiji period (1868–1912), coffee was introduced to Japanese guests by Dutch traders who maintained a trading depot at Deshima in Kyushu. The Japanese visitors did not like it much.

Coffee was merely a curiosity until the early nineteenth century when Japanese sailors and soldiers in Hokkaido started needing it as a cure for dropsy. In the late nineteenth century, it was adopted by the Japanese elite along with other Western fashions. But coffee really took off in the 1950s when milk coffee, particularly the varieties sold in cans, became popular after the invention of refrigerated vending machines. Today, coffee has become one of the most, if not the most, common drink in Japan. In addition to vending machines, coffee is served in most offices and homes to visitors and others alike, and in coffee shops.

Japanese coffee shops are an institution that is always worth exploring. Given the small size of most Japanese homes, coffee shops have become public sitting rooms, where businesspeople, friends, and lovers can meet and spend hours. While many coffee shops are part of large chains, many others are run by their owners to suit their own preferences and tastes. There are rock coffee shops, classical music coffee shops, comic book (manga) coffee shops, and others catering to almost any possible ambiance. Most coffee shops stock an impressive array of beans from all over the world and will grind to order. Some coffee shop owners carry their meticulousness with the beans to extremes by roasting the beans themselves just before brewing. Though the coffee shop industry is in decline, largely as a result of the generic, characterless image of giant national companies' shops falling out of consumer favor, there are still more than 50,000 such establishments throughout Japan and they have become such an ingrained social fixture that they are unlikely to completely disappear. If anything, it is those shops that tempt the jaded consumer with unique offerings in furniture and interior styling, tableware, music, food, or as mentioned above, in consummate attention to the minutest details of coffee and tea service—from procurement to preparation—that are now in the ascendant.

Today the Japanese drink enormous amounts of coffee. It is provided at home for breakfast in greater frequency than tea. It is available from coffee shops in elegant chinaware, or as prewarmed cans from automatic vending machines. And it comes, of course, in a bewildering variety of qualities, flavors, enhancements, and types. A study of vending machines found more than 40 different varieties of coffee sold in automatic vending machines alone.

Tea

At the other conceptual pole from alcohol is the refined world of tea. Of course, tea is drunk as an everyday drink by many Japanese, whether with meals or on its own. Some tea is very plebeian indeed: a greeny-brown drink made from the cheapest twigs and leaves called *bancha*, but expensive and refined teas are in high demand and can be found anywhere.

The epitome of tea is in the first plucked leaves in spring. The top three leaves of blanched bushes (surrounded by straw mats to prevent direct sunlight) are picked by hand and dried in a kiln. This earliest crop is the choicest, highest quality tea and is sold as green dew (*gyokuro*). A proportion is set aside and ground into powdered form to give *matcha* for use during the tea ceremony. True connoisseurs eagerly await the precise moment in spring when the tea bushes (*Camellia sinensis*) give forth their new leaves. Parties of connoisseurs descend upon the tea plantations in places such as Uji near Kyoto and Izu not far from Tokyo, where the best tea is grown. Equipped with charcoal braziers or gas burners, they boil the local water and infuse tea from the fresh leaves as they are plucked and brought directly to the pot by the farmer. If the weather is clement, the atmosphere created by the long caterpillar shapes of the neatly trimmed tea bushes crawling over the hills adds to the flavor. The arrival of the new tea—*shincha*—is greeted all over Japan with as much anticipation as Beaujolais Nouveau (which also has a great following in Japan). Tea shops and tea merchants advertise its arrival, and everyone who cares to, gets to taste the fresh breath of spring.

To add to choice, since China has become one of Japan's major trading partners, Oolong tea (semifermented from Fujian Province, China), prized for its medicinal and health-preserving qualities, has become a major favorite. Whether drunk hot or cold, in a posh coffee-shop (where tea is meticulously prepared from leaves and never tea bags) or from a corner vending machine, Oolong tea is drunk by the gallon by people of all ages and classes.

This delight and pleasure in the sensuous qualities of tea has a mythical-religious side to it. Legend has it that Boddhidarma (Daruma in Japanese), founder of the Zen sect in China during the first millennium C.E., was trying to meditate in order to overcome bodily weakness and enter a state of enlightenment. His weak body, however, fell asleep. When he awoke, the sage, enraged by this betrayal, tore off his own eyelids and threw them to the ground. The Buddha, perceiving his disciple's distress, caused a wondrous bush to grow. From its leaves, he said, a wonderful drink can be brewed that will banish sleep. Thus tea came into being.

The Tea Ceremony

Tea is so important in Chinese and Japanese cultures, that special events—tea ceremonies—became an important part of cultural and religious life. In Japan, this type of tea ceremony is called *chanoyu* or sometimes simply "Tea" (*O-cha*) (see also chapter 6). Finely ground green tea powder (*matcha*) is measured into a warmed drinking bowl. To this is added boiling water, which is then briskly whipped with a special bamboo whisk. The resultant drink is a frothy grass-green, rather thick liquid. Tasting like freshly-mown grass smells, it is slightly astringent and refreshing. Many Japanese drink this in preference to any other drink when eating traditional confectionery.

Significantly, not only the drink, but its utensils are expected to be things of beauty and aesthetic charm. Humble items such as the tea scoop, cut and shaped from a sliver of giant bamboo, may be named and treasured for generations. This of course goes double for the larger and more elaborate tea utensils such as iron kettles (*tetsubin*), tea-powder caddies, and above all tea bowls.

Tea Ceremony Utensils

Two contrasting stories from Japanese history illustrate the importance of these utensils. A certain general during the Civil War era (the fifteenth and sixteenth centuries C.E.) was in possession of a famous tea bowl. Defeated in battle, he retreated to his castle. The castle was besieged, and knowing his end was near, the general had the tea bowl brought to him. Crying that it was worth more than his life, and that he would never let it fall into the hands of the barbarians besieging him, he clutched the utensil to him and set fire to his hall, destroying the bowl and himself together. In another story, a certain warlord during the same era was besieged as well. He, too, knew the odds were hopeless. He called down to the leader of the besieging forces somewhat as follows: "I know you are an honorable and discerning opponent. You know as well as I do that the only way you can take this castle is to burn it to the ground. I do not, however, wish my priceless antique tea set to be destroyed. Knowing that you are a cultured man and a connoisseur, I therefore beg you to accept it, and treasure it over your life, as I have." Saying this, he had the carefully wrapped set lowered to the besieging general's hands, then fought to his death.

Tea utensils are still made today by named and famous artists and by unknown artisans throughout Japan. A village in the mountains near Kyoto still makes much of its income from the exacting manufacture of tea whisks. And many tea utensils, as the preceding stories show, have become collectors' items, trading for tens and even hundreds of thousands of dollars.

This humble drink has had a major effect on the material culture of Japan. The cultivation of tea and its ritual drinking has brought with it surges in the production and artistic direction of Japan for centuries. Fine brocades, woodwork, metal kettles, bamboo tea stands, traditional architecture, traditional painting, traditional poetry, and many other artistic endeavors are all elements interwoven into the tea ceremony and have developed, changed, and flowered by this association.

FOOD SOURCES

Japan's population is now predominantly urban—only about 10 percent of Japanese live outside cities, and the proportion of farming households is probably no more than half of that. Japanese farms today are productive, due to a mix of hard work, careful balancing of nutrients and crop rotation, and micromechanization, but they are hardly efficient in economic terms: raising a given weight of almost any agricultural product in Japan is much more expensive, often double or more the price in either a mechanized agricultural system like that of the United States or a human-intensive agricultural system like China's. On the other hand, from the point of view of a food lover, it has to be admitted that the Japanese claims for quality of their foodstuffs are (almost) always born out.

There are several factors that maintain this food price inflation. First, Japan's electoral districts are skewed toward farming districts. As a consequence, farmers have relatively more electoral power than do urban dwellers. Second, after some bitter experiences during and after World War II, the Japanese government decided, as a matter of national security policy, to ensure sufficient domestic supplies of food staples: rice and soybeans particularly. Finally, in an effort to protect the farming population, the government erected a number of nonmonetary trade barriers for food products. Rigid inspections (similar to those of the U.S. Department of Agriculture), tough regulations, and restricted ports of entry ensured that imported foods would only arrive in a slow trickle. The joint pressure of domestic consumers wanting a better deal and foreign suppliers wanting access to the market has eased some of those restrictions. Though many of these barriers have been removed, they have by no means vanished.

Another factor in the way Japanese food is produced is the strength and nature of the Japanese farm work force.

The number of people engaged in agriculture is steadily declining, relative to the total population. In 2000, the national total of economically active people was 63 million. Of these, a little under 3 million engaged in agriculture (around 5 percent of the working population, around 3 percent of the total populace).

Most farms are small, family-run concerns about one to two hectares (2.5 to 5 acres) in size. Larger farms can be found in Kanagawa Prefecture just north of Tokyo and particularly in Hokkaido, where farms can be around 25 acres. The small size of the farms has required the development of specialized tools and machinery. Most farmers have a utility vehicle: a small gasoline motor mounted on two wheels to which different machinery—plow, weeder, cart—can be harnessed. Farms in the flatlands that have rice acreage will usually also have a tiny (about four feet, or 120 cm, high), hand-guided rice-planter and harvester combine. Larger machinery is of course available as well, but hardly common. Few Japanese farms raise animals. Hokkaido, where farms are larger and generally unsuited for rice cultivation, raises cattle for meat and milk. Some other areas such as Matsuzaka are famous for their hand-reared meat cattle.

The restrictions on land usage have led Japanese firms to explore the possibilities of raising food hydroponically (that is, in water). Lettuce, flowers, and luxury fruit are raised in hothouses and in other innovative systems, such as on pierced metal hydroponics sheets. With declining numbers of agricultural workers, innovative resource-saving methods have been introduced. In precision agriculture, robotics and bioinformatic technology enable traditional labor- and time-intensive farm operations to be automatically performed. In essence, this makes agriculture feasible as a part-time occupation, and perhaps more attractive as an incentive for young Japanese to stay on the land, instead of seeking their livelihood in over-crowded urban areas.

Rice Production

Rice is undoubtedly the major crop in Japan in terms of prestige, even if the actual production and consumption volume has been steadily declining in the past few decades. The type of rice grown and preferred in Japan is the Japonica type, short-grained and lustrous, with a vague sweetish aftertaste when cooked.

In 2001, Japan grew 11.3 million metric tons of rice, most of it on small farms, some on large agribusiness tracts. Total consumption of rice today is less than 110 pounds per person per year. In contrast, during the nineteenth century, annual consumption of rice per person was about 330 pounds; and the traditional premodern rice ration for an adult man was 396 pounds of rice per year. More than half a million tons of rice are imported yearly: Japonica-type rice from the United States (mainly California), Australia, and China. Indica-type rice from Thailand is imported mainly for industrial or cheap chain-restaurant use, as well as animal feed.

Artificially flooded fields—paddies—are created by channeling water between dikes. The paddies are deep plowed in the dry season after the rice harvest (around October), heavily fertilized, and flooded come spring. In the early spring, selected rice seed is sown compactly in wooden beds until the seedlings are about six inches high. The paddies by then have been plowed and soaked until they are little more than deep bogs. The seedlings are separated and planted about a hand-span apart by small specialist machinery planters. In the past all this back-breaking work was done by hand. Now the landscape of rural Japan is dotted by miniature planters and harvesters during the busy seasons. Some farmers will still plant part of their field by hand in the traditional way: it gives them a feeling of being close to their ancestors and to the land, and, say some, handplanted rice often tastes better than its mechanically planted counterpart.

For the first few months the fields remain flooded. The farmer must go about, discouraging weeds and pests. The paddies, viewed from afar, look like a giant lawn crisscrossed by raised pathways (the dikes). With summer, the fields are drained so the grain can ripen. At the tip of each stalk cluster grains of rice, each on a separate twiglet. Provided there has been no upset—a typhoon, grasshoppers—the fields will turn golden in late August. The rice is then harvested and piled in stooks to dry: many areas of Japan have their own unique pattern of piling the rice.

The grain is separated mechanically from the panicle (the stalk and twiglets that hold the grain). Rice straw has many uses—for rope and string, for weaving mats to hold the rice grain, and not the least, for the weaving of *tatami* mats that floor traditional houses—and is considered an important part of the crop. The rice grain is then milled at a commercial or neighborhood mill to remove the husk, and can be eaten as wholegrain brown rice (*genmai*). Further polishing with talcum powder removes the brown covering (and rice germ) and produces the familiar white rice.

Japanese prefer rice from a named location for household consumption. Named varieties, such as top-ranked *Koshihikari*, developed after intensive research and development in the 1920s for more productive and tastier rice varieties, are sold at a premium, as is the first newly harvested rice. Though rice is grown virtually all over Japan, except for the northernmost half of Hokkaido, the best-tasting rice comes from specific areas such as Niigata and Akita prefectures. (It is worth noting that both areas are noted for the quality of their water, as well as their rice wine. Not surprisingly, pure water and good rice are the requirements of quality rice wine.)

Rice grains are usually white, but there are also red, green, and black varieties. These are grown in very small quantities. Glutinous white rice (*mochi gome*) is also extensively grown for confectionery and festive cookery use.

Varieties of traditional grains are raised as sidelines by many farmers. One can still get *kibi* (a type of millet) to flavor dumplings and *awa* (another type of millet) for rituals. Maize (corn) is grown as a vegetable: large cobbed, black-kernelled sweet corn is a summer snack sold from street barrows. Corn for industrial use—alcohol and beer, oil, cornstarch—is usually imported.

Vegetable Production

Soybeans are raised throughout the country. The major growing areas are Hokkaido and northeastern Honshu. Insufficient quantities are grown domestically, so that close to 95 percent of the supply is imported from the United States, Canada, and China. In 1990, 4.7 million tons were imported to supplement domestic production of 220,000 tons. About 80 percent of the soybeans go into oil production, with the rest going for food-stuffs.

Japanese farmers grow an enormous array of vegetables for the table. Vegetables in Japanese cuisine include the familiar and ubiquitous Chinese and Western cabbage, carrot, potato, cucumber, and tomato, as well as unfamiliar ones, such as various types of green leaves, stalks, roots and tubers, and edible flowers. Some of the more common vegetables grown are summarized in table 2.3. Overall, Japanese farmers raised about 12.5 million tons of varied vegetables in 2001.

The most important family of vegetables in Japan (as well as elsewhere) besides the legumes is the *brassica* or cabbage family. This includes the cabbages and radishes, and it is these two main types of vegetable that feature in many meals in one form or other. The *brassicae* are easy to cultivate, they yield good returns, and, no less importantly in rural Japan, they yield well into the winter providing people with fresh greens throughout the cold season. Made inaccessible when snow-covered, they quickly recover in spring to provide early greens.

Most farmers and many small-town households have a patch of vegetables in which they will grow cabbages (Chinese and Western), giant radish *(daikon)*, squash, cucumbers, tomatoes, leeks, Chinese chives *(nira)*, perilla, and many others. Commercial farms grow long rows of vegetables under plastic canopies, protecting the crop and ensuring its perfection.

Vegetables are nurtured carefully to ensure unblemished, uniform shapes. Cucumbers are straight and even-diametered, harvested before they set seed and become watery. Chinese or Western cabbage leaves are

Table 2.3
Cultivated Vegetables

Edible Part	Vegetable
Leaf	Chinese cabbage, cabbage, lettuce, spinach, spring chrysanthemum (*shungiku*), *komatsuna*, *takana*, *nozawana*, mustard, perilla (*shisô*), parsley, Chinese chives, trefoil (*mitsuba*), jute (*moroheya*), native regional and Chinese varieties of the cabbage family (Kyoto's *kyona*, Tohoku's *kukitachina*)
Stalk, young shoot	Asparagus, bamboo shoot, *udo*, celery, fern (*warabi*), Japanese butterbur (*fuki*), *zenmai*, Japanese leek, Japanese parsley (*seri*)
Root, tuber, bulb	giant radish (*daikon*), turnip, carrot, lotus root, ginger, radish, beet, Japanese horseradish (*wasabi*), devil's foot root (*konnyaku*), mountain and other yams and taro (*imo*), Chinese artichoke, lily bulb, garlic, onion, potato, sweet potato
Fruit	Cucumber, squash, various gourds, tomato, eggplant
Flower	Chrysanthemum, *myoga*, artichoke, broccoli, cauliflower, *nanohana*

compact and even. Giant radishes do not taper toward the root, but are evenly cylindrical throughout.

The major vegetable growing areas in Honshu are Chiba and Ibaraki prefectures on the Kanto plain near Tokyo; and Mie, Shiga, and Kyoto prefectures in the Kansai area (which includes the Osaka-Kobe-Kyoto conurbation).

Fruit Production

Apples are commonly grown, whether bright red, crisp Star Fuji with a honeyed center, or giant pink Mutsu varieties, large enough for a family to share, in northeastern Honshu. Grapes for wine and for the table are grown widely, the major area being Yamanashi Prefecture just north of Tokyo, and other mountain areas. Peaches and other fruit such as cherries are grown, the latter in the colder prefectures of the northeast. There are pineapples from Okinawa and perfect melons, strawberries, and mandarin oranges (*mikan*) from Shizuoka prefecture, grown in the shadow of Mt. Fuji.

Loquats and oriental or Asian pears are local fruits that are not so well known outside Japan. Figs, quinces, and Japanese apricots (*ume*) are made into preserves and the latter two also into sweet liqueurs. Fruit, like vegetables, is expected to have a perfect appearance: fruits with blemishes are disdained by most customers. Cherries are packed so that the almost unnoticeable indentation on each fruit all face the same way in a box, and the uppermost fruit polished. Melons are supported on a bed of straw so they grow into perfectly round shapes. Some watermelons are grown in forms so they are cube-shaped rather than round. A few wild fruits such as the fruit of the akebia vine (*Akebia quinata*), pawpaw (*Asimina triloba* imported from the United States as an ornamental tree, now growing wild in some places), native grape, and raspberry are occasionally collected and sold at markets, more usually consumed at home.

Fishing and Aquaculture

Another major source of food, and one that characterizes Japanese food more perhaps than any but rice and soybeans, is the sea. The sea is both fished and farmed, yielding millions of tons of food products aptly termed "delights of the sea" (*umi no sachi*). There are extended fish farms in the Seto Inland Sea and elsewhere along the deeply indented coastline.

Coastal fishing, particularly in the nutrient-rich waters of the Black Current (Kuroshio) that runs past the eastern coast of Japan has been documented from early history. It brings with it annual bonanzas of deep-sea fish: herring, tuna, mackerel, squid, and bonito are among the most popular. Japanese coastal fishermen bring in hundreds of species of fish, including sea-bream (*tai*), puffer fish (*fugu*), and squid. Deep-sea trawlers trailing miles of nets and lines roam all the oceans of the world. All of this is not without ecological cost, and the Japanese have been accused numerous times of visiting ecological destruction on other seas than their own in their pursuit of tasty tidbits. Overall, the Japanese fishing industry landed over five million tons of fish and seafood from all species in 2000 alone and purchased more from other fishing fleets.

In addition to fish, the Japanese catch many other forms of marine life. Shellfish—oysters, clams of various species, and abalone—are very popular, as are a large number of species of crustaceans, from tiny shrimp to giant spider crab. In late winter, piles of snow crab and hairy crab (*kegani*) grace every corner of the markets in the fishing ports of Hokkaido in the north.

The Japanese not only hunt wild fish, but since the 1970s have also farmed marine fish. Yellow-tail, a kind of jack, have been farmed in the Seto Inland Sea, as well as other sea fish. Freshwater aquaculture of carp, trout, and eels is widespread throughout central Japan. Laver (*nori*) and kelp (*konbu*) and *wakame* seaweed are raised commercially. Other forms of marine algae and vegetables are collected on a semicommercial basis, as are several varieties of shellfish.

Meat and Animal Products

The Japanese were introduced to beef-eating largely by British merchants who arrived in the country in the late nineteenth century. The native cow (*wagyu*) did not yield much meat and was usually used as a beast of burden or plow. As a consequence, the *wagyu* had a more uniform distribution of fat than European or American breeds. Distribution of fat cells within the muscle, called "marbling" is closely related to the quality—taste and texture—of the meat. Japanese farmers were thus poised, almost by accident, to provide the best (and most expensive) beef in the world. Farmers have also tried various ways of improving the quality. Cattle are fed on *saké* and beer lees to improve their appetites (and because these make good, cheap feed). There is still argument as to whether this practice, as well as the common practice of massaging the beasts, does anything to improve the flavor or quality. Whatever the case, a pound of well-marbled *wagyu*, the pink meat laced with a delicate tracery of white fat, can sell for ¥21,000 (about $180) at a luxury butcher. Most house-

Table 2.4
Domestic versus Imported Consumption of Livestock, Milk, and Dairy
Products (FY 2000)

Item	Domestic (in 1000 tons)	Import (in 1000 tons)
Beef	520	1,055
Pork	1,255	952
Chicken	1,195	686
Egg	2,540	121
Milk for drinking	5,005	0
Milk for dairy products	3,308	3,952

Source: Food Policy Division, General Food Policy Bureau, Ministry of Agriculture, Forestry and Fisheries, *Food Balance Sheet* (Tokyo, Dec. 19, 2001).

holds, of course, make do with far less-expensive meat. But even imported Australian, U.S., and Canadian meat can be quite expensive: $9–11 per pound is not unusual. As a consequence, meat portions in Japan tend to be small, and meat dishes run to thin strips or slices, rather than large steaks or roasts.

The Japanese milk industry produces milk from hybrids of native cattle (*wagyu*) and imported dairy breeds. And in the past 20 years, a flourishing cheese industry, some of whose products rival their French originators, has developed in the Nagano highlands of central Honshu and in the northern island of Hokkaido.

Imported Products

Though the Japanese government has tried to see to it that the basic foodstuffs, and the ability to produce them, are always present, much of the modern Japanese diet comes from abroad. This is partly due to conflicting demands upon agricultural lands, a growing proportion of which are being used for domestic and commercial building. Lack of agricultural workers (some hamlets have been virtually depopulated due to low birthrate and migration to the cities; in others, bachelors are finding it impossible to find wives and have started marrying women from abroad) is another major factor.

The Japanese pride themselves on the quality and taste of their rice. Nonetheless, for a number of reasons, the Japanese have been importing rice from abroad—California, Australia, and Thailand—for several decades. The reasons for this are complex. Partly it was pressure from exporting countries, such as the United States and Australia, to lower tariff barriers to their produce. Partly it was attempts by the Japanese government to cooperate with Third World countries such as Thailand. There was also domestic pressure to lower the cost of rice—particularly for industrial uses such as making crackers and packed lunches,where the Japanese consumer was less concerned about taste and appearance, and more about the price of the final products.

In the past 50 years, there has been a massive increase in the consumption of bread and baked goods. Japan can grow little wheat, and certainly it cannot compete with the large wheat exporters such as Australia, the United States, and Canada. Therefore, much of the wheat eaten by Japanese is imported.

Much as in the case of rice, the Japanese government was reluctant to open its market to meat and meat products from abroad. Pressure from consumers, on the one hand, and producers—Australia, the United States, and Canada again—on the other opened the barriers, and meat from those countries is now more readily available. Many of the producers from abroad have had to modify their products to suit Japanese tastes, but the overall benefits to the consumer and the lowering of overall prices have been largely accepted. The import of meat has also meant that there is a greater vertical segmentation of the meat market, so that both cheaper cuts and meat products and more expensive ones are sold to customers with different tastes and pockets.

Japan can also no longer sustain its own demand for fish, and with the end of World War II, Japanese trawlers once again ventured onto the high seas. The new Law of the Sea regime ensured that most countries would have a share in the world's fish resources. Whereas before these resources went to those with more power and technology at their disposal, nowadays they must be paid for. Thus Japan imports large quantities of fish— particularly those in high demand such as bluefin tuna—from countries such as Morocco, New Zealand, Argentina, Chile, Alaska, and other places where these fish abound. Japan's import of fresh and frozen tuna alone was about 310,000 tons in 1999. Squid imports totaled about 63,000 tons, and cuttlefish imports were about 44,000 tons, half of this latter sourced from Thailand.

While Japanese farmers try to grow all varieties of fruit in demand, this is not always possible. Many varieties of fruit are imported from abroad, including navel oranges and grapefruit from Florida, kiwi fruit from New Zealand, apples from New England, bananas from South America, and pineapples from Hawaii. Some of these fruits end up in products such as jams and cookies; others are sold on the open market and can be found throughout Japan.

FOOD SUPPLIERS—SHOPS, SUPERMARKETS, FARM COOPERATIVES, AND HOMEMAKER CO-OPS

In Japan, as in all other technologically developed societies, most people source their food from a variety of retail outlets. Behind those retail outlets lies a complicated system of wholesalers and intermediaries.

Supermarkets look very much like their counterparts elsewhere, though the range of foods is of course different. Small neighborhood stores including one or more greengrocers, a fishmonger, rice merchant (who also sells vinegar and oils), Japanese confectioner, florist, pharmacy, grocer, and butcher are usually clustered in shopping streets called *shôtengai*. Convenience stores, often open 24/7, have become an essential part of modern urban life, and catering to singles or the emergency buyer, they sell everything from a pack of two apples or a styrofoam tray of *sushi* to slush puppies in insulated cups.

Many urban centers also have a small traditional market, though these, alas, are becoming scarcer. Large ones such as the one at Tokyo's Sengokuchô quarter occupy several blocks. Smaller ones might consist of little more than a covered alleyway. There one can find old-fashioned pickle shops with barrels of assorted pickled vegetables and fruit, fishmongers, butchers, and sellers of anything anyone could desire. One of the most attractive features is the traditional cries of the sellers—rhyming and musical—who try to entice shoppers to their open stalls. Major department stores, such as Seibu, Mitsukoshi, or Isetan in Tokyo and other metropolitan areas will have one or more floors devoted to food and drink, fresh as well as preserved and ready-to-eat foods of all kinds. The stalls in these food floors aim to replicate the ambiance of traditional market stalls, and there will be a wider variety of choice in ingredients from all parts of the country, as well as the entire world, than can be found in neighborhood shopping streets. More and more Japanese working women find the ready-made food at these department store food floors a boon and on their commute home will shop for dishes to augment the rice and soup that they themselves will prepare for the evening meal.

Mail-Order Food

Ordering food by mail is part of a lengthy Japanese tradition of marketing food at a distance. These days, one can order from extensive and mouth-watering catalogs put out by the Japanese Post Office and major department stores, and within hours, the delicacy will be delivered to the desired address. The range is enormous, encompassing preserved Japanese and Western foods, fresh fish, liquor, and even *sushi*. Japanese people make particular use of this service during the two gift-giving seasons of mid-summer and the New Year. And, of course, the nationally distributed catalogs have many local competitors as well.

Homemaker Cooperatives, Direct-Farm Sales, and Health Foods

Many Japanese consumers, particularly homemakers, have become increasingly worried about the consumption of industrially processed food. And in some Japanese neighborhoods, homemakers have organized themselves into buying clubs, which purchase certified organic foods directly from farmers who participate in the project. Several national organizations sponsor this activity, providing introductions and certification for the farmers. In parallel, since many rural communities have been losing residents drawn to the cities, small communities have established one-to-one relationships with former residents or their descendants. When such relationships are established, the former rural people can receive monthly packages of fresh food from the countryside, accompanied often by newsletters describing what is going on in the community and the life "back on the farm."

Vending Machines

Vending machines are an omnipresent sight in towns and the countryside alike. These machines can be found everywhere (including, it must be added, some very inappropriate places such as shrine groves). The machines tend to cluster together, like members of a gang hanging out on street corners. Impossible to miss, they are lit with bright neon facias. Some have a game built in: a simplified roulette, the winner getting an extra drink of choice.

Vending machines mainly sell canned and bottled drinks in bewildering variety: there can be close to 200 different varieties of drinks sold on any given city block. The machines also sell snacks, magazines, noodles, rice, sandwiches, cakes, beer, *saké*, and pickles. Some people in Japan suffer from severe inability to tolerate social contact, and for them the vending machines provide a source for some, perhaps even much, of their food.

Gifts

The two formal gift-giving seasons—in mid-summer and the New Year—are a source of some of every Japanese household's food supply. Gift boxes of household items such as soap, oil, and vinegar as well as luxury items such as preserved meat and fish, biscuits, and cakes are sold in super-markets or through mail order. These may be passed along, but in smaller households, such gifts often provide access to luxuries that could not oth-erwise be enjoyed. Other gifts of special or local produce are provided by neighbors, friends, and family members when returning from a trip. With the rise of travel by the Japanese populace in the latter half of the twenti-eth century, these gifts (omiyage) have become a source of knowledge about, and experiences of, faraway and special local luxuries.

CONSUMER PREFERENCES

Japanese consumers are extremely brand-conscious, and Japan has become, since the 1990s, the fashion capital of much of Asia. This fash-ion- and brand-consciousness affects purchasing patterns in all areas of consumer life, including food. Some consumers buy only a particular brand or kind of rice, soy sauce, and soybean curd (tofu). Meticulous at-tention is paid to the visual appearance of food products. Vegetables and fruit, fresh meat and fish are perfect and uniform, their exteriors unblem-ished. Each item is well formed and identical in size to others of its kind. The high prices paid by Japanese consumers for food reflect the high cost to producers in adhering to these strict quality criteria. In their partiality to fresh-caught fish, there are finicky consumers who willingly pay up to three to four times the cost of frozen equivalents of comparable quality. As discussed above, top-quality Japanese beef retails at astronomical prices, reflecting the Japanese consumer's predilection for evenly marbled, fork- (or to be more apt, chopstick-) tender meat.

Domestically grown produce is preferred to imported, not only in terms of quality and taste, but also safety. In a 1999 food survey, 81 percent of re-spondents regarded Japanese-grown produce as fresh, 77 percent regarded it as high-quality, and 90 percent regarded it as safe. Nearly 50 percent would not buy imported apples; and 41 percent would not buy imported poultry. Fruits and vegetables, such as oranges, garlic, and sweet peppers, were acceptable if their quality was good.

With the high literacy rate and multiple communication media, Japa-nese consumers are very well informed and up-to-date with the latest trends. There is a preponderance of magazines and Web sites for all age groups catering to miscellaneous leisure activities, and food—its prepara-tion, consumption, source, and venue—features quite heavily. A related leisure activity, travel, also by necessity includes food, as whether touring domestically or internationally, the Japanese preference for gifts to take back home is for renowned local delicacies.

When it comes to food gift-giving, the quality criteria go up several notches. To keep already perfect and unblemished muskmelons, large-sized peaches, or plum-sized seedless Kyôho grapes at the peak of perfection, each is cradled in an inflated styrofoam net. Japan is the Land of the Gift, inasmuch as gifts are expected in almost every social occasion and, as mentioned previously, there are two specific gift-giving seasons (mid-summer and the New Year). There is therefore much pressure to procure the perfect gift. Foods—particularly the rare, the unusual, and the special—are greatly appreciated. Thus, food gifts are constantly circulating, from utilitarian packs of dried laver or mushrooms, to large bottles of name-brand cooking oil, choice biscuits or brandy-soaked fruitcake individually wrapped in individual portions for tea- or coffee-time, wines, or jams and fruit preserves.

3

Cooking

As in most societies, cooking in Japan is done in particular patterns. This chapter explores *who* does the cooking and *how* cooking is done. Among other issues, this chapter examines the role of homemakers and professional chefs in their respective domains. It also takes a peek into the Japanese domestic kitchen, which in some ways is distinctly different from the kitchen you may be familiar with. Finally, most of this chapter is devoted to a description of the various types of foods the Japanese eat. Fortunately, Japanese chefs have developed specific categories of food preparation for the construction of meals, and this chapter roughly follows that arrangement.

WHO COOKS?

Japanese people experience their first food and develop many, if not most, of their food likes and dislikes in the home. As in most cultures, day-to-day cooking is usually done by housewives. In traditional Japanese culture, the position of the housewife is a very powerful one in many ways. Her position is symbolized by the possession of the rice paddle (*shamoji*), the flattened wooden spoon-shaped scoop that is used to dish out rice. *Shamoji* are associated with the thunder god and indicate how powerful the housewife was ritually. In modern Japan, the wife is supposed to control the purse strings: she receives the husband's pay packet and allocates him some pocket money, reserving the bulk of the income for the household budget. In practice, this may not be the case, but the

Modern Japanese husband in kitchen.
Courtesy of the authors.

implication of homemaker power is there. Nowadays rice paddles are made of plastic and come with every rice cooker, but many households still retain *shamoji* that are given as talismans by the neighboring Shintô shrine and are used on special occasions. To this day, some rural house-holds make an occasion of the transfer of the *shamoji* between an older woman and her daughter-in-law or daughter, when the young woman fi-nally assumes her duties.

Japanese eat out a great deal, so the other major figure in food is the pro-fessional chef. Professional chefs come in many types, specializations, and even grades (like many Japanese arts, chef schools award graded ranks to their trainees). As in most traditional arts, there are schools of cooking,

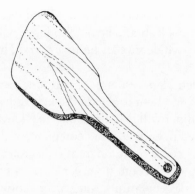

Shamoji (Rice Paddle)

and a high-quality chef is usually able to trace his "lineage" from pupil to student for many generations. Chefs tend to rule their kitchens with iron hands. In the imperial court, the position was of considerable importance, and to this day there are annual ceremonies in Kyoto in which traditional chefs from imperial cooking lineages display their cutting skills on fish caught for the event.

Professionalism and perfection are central to Japanese ideas of service. Japanese customers can discern, by visual, auditory, and of course, taste cues what to look for. An instructive course in how to select a good restaurant is provided by the Japanese film *Tampopo* (1985). In the film, the heroine, who owns a failing noodle restaurant, is taught by her guide, the truck driver, what the essence of a good chef means. He takes her to see a variety of good and bad establishments, showing her (and the audience) what goes into making the Japanese ideal. Briefly summed up, the perfect cook (in addition, of course, to cooking well) must be able to please her or his customers: every customer must be observed minutely and their preferences and reactions noted. Every movement of the cook must be choreographed and timed to perfection. The seating and tables, the shape and size of the bowls, must all make the customer feel as comfortable from the first sitting as if he had been visiting the establishment for years.

Visiting a Japanese restaurant is an experience in total pleasure. One is greeted at the door by cries of "*Irashaimase*" (welcome) and the good customer can tell immediately if these cries are full of vigor and sincerity or mere utterances devoid of content: in the former case, the food is likely to have soul, in the latter, it is likely to be mere fodder to fill the belly. The dining room must be arranged to please the eye and occupy the customer for the brief time between ordering the food and its delivery. In fact, a really good restaurant cook should be able to judge what it is the customer wants. As Tampopo's guide says "Is he in a hurry? Hungry? Willing to try something new?"

Most chefs in high-class restaurants will also provide a chef's choice (*omakase*). That allows them to create the best dishes in their repertoire. In such a case, the diner will be "subjected" to a lengthy string of delicate dishes, each designed to enhance and complement the one before it.

Professional chefs come from different backgrounds and pursue different interests. Many chefs come from generations of chefs: families that have supplied food for generations, sometimes centuries. In such families, one has the feeling of great continuity. Any current head of a cooking school (the position is inherited) is expected to provide guidance for the junior members, and there is an attempt to maintain some sort of uniformity, or at least unity, in the way certain dishes are cooked and served.

Of course, there are many small-time cooks in the tens of thousands of food outlets throughout Japan. Such cooks range from the indifferent to the sublime, as they do in any country. However, the training of any cook in Japan is an arduous business. In Japanese tradition, the best way to learn a craft is by lengthy apprenticeship. It is of course possible to go to a cooking school as well, but even a cooking school graduate would expect to spend several years as a rather subdued junior in some cooking establishment. Chefs often move about from one restaurant, bar, or eating place to another, until they eventually settle for some time at a place they fancy. So common is the idea of the wandering chef that there are even several comic books whose main character is a wandering cook. Their adventures generally have to do with creating the perfect dish, struggling with inner deficiencies which are overcome with hard work, or learning from a hidden master.

THE KITCHEN

In many apartments, the kitchen is little more than one side of the dining/living room (or LDK as Japanese estate agents have it). The kitchen area is small and rarely offers sufficient room for more than one person to work comfortably. Most kitchens have relatively modest cooking arrangements. Hot water is still often dispensed from a gas boiler over the sink. Refrigerators are generally tiny by U.S. standards, and working surfaces are very limited. Cooking is done on a countertop gas range. Built-in ovens are rare, though houses and apartments built in the past 20 years sometimes have built-in ranges and ovens. Countertop labor-saving devices, including ovens, have proliferated. There are no garbage disposals: Japan has a strict set of separation rules that mean that different kinds of waste must be disposed of in different ways. Limited storage and chilling space also means that many households must do their food shopping on a daily basis.

In the past 20 years, there has been something of a revolution both socially and technologically. Fewer husbands can now boast that they have never seen the inside of the kitchen (as their fathers would have), and more labor-saving devices have come to the home-cook's aid. Women have benefited from both revolutions, though the burden of cooking still falls largely on them.

Utensils

Cooking utensils around the world fulfill similar functions. But given cultural differences, the implementation of these functions can differ significantly. This is definitely the case with the Japanese kitchen. Bowls are

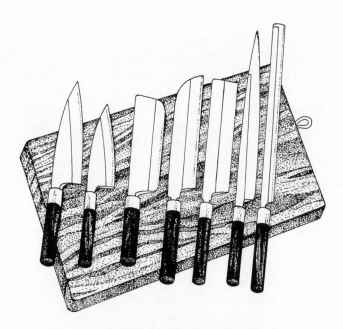

Array of *Hôchô* (Kitchen Knives)

used for mixing and storing, knives for cutting, and a variety of pots and pans for heating foods. Most of these are quite familiar, and, given the vagaries of modern manufacture, look very much like your own. But in addition, the Japanese kitchen contains several particular utensils that are unlikely to be found anywhere else.

Japanese kitchens use a large variety of knives. Rectangular knives with very thin blades are used for slicing and peeling vegetables. Thicker triangular blades are used for meat and fish. The edges of these tend to be beveled on one side only, which allows a better control of the cut. Most kitchens will have at least one vegetable knife and two of the triangular blades: a short one for smaller fish and cuts, a long one for long smooth slicing of items such as *sashimi*.

Long chopsticks for cooking—stirring, whipping eggs, frying—and shorter ones for eating at the table are the most common implement. Table chopsticks are made, of course, of many materials: plain wood, lacquered wood, bamboo, or plastic. But little exemplifies the sensory impact of Japanese food like a pair of chopsticks newly cut from a piece of green bamboo: the green outer surface brightly evocative of freshness, the smell redolent of growing things, and the texture, barely noted by the teeth, but adding immeasurably to the eating experience.

One unusual item of kitchenware (in fact, as one scholar has pointed out, an indispensable part of *all* of Japanese culture) are small towels (*tenugui*). These have multiple uses in Japanese society. Wrapped around the head they serve as sweatbands, but, more importantly, they symbolically indicate great effort: "to put on a headband" is the Japanese equivalent of the Western "roll up your sleeves." In the kitchen, *tenugui* have multiple uses. They are used obviously for wiping dishes and utensils, and, freshly washed, squeezed dry of water, serve as wiping towels (*shibori*) for diners before or after meals to cleanse their hands and faces.

Electric Utensils

Given the significance of the Japanese electrical goods industry, it should not be surprising to find that the average Japanese kitchen overflows with countertop electric devices. Pride of place goes to the electric rice cooker. The most modern versions are equipped with timers and will keep rice warm for a day. Like the *shamoji*, the rice pot is the province of the housewife, and many men still have (or claim to have) no idea how to work it. Significantly too, it is used for rice alone: several decades ago, an

Rice Cooker

American company tried to sell a rice cooker that could also be used for baking, but had no takers. The rice pot is still sacred.

Countertop microwave and combination (microwave and convection) ovens are a common feature, since many home cooks now bake their own Western bread and cakes. By extension, bread-makers and electrical blenders and food processors have also become common. Electrical *mochi*-makers (which cook, then pound glutinous rice into doughlike consistency) are probably less familiar to non-Japanese.

There is also a growing number of Western plates, utensils, and pots as more and more Japanese come to eat Western foods and as homemakers, carefully following instructions in fashion magazines or cooking courses, try out Western foods on their families. Thus, in addition to sets of Japanese utensils, there might be a parallel set of plates and Western utensils for such items of diet as curry rice, sandwiches, breakfast cereals, and coffee and Western foods.

Low-tech developments of traditional items have a place in the Japanese kitchen as well. As noted in chapter 2, pickled vegetables are an important element in Japanese meals. Many homemakers still make their own, and many kitchens are equipped with a pickling container: a lidded plastic container with a screw that pushes down a slotted plate allowing pressure to be put on the pickles and ensuring they are immersed in the pickling medium.

Table 3.1 gives some idea of the utensils to be found in an average Japanese kitchen in addition to the ones discussed in detail above.

Table 3.1
Kitchen Utensils and Their Uses

Utensil	Japanese Name	Description
chopping board	*manaita*	Modern chopping boards are made of polyurethane impregnated with fungicide. Old-fashioned ones of a single slab of wood can still be bought.
colander	*zaru*	A basket with a thin weave for draining foods cooked in water, such as noodles. *Zaru soba* is a popular form of summer noodle, drained and served cold on a *zaru* with a dipping sauce and various garnishes.
grater	*oroshigane*	Usually made of ceramic with raised serrations on a flat surface, it is used for grating radish, horseradish, etc. Metal ones are also available.
griddle	*teppan*	An iron plate traditionally placed over charcoal. Many modern houses have an electric one that can be placed in the middle of the table for *teppanyaki*.
katsuobushi grater	*katsuobushibako*	Unique to Japanese food preparation, this is an inverted wooden plane fitted over a box into which gratings from *katsuobushi*, looking somewhat like pencil shavings, fall. The box is about 3 inches square by 6 inches long.
knives	*hôchô*	Various sizes and shapes. A rectangular thin–bladed one for cutting vegetables. Long and short triangular blades for fish and meat. Small thin blades for trimming and boning fish.
mortar	*suribachi*	Ceramic bowl with its interior deliberately roughened. Material to be ground such as sesame seeds or beans are grated using a wooden pestle (*surikogi*). A pounding mortar (*usu*) such as the kind used to pound *mochi* is no longer a household implement.
pot	*nabe*	In traditional parlance, this meant a large cooking pot of ceramic or iron used for stews or simmered dishes. Today it can mean any pot or skillet, including a frying pan. Most kitchens have them in two or three sizes.
rice box	*komebitsu*	Modern ones are made of plastic and have a push-button spout to dispense the right amount of rice for the number of servings desired. Traditional ones were of fragrant wood and bound with bamboo.
rice-serving container	*ohitsu*	Lacquered wooden flat-bottomed and lidded bowl for bringing rice to the table. Some have an attachment to clip the rice-paddle to the side. Today, like many other utensils, it is unfortunately often made of plastic.
rolling pin	*membô*	Necessary for anyone making noodles by hand, and, of course, in the modern Japanese household, for rolling out dough for Western–style pies and cookies which are tremendously popular.
sieve	*koshiki*	Very important for many uses such as removing *katsuobushi* and tea dregs. Smaller ones are used for removing bits of batter from hot oil, large-mesh ones for taking noodles out of boiling water.
sushi-rolling mat	*makisu*	A small mat of thin bamboo slats used for rolling *sushi* rolls.
table top gas burner	*konro*	A small burner fed with bottled gas. Used for cooking *sukiyaki* and other pot-dishes.
whetstone	*toishi*	Particularly important in a cooking culture that gives a great deal of precedence to proper cutting of food items. There are many different grades, and they often come as a double whetstone, coarse and fine.

COOKING METHODS

See table 3.2 for a list of the basic food preparation methods discussed in more detail in this section, as well as the Japanese word describing each. The order in which the foods listed in table 3.2 are served in a formal meal depends on a number of factors, not least of which is regional preferences. For convenience, table 3.2 and this chapter present them in alphabetical order by Japanese name; chapter 5 of this book offers a discussion of the serving order of foods.

Preliminaries

To preserve the natural flavors and colors of foods and to present them visually in the best possible way, authentic Japanese food preparation often requires extensive preprocessing before cooking actually starts. Many favorite Japanese foods require that the cook start by leaching them of alkaloids that make them bitter. This is particularly true of mountain vegetables. Many of those must be treated with repeated washing in fresh water. Other, more stubborn cases such as fiddlehead ferns must first be soaked for a while in lye water to remove the bitterness. After several washings in fresh water, they are ready for use.

Preserving the color of natural foods is another issue Japanese cooks take seriously. One common method is to refresh blanched vegetables by quickly plunging them into cold water. This preserves and even enhances the green color of various cooked leaves and beans. In addition, the plunging method ensures that the vegetables are not overcooked.

The art of cutting is one that has been developed to perfection in Japanese cooking. Cooking schools and cookbooks teach the art of cutting and of preparing the cook's knives. Japanese knife-making, an art that

Table 3.2
Cooking Methods

Japanese Term	English Meaning
aemono	Dressed cooked salads
agemono	Deep–fried dishes
gohanmono	Rice and rice-rich dishes
mushimono	Steamed dishes
nabemono	One-pot dishes
nimono	Simmered dishes
shirumono	Soups and stock-simmered dishes
suimono	Soup, always based on a clear stock
sunomono	Vinegared foods and vinegared salads
tsukemono	Pickles
yakimono	Grilled foods, directly over coals or on a griddle

originated before the formation of the Japanese state and reached a perfection not seen anywhere else, is closely related to the art of sword smithing, for which Japan is world famous. In traditional knives, a wide layer of hard but brittle steel is protected by a layer of softer iron. This makes the cutting edge asymmetrical: an obstacle to the novice, a boon to the expert who can manipulate the asymmetry to produce a variety of subtle differences in different cuts.

Cuts have been developed to suit the characteristics of each type of vegetable and the cooking requirements for each dish. While the most conspicuous type of cut is the decorative, in particular the fashioning of crisp vegetables, such as carrot, giant radish, and turnip, into pleasing shapes that adorn many dishes, other types of cuts are not merely a matter of aesthetics. Many dishes require that a vegetable (or fish) be cut in a specific way to encourage even transmission of heat, ensure uniform distribution of flavor, and to showcase natural textures. An asymmetrical and diagonal cut (*rangiri*) made by rolling a vegetable during cutting will create more facets than achieved by static square cutting. The greater number of vegetable surfaces created thereby exposes more of the vegetable to the hot cooking liquid, thus resulting in more rapid cooking time.

Another kind of cut ensures even distribution of heat through vegetables that, for aesthetic reasons, are best kept in large pieces during cooking. An example is giant radish, which is usually cut into fairly thick cylinders for a stew called *furofuki daikon*. A cross-cut called a hidden cut (*kakushi hôchô*) is made on one end of the radish cylinder, without going through to the other end, up to about three-quarters of the cylinder. This cross-cut, which will not be apparent to the diner once the vegetable has been placed on a dish and topped with sauce, allows the cooking liquid and heat to evenly pass through the thick vegetable. The cut also makes it easier for the diner to eat, as it serves as an access point for the diner's chopsticks and enables easier breakdown into bite-size pieces. A variant of the hidden cut is called a tea-whisk cut, usually made to baby eggplant cooked whole, that is, including stalk and the green calyx that surrounds its narrow neck. The sharp tip of a knife is slipped into the eggplant from its midpoint to the widest part, without cutting through to the bottom. The cut is repeated at quarter-inch intervals all the way around the eggplant. The result is a fanciful rendition of the bamboo tea whisk used during the tea ceremony. However aesthetic this cut is, it is also functional, as it makes the cooking liquid enter the vegetable faster, again decreasing cooking time as well as evenly distributing flavor.

There are many cuts used for adorning food and entire books are devoted to the subject in Japan. Inspiration for the shapes comes from popular natural symbols—plum and cherry blossoms being the most common. New Year icons furnish the greatest number, ranging from arrows and bells to the three classical auspicious symbols of bamboo, pine, and plum.

The vegetable that yields most readily to the decorator's knife is the giant radish. It is cut and peeled into a cylinder slightly shorter than the knife blade is long. The chef then uses a thin rectangular blade to shave off a long strip about 1/16th inch thick the length of the cylinder, looking somewhat like unrolling a paper scroll. The strip, which can be several yards long, is then doubled and shaved crosswise, creating long noodle-like threads which serve, for instance, as bedding and garnish for *sashimi:* an attractive decoration that is crisply edible as well.

Cutting Fish and Meat

The single most important skill in dealing with fish (besides choosing the freshest one for the season) is the ability to cut it properly. Each type of fish has its own special needs, and the good cook will be equipped with a series of very sharp knives and a great deal of practice to get the cut perfect.

As in most things of this nature, the Japanese have devised a series of proper procedures—*kata*—to perform cutting properly. The angle at which the knife is held, the stance of the cutter, the proper grip on the knife, and knowing how the blade will move inside the flesh are all important aspects that must be attended to. The result is perfectly cut, clean-edged, evenly sized bites of fish flesh, whether raw or cooked. One good way to see whether the cook is a good one is to examine the cut, say professional chefs. It must be clean, with no ragged edges. The cook must not use a sawing motion, just a single long stroke. And each type of preparation must have the right cut for that particular dish. Cutting fish for *sushi* is quite different from cutting for grilling, for instance.

Because of the importance of cutting, a chef is usually titled *itamae* (behind the counter), meaning the one responsible for the actual slicing of fish into its components. Imperial chefs, and specialist chefs at some Shintô shrines in Kyoto, still carry out an annual ritual of slicing fish, where the expert chef, using nothing but a pair of large chopsticks and a sharp knife, dismembers and prepares a large fish, usually a bream, for offering to the deities. These rituals have been carried out annually since the eighth century, and they highlight the importance of both freshness (the fish must be live) and of knowing precisely how to handle the knife.

Salads

Salads (*aemono*), generally speaking, are raw or parboiled vegetables on their own or mixed with seafood or other ingredients and dressed with a sauce. *Aeru* means "to dress with condiments."

Miso, tofu, or crushed seeds and nuts are most commonly used to provide body, thickness, and flavor to the sauce, with various proportions of rice wine, cooking wine, soy sauce, and sometimes stock blended in. The resulting thick sauce is mixed gently with the salad ingredients just before serving so that the sauce does not separate or weep. Examples of *aemono* are parboiled baby shallots in walnut and *miso* dressing or beef strips with green soybean and tofu dressing.

While *aemono* is the generic term for all dressed traditional salads, those that are dressed with vinegar are separately referred to as *sunomono*.

Aemono fill a role somewhat like the *sorbet* of the traditional French dinner: a mouth cleanser that prepares the diner for further adventure. Or, in Japanese, "to rest the chopsticks." The taste of *aemono* dressing ranges from faintly sweet to decidedly sweet.

Fried Dishes

Like most people everywhere, the Japanese are fond of fried foods (*age-mono*). French fries are found throughout the country, and doughnuts are as popular as they are in the United States. But there are some special methods of frying food that are particularly and characteristically Japanese. Three frying methods are used for different results in the Japanese kitchen.

Chinese frying (*kara-age*) is a technique whereby the food to be fried—small fish or chunks of larger fish, chicken nuggets, or tofu—are dusted with corn starch and some grated ginger, then fried. "Naked" frying (*su-age*), where the food, without a batter, is placed in direct contact with the hot oil, is used for harder foods and ones where seeing the skin is important, such as eggplants, whose purple skin adds much to the visual appeal of a dish, or fish with attractive skin such as mackerel. Batter frying (*koromo-age*) coats the food with a light, very cold batter. This technique is best known in the form of *tempura* and *tonkatsu*.

Like the British, for example, the Japanese fry fish. But there is more than a little difference in the result. *Tempura*, it is said, was a Japanese adaptation or imitation of a dish that Portuguese sailors brought with them from Europe. In the Japanese version, small chunks of fish and vegetables are dipped into a very light, cold batter, then fried in deep oil. Until the middle of the past century, *tempura* was a street food, sold by vendors from small baskets. Now no longer sold from street barrows, most restaurants, even noodle shops, serve *tempura*. *Tempura* served at noodle shops will usually have a darker and heavier batter than that served elsewhere. The best, the lightest, and the most delicate *tempura* with the freshest ingredients will always be served by a restaurant specializing in just this way of cooking. At a *tempura* restaurant, there will be no hint of any oil whatsoever in the subtlest of coatings, functioning merely to protect the freshness of the ingredients from direct contact with the hot oil. Another adaptation of a European original is a deep-fried battered pork cutlet (*tonkatsu*).

Vegetable and Shrimp *Tempura*

- 8 prawns (shrimp)
- several sweet potatoes
- small Japanese eggplants
- 1 egg
- 4 perilla (beefsteak plant, or *shisô*) leaves
- shiitake mushrooms
- 1 cup fine flour
- 1 cup ice-cold soda water
- oil for deep-frying. (Any cold-pressed, refined vegetable oil or blend [rapeseed, corn, rice, or soybean]. Do not use olive oil, peanut oil, or animal fats because of their dominant flavor.)

For dipping sauce:

- grated *daikon* radish
- grated fresh ginger
- 1/4 cup each of soy sauce and *mirin*
- 1 cup *dashi* stock

Warm stock, soy sauce, and *mirin* liquor in pan. Divide into dipping bowls. On separate small plates mound grated radish and top with a cone of grated ginger. The garnish is to be mixed in the sauce by each diner just as food arrives.

Before starting, prepare for each diner a plate, or, ideally, a *zaru* bamboo basket, lined with one sheet of unglazed, white paper folded in half.

Peel prawns and remove the veins. Leave tail tips intact. Cut sweet potato into 1/8-inch thick slices. Cut eggplant into tea-whisk shape by slicing lengthwise half-way down the vegetable in several parallel cuts about 1/8 inch apart, so the pieces are all still attached, then fan slightly like card deck.

Mix egg and ice-cold soda water to make one cup. Add the flour. The mix should be lumpy, and plenty of pockets of unmixed flour is fine.

Heat oil slowly to about 338°F. Test with a drop of batter: frying should be rapid, but not browning or burning. Starting with prawns, dip pieces into batter. Slide carefully into hot oil. When golden brown, remove and place on metal draining rack, then immediately onto a plate. Once prawns are done, repeat for vegetables. The oil should be slightly cooler: slightly below 338°F is fine.

Stuffed Baby Eggplants

- 1 or 2 small (preferably, sweet Japanese) eggplants per person
- 3 oz. finely chopped shrimp meat
- 1 spring onion, finely minced
- 3 1/2 oz. minced pork
- 1 tsp. cornstarch
- 1 Tbs. grated ginger
- oil for deep frying

Cut each eggplant lengthwise to about one-third of the way from the stem end. Repeat cut at 90 degrees to make a cross. Widen gap carefully, then salt exposed flesh. Mix meat, shrimp, onion, ginger, and cornstarch. Form a rough ball (about 1 Tbs.) of the mixture, and stuff the eggplants. Dust with some more cornstarch.

Heat oil to about 330°F. Slide eggplant carefully, one or two at a time, into hot oil until flesh is tender. Drain and serve.

Rice and Rice-Based Dishes

Rice is best eaten on its own, and is accorded a great degree of respect in Japanese cooking. Each grain will not be loose but will have a moist sheen. The rice will be just slightly sticky to the touch. When moistened with some water, the grains do separate easily from the others. However, there are dishes in which pure white rice is mixed with other foods. This may be in the form of *chirashi-zushi*, an unpressed *sushi* of rice, vegetables, and pickled fish, somewhat like a cold pilaf or rice salad. It may also be a dish required for all celebratory occasions—*sekihan*, or red rice—where *azuki* beans are cooked with sticky rice to produce the pink-colored rice that means "festival" to any Japanese.

Gyûdon or Oyakodon

- 1/2 cup chicken breast per person, cut in cubes, or the equivalent *thinly* sliced good beef
- 1 1/4 cup *dashi* (or substitute a very light chicken bouillon) stock
- 4 Tbs. Japanese dark soy sauce
- 2 Tbs. Japanese light soy sauce
- 4 Tbs. *mirin, saké*, or dry sherry
- 2 tsp. sugar
- 2 cups leeks, cut into thin diagonal rings
- 4 eggs, lightly beaten
- bowl of freshly cooked hot rice per person

Bring the stock to a light boil. Add the soy sauces, liquor, and sugar. Add the chicken or beef, reduce the heat and simmer for five minutes. Stir in the leeks and allow to stand for one minute. Add the beaten eggs and allow to stand for a further two minutes. Carefully stir once. Pour meat over rice in each bowl.

Flavored steamed rice (*takekomi gohan*), in which additional ingredients are boiled together with the rice, is next in popularity to plain cooked white rice. Depending on the additions chosen, the rice is given color, texture, and a festive appearance. This way of cooking rice is not often encountered in home cooking. It is most often seen in Buddhist vegetarian menus, where the dearth of meat- or fish-based dishes is an incentive to the cook to devise ingenious means of tempting the diner.

Rice balls (*onigiri*) have been the Japanese equivalent of sandwiches for centuries. Fresh cooked rice molded around a stuffing is the quintessential picnic or travel food. A common filling is a soft, meaty pickled plum (*umeboshi*): tart, aromatic, and salty. The plum pickle helps preserve the freshness of the rice and was the traditional filling for long journeys. Other popular fillings are salted cod roe (*tarako*) or grated dried bonito (*katsuobushi*). Rice balls can be shaped in triangles as well, and a small rectangle of crisp dark green seaweed (*nori*) is sometimes wrapped at its middle to facilitate being eaten by hand.

Rice is sometimes eaten in the form of a rice soup or gruel. *Okayu* is rice gruel, flavored with pickled vegetables or fish or eaten on its own with a side dish of pickles or fresh vegetables. *Zosui* is an upmarket version, with fresh crabmeat and other seafood simmered with the stock-flavored rice and garnished with the mild parsleylike trefoil.

Tea-based rice soup or *ochazuke* is a more unpremeditated version of rice soup. Its origin is the customary respect accorded to rice. Traditionally regarded a gift of the deities, rice has great ritual and physical importance. Most traditional Japanese to this day shudder at the idea of wasting any bit of it. But what is one to do with the odd grains of rice that are stuck in the rice bowl at the end of a meal? The solution was to pour a little bit of tea into the bowl, scrape off any remaining rice with one's chopsticks into the tea, and then drink the tea, dregs and all. Gradually this custom has evolved into a dish of its own. Many elderly Japanese will still perform this action at the end of a meal. In the tea ceremony and in Buddhist monasteries, a teapot of hot water is served at the end of the meal for the same purpose, as well as for cleaning one's own eating bowl. *Ochazuke* can be, and in fact has become, quite an elaborate dish, far from its humble origins. Rather than simply tea, stock is added. Instead of just a few grains of rice, it has become a proper helping. Flavored with pickles, vegetables, or even meat and fish of the diner's choice, it can be a full, one-bowl meal. Add some sesame seeds, some crisp, crumbled seaweed, and it is considered a weapon against drunkenness, and as such is served at the end of drinking parties, both to indicate the end of the drinking, and to help the inebriated recover.

Pounded Glutinous Rice

Some rice varieties, when cooked, become very waxy or glutinous, owing to a low proportion of starch. The higher the starch or amylose content, the fluffier and looser the individual cooked kernels. The regular rice eaten at Japanese meals has an intermediate starch content, which results in soft cooked grains with a slight tendency to adhere to one another. Low-starch or glutinous rice is sought after for making sweets and for festive rice dishes in Japan, as in most Asian countries.

In contrast to regular rice, which is cooked by a combination of boiling, simmering, and steaming, glutinous rice is merely steamed for 20 to 25 minutes. When done, it is taken and pounded (traditionally in a wooden mortar made of a hollowed-out log), resulting in what is called *mochi*. What emerges is a sweetish, very sticky dough, the consistency of stiff chewing gum. *Mochi* is beloved of young and old. It is distributed to neighborhood children when a new house's roof is put in place. It is given as take-away gifts at weddings, and thrown to crowds at festivals. Dipped into sweet bean jam it makes a sumptuous confection. Dried, *mochi* was a hard-times treat, which kept for many months. It would become rock hard, looking somewhat like a small, badly made ceramic tile. Inedible in its natural state, dry *mochi* toasted carefully over coals (or in a grill) puffs up. The outside crisps, and the inside softens. Somewhat like marshmallows, the inside is gooily good, the outside toasty-crunchy. *Mochi*-eating is not without its dangers, especially to the elderly, who can choke on the chewy sweetmeat.

Mochi is a ritual food par excellence. The sound of the pounding mortar is reputed to scare away demons, and whether it does so or not, the evocative sound is enough to bring out droves of people expecting a treat. Traditional pounding requires two people. The warm cooked rice is placed in a mortar carved from a tree trunk. Holding a heavy wooden mallet, a man (usually) pounds the mixture in a steady rhythm. A woman (usually) moves the mass about in time to the pounding, to provide an even kneading. Sometimes they get their timing wrong. In such a case, the pounder is required in many places to strap the mortar to his back and climb with his burden over the roof of the nearest house. The ambiance of the *mochi*-making is one of jocular gaiety and lightheartedness, and in the process, many jokes (some suggestive) produce hilarity and good-natured teasing as people wait for their share and their turn at the mallet or mortar.

Red Rice

A common way of preparing rice for celebrations comes down from the Heian period (794–1185) and possibly before. Red rice (*sekihan*) is one of the remaining descendants of the many types of festive colored rice dishes dating from that period. Lightly cooked small purple beans (*azuki*) and their purplish liquid are added to the rice and cooked together. The beans dye the rice a pink-purple color and both flavor the rice and make it stickier than normal. Red rice can be shaped into many different forms, or it can simply be placed in a box or a mound for consumption. It is a necessary element of many Shintô shrine celebrations, not only as an offering to the deity but also because by partaking of it, the participants in a ritual are regarded as having shared a meal with the deity.

Alternatively, red rice can be achieved by cooking the rice with a bit of stock and some finely minced pickled plum. This, too, dyes the rice the desired color, but less flamboyantly than the beans. Red rice is not, of course, common fare but is normally used for special occasions: rituals, weddings, or other special occasions where rice represents a small portion of the quantity, but a large portion of the significance, of the celebratory meal.

Steamed Dishes

Steaming is an excellent way of preserving flavor and uniform color. Steamed dishes (*mushimono*) can include fish and vegetables steamed together, often in a sauce of ginger, soy sauce, and *mirin*. Pride of place in the steaming shelf goes to a steamed soup custard called *chawan-mushi*. This steamed custard is based on a mixture of eggs, *mirin*, and *dashi*, to which the cook might add fragments of marinated chicken, vegetables (strong-flavored herbs counteract the blandness of the dish), gingko nuts, and lotus root. The art of making a good *chawan-mushi* is the art of balance: ensuring that blandness is counteracted with bursts of flavor, and that the softness of the custard is balanced by tasty nuggets that give one's teeth something to work on.

Steamed Savory Custard (*Chawan-mushi*)

- 3 eggs
- 2 cups *dashi* stock
- 1/2 cup white chicken meat cut into thin strips
- 8 small peeled shrimps
- 1 lily bulb
- 4 trefoil leaves (*mitsuba*)
- 4 *shiitake* mushrooms
- 8 shelled gingko nuts
- 1 1/2 tsp. soy sauce
- 1 tsp. of salt
- 1 Tbs. *saké*

Beat eggs with stock, soy sauce, and *saké*. Cut each strip of chicken into four pieces and sprinkle lightly with soy sauce. Cut off inedible stem ends of mushrooms. De-vein shrimp if necessary and poach lightly. Cut lily bulb into four.

Distribute dry ingredients evenly among four individual small, deep, heat-proof bowls. Deep tea-bowls (*chawan*), or large, handle-less tea-cups, can be used if you have no *chawan-mushi* bowls. Pour in egg mixture. Place trefoil leaf on top. Place in large steamer *above* water. Close lid and steam for 15 to 20 minutes. The result should be firm but wobbly on top, soupy at the bottom.

Pot Dishes

Cold weather, which can be *very* cold, particularly in central and northern Japan, has brought about the invention of a number of different "pot dishes" (*nabemono*). These dishes are also determined by regional technical specialties: iron pots and ceramic pots were popular in different parts of the country, depending on regional technology and industry in pre-modern times. The eastern coast of northeastern Japan has been famous for centuries for its ironwork, and, unsurprisingly, most pot foods there are made in the cast-iron pots that were the area's specialty. Around the Inland Sea (*Seto-nai kai*), where potteries were common, and the weather less brutally cold, *nabemono* are made and served in large ceramic pots.

The large variety of *nabemono* owe their existence to the simplicity of the dish. Generally, they fall into two types. On the one hand are dishes cooked in a pot in the kitchen. Mostly these are hearty stews for the winter. These *chirinabe* vary from place to place, including fish such as cod, meat, chicken, and always a plenitude of vegetables stewed for a brief period in stock and served with dipping bowls of soy sauce or the juice of Japanese limes mixed with *tamari* into a sauce called *ponzu*. The second type belongs to a lengthy tradition of cook-your-own, a tradition that extends over several different cooking methods. In dishes such as *sukiyaki* (probably best known to the non-Japanese) and *shabu-shabu*, diners cook thin slices of meat and vegetables in a greased flat iron pan (*sukiyaki*) or in boiling water (*shabu-shabu*), then help themselves to the cooked food. The juices that collect in the pan are supplemented (or in the case of *sukiyaki*, deglazed) with *saké* and stock, and noodles or rice cakes are cooked in the flavored liquid to end the meal.

Perhaps the most interesting of *nabemono* is *chanko-nabe*. This is the dish used to put meat and weight onto sumo wrestlers. The wrestlers consume huge amounts of this dish as a staple. Its most prominent characteristic are the large cakes of *mochi*, which are required to give the wrestlers their strength. Early in the morning, once they have finished their training, apprentice wrestlers go about preparing a huge pot of *chanko-nabe*.

Udon Noodle Bowl

Recipes vary, including meat, chicken, fish, seafood, *hakusai* cabbage, leeks, and kelp. Two ingredients are considered, however, to be absolutely necessary. Large cakes of *mochi* (pounded rice) are always included, since the experience of trainers shows that this puts meat, rather than fat, onto the wrestlers whose weight is an important factor in victory. The second element is *shiitake* mushrooms, which wrestlers believed (and it has since proven to be the case) counteract arteriosclerosis. So important are *shiitake* to the diet that one of the prizes given during the bimonthly national Grand Sumo tournament is a huge glass trophy cup, about five feet high, full of these dried mushrooms: presumably enough to last the wrestler until the next tournament, two months away.

Simmered Dishes

Simmered dishes (*nimono*) are an important category of Japanese cooking. The objective is to impart flavor to a food without loosing its essential sensory characteristics: taste and shape. The simmering liquid is most often some form of *dashi* stock. *Saké, mirin,* and soy sauce are common additions, depending on the food to be cooked. The food is placed in a ceramic pot and gently allowed to simmer for as little as a minute or two, or as long as several hours. Often simmering is the second step after blanching (particularly for bitter vegetables), frying, or grilling. The food is kept under the liquid by the use of a lid with a smaller diameter than the pot. Usually made of cedar wood, such a lid gradually assumes a seasoned flavor which it imparts to the food.

Soups

The foundation stock of Japanese cooking, *dashi,* can be consumed on its own as a clear soup or as *miso* soup. Both *miso* soup and clear soup are based on *dashi* stock. Vegetarian soups for Buddhist cooking are based on dried brown mushroom (*shiitake*) and laver (*konbu*). Though fish stock (*ichibandashi*) is the heart of Japanese soup dishes (and many other dishes as well), its delicacy means that sometimes something stronger is necessary for a soup dish. This is accomplished by adding a third ingredient to the *katsuobushi-konbu* alliance. *Niboshi* are tiny sardines that have been dried whole. The addition of good *niboshi* (they go off quite quickly) to a stock ensures a stronger, more robust flavor. This kind of stock might be used as the basis for a *misoshiru* or for a robust sauce or stock. The *niboshi* themselves might be discarded like *katsuobushi* after it has yielded its essence, or fresh *niboshi* may be added as a garnish to the soup.

The standard Japanese soup that accompanies most meals in traditional Japanese cooking, however, is *miso* soup. *Miso* soup or *misoshiru*, otherwise known as *omiotsuke* (honorable flavor enhancer) permits almost infinite variation and is made by the addition of fermented soybean paste (*miso*) to a *dashi* stock. Everyone and every household has their own preferences. *Miso* soup is an energy-giving food: combined with rice, it makes a complete and healthy meal. Protein is supplied by the soy beans that have been fermented in the *miso* paste, carbohydrates by the rice, and vitamins and minerals from the soup vegetables.

Some households use only one type of *miso*, but chefs prefer to blend different kinds and colors—red, white, dark—to achieve a harmonious balance. Pale *miso* soup is favored in western Japan, while darker *miso* in Tokyo and the north. And the types of garnishes that can be added are almost innumerable. Most popular are cherrystone clams, small tofu cubes, and seaweed. Garnishes are limited to two or three different items, chosen according to season and contrast of texture, shape, and taste. One of the items is usually chosen for its scent, thus a few fresh *shiitake* mushroom slices, chopped spring onions, or a spoonful of fermented soybeans (*natto*) might grace the soup. *Nameko* mushrooms, jute leaves (*moroheya*), or small parboiled taro tubers might be added to contribute their slipperiness, a desirable food quality. Among other garnish choices are strips of bamboo shoot, fancy cuts of giant radish, leeks, lotus root, molded fish paté, or dried gluten (*fu*) molded in celebratory shapes.

The garnishes are chosen with restraint so as not to overwhelm the background flavor of the *miso* soup itself. Overall, exploring the variations of *misoshiru* is such a delight that it never palls.

Misoshiru

- 4 cups *dashi* stock (either first or second stock, as discussed in chapter 2, depending on the strength of flavor desired)
- 3–4 Tbs. *miso* (one, two, or three types of miso, depending on choice: blends depend on individual preference)

For each person:

- 10 cherrystone clams, or
- 1–2 leaves trefoil, or
- 10 small tofu cubes, or
- 1 cut *shiitake* mushroom, or
- 1–2 *wakame* seaweed pieces

Add a few Tbs. warm stock to the *miso* in a bowl. Using a pair of chopsticks or a wire whisk, mix stock and *miso* to a thin paste, adding stock as necessary. Heat stock and add softened *miso*. Simmer gently, then add the garnish until warmed through. Be careful *not* to boil the soup or it will turn bitter. Serve in individual bowls (preferably lacquered wood, which keeps the soup at the right temperature) with a few pieces of garnish in each bowl. To drink, stir bowl once with chopsticks so the *miso* mixes with the stock.

Clear soup *(suimono)* is the other type of soup. In its most refined form, *suimono* is simply a *dashi* stock enhanced by adding a few bits of green—trefoil is one example—to float on the surface. When this clear soup is served in a black lacquered bowl, the leaves appear miraculously to be suspended on air. Often a few white mushrooms *(enokidake)*, small clams, or a piece of bream or cod cheek will garnish clear soup. This clear soup is made from fish stock, a fact that comes as a surprise because it tastes of the mildest chicken consommé.

Vinegared Dishes

Su is vinegar, commonly made of rice and thus much less acidic than Western vinegar. The term *sunomono* applies only to vinegar-dressed traditional Japanese salads. Western-style salads dressed with vinaigrette are called *sarada*. *Sunomono* might be a simple dish of blanched spinach or fresh raw purple and white seaweed, or an elaborate mixture of julienned carrots, giant radish, and raw fish. The dressing can be elaborated and smoothed by the addition of a tiny bit of sugar and some sesame paste.

Red and White Salad

- 4 cups or so sliced *daikon* radish (see below), about half of one radish
- 2 cups sliced carrots (see below)
- 1/4 cup *dashi*
- 1/4 cup rice vinegar
- 1 Tbs. sugar
- 2-inch piece *konbu* kelp

Make the sweet vinegar at least half a day earlier: heat *dashi*, add vinegar, dissolve sugar in liquid, allow to cool.

Slice vegetables into thin, narrow rectangles (about 1/8 inch by 1/2 inch by 2 inches). Place in bowl, salt thoroughly, then knead with hands for about five minutes. Radishes will turn translucent. Squeeze vegetables gently and discard all liquid.

Transfer to clean bowl, add one-third of the sweet vinegar. Mix again with hands, then lightly squeeze out vinegar and discard. Add rest of vinegar and kelp, mix, and allow to rest for at least a day before eating as a small side dish at room temperature.

Pickles and Preserves

Pickles, historically speaking, were for many people the only food to supplement the carbohydrates they ate. They were also absolutely necessary because they allowed most people to maintain a food supply over the winter, when fresh vegetables and other foods were scarce. The traditional food of the poor in rural Japan during the harsh winter months when nothing grew consisted of three things: hot water, cooked rice or millet, and pickles. So it is not surprising to find that pickles are a major item of diet in Japan, accompanying almost every meal, from breakfast to dinner. They are so popular that in rural areas, guests may be given a small plate of pickles and a cup of tea as a snack! And in traditional Japan in some areas, a girl was considered eligible for marriage once she could cook rice perfectly and make pickles. To this day, women in rural households in particular pride themselves on their pickles. Japanese pickles come in two broad categories: *shinko* (short pickles) and *tsukemono* (long pickles, though the word is also used to mean pickles in general).

Short Pickles

Most homemakers have a small pickling container at home. These are made of transparent plastic today (in the past they were wooden barrels), fitted with a lid with an internal screw ending in a perforated foot. Quick-pickling—cucumbers, eggplant, cabbage, or what have you—vegetables are thinly sliced and heavily salted in the box. The lid is fixed, and the screw brings the perforated foot down on the vegetables inside. In an hour or so, the liquid has been extracted from the vegetable, and the simple *shinko* is drained and rinsed from excess salt, ready, either on its own or with a sprinkling of vinegar, to be added to the family meal.

Pepper-Stuffed Cucumber Short Pickle
- 4 cucumbers or straight gherkins
- 8 banana peppers or Japanese *shishito* sweet peppers
- salt
- 8 green perilla leaves (*aojisô*)

Top and tail the cucumbers. Open the peppers lengthwise and discard seeds and stem end. Sprinkle cucumbers with salt and allow to stand for a few minutes. Then rinse briskly in boiling water. Cut each cucumber into two (the pieces should be large enough to enclose the peppers). Hollow out the cucumbers. Roll each pepper up tightly (or cut into strips lengthwise) and stuff the cucumber cylinders. Wrap each cylinder in a perilla leaf and pack into the bottom of a flat-bottomed bowl, or, if you are fortunate enough to own a Japanese pickling jar, use that. Salt liberally. If there are more cucumbers, create a second layer. Cover with a loose lid smaller than the diameter of the bowl (a strong flat plate will do) and lay a heavy weight on top (or screw down the plate of the pickling jar). Allow to rest in a cool place for two hours. Consume immediately: this is a short pickle and will not keep for more than a day.

Long Pickles

Long pickles, intended for preservation over a long time, are made in small local pickle factories and in giant industrial complexes as well. Few people make their own long pickles these days because the process is lengthy, great care must be taken, one needs room, and the process can be very smelly. The vegetables—Chinese cabbage, *daikon*, gourd, cucumbers, eggplant, and many others—are first dried, or sliced then dried. To this day, travelers in rural Japan can see racks of drying vegetables tied together by rice straw hanging under the eaves of many houses. The dried vegetables are then put into the fermenting vat with one of the common fermenting agents—rice bran *(nuka)*, miso, saké lees—and salted heavily. They are then allowed to rest and ferment for an appropriate period. Miso pickling results in a dark, gnarled pickle with a strong miso flavor. The pickle will keep for years in a refrigerator. The flavor depends, of course, on the kind of miso used. The residue of saké-making, *nuka* is a brownish, alcohol-scented cake. This is broken up and the vegetables immersed in it for a lengthy period of time. Such pickles, too, are the province of the professional pickle-maker. Before eating, the *nuka* must be rinsed off, but the resulting fragrant pickle is well worth the wait.

Above and beyond all pickles, however, the apricot-plum *(umeboshi)* reigns supreme. The fruit itself (not a plum but a kind of apricot, *Prunus mume*) is a rather small, strongly scented but insipid fruit. However, dried and preserved in salt and red perilla *(akajisô)* leaves, it becomes a pickle that accompanies every breakfast and many other meals. Some people favor the tiny (about the size of your little fingernail) crunchy ones, others prefer the larger (plum size) squishy ones. Whatever the texture, the flavor is a mixture of sour and intense salt. The *umeboshi* gives rise to one of Japan's eponymous dishes: *hinomaru bentô*.

Hinomaru Bentô

The name of the dish—*hinomaru*, or rising sun—is a tribute to the Japanese flag, and the dish was invented as a patriotic gesture in the early twentieth century.

- 1 flat lunch box
- 1 serving plain cooked white rice
- 1 large pickled plum (*umeboshi*)
- 1 tsp. light rice vinegar (or mix 1/2 tsp. white vinegar with same amount of water)

Flavor rice with vinegar, mixing thoroughly. Press rice flat in box. Center plum in middle of rice. Serve immediately, or seal and take along for a picnic or for eating later.

Daikon is most often made into *takuan*. After peeling, the giant root is allowed to dry in a well-ventilated space. In several months, it loses about 60 percent of its weight and bulk. It can then be pickled in many ways. The most common is to store it in a wooden barrel full of either *saké* lees or, more commonly, rice bran and salt. In the north, it is most often smoked before pickling, and it is possible to pickle it in just salt.

Chinese cabbage is often made into *kimuchi*, a pickle of Korean origin that has now become a Japanese staple. Coming in mild, hot, or fiery, depending on taste, the *kimuchi* is flavored with garlic, red peppers, and small shrimp. In Korea until a few decades ago, every rural household in the winter had several large black jars stuck in the compost pit, to keep the temperature even for the fermentation of this Korean staple. Japanese homemakers eschew the compost heap, but otherwise follow the traditional recipe.

Grilled Dishes

As in other societies, the foundation of all cooking methods is to be found in grilling over open fires. In Japan, grilled dishes (*yakimono*) can be prepared over a charcoal fire, and many foods—fish, chicken bits, vegetables, mushrooms, glutinous rice cakes—are grilled this way. The word *yakimono* also refers to what we would call dry-frying or searing. Many such dishes are adoptions of foreign foods. Thus stir-frying was adopted from Chinese origins but flavored and prepared the Japanese way, with thin strips of meat or vegetable, quickly cooked and flavored with soy and *mirin*.

Whole or sliced fish are often served as *yakimono*. One of the most common ways of preparing medium-size fish is simple salt grilling. This is a particularly good way of preparing delicate-fleshed river fish such as sweetfish (*ayu*) or trout, and even sea fish such as mackerel (*aji*) or sea bream (*tai*). By scattering salt heavily on the tail and fins, it is possible to ensure that they will stay crisp and erect, and a good cook will also impart to small fish such as *ayu* a sinuous curve as if it is still swimming. Some larger fish can be grilled as well. An excellent example is *katsuo-tataki*. Reputedly a favorite of Katsu Kaishu, a *samurai* who founded the Japanese navy, it is a specialty of Tosa on the island of Shikoku. This area has traditionally been home to a large *katsuo* fishing fleet, and the dish arises from that fish's annual visit in the autumn. The fresh fillet is cut off the fish. It is then quickly charred on the outside so the flesh becomes black and ashy. Sliced like a loaf of bread, the inside is a bright red. Slices are dipped into a *ponzu* sauce with minced shallots or spring onions. There are few more delightful ways of eating fish, and few fish that receive as much appreciation.

Seared *Katsuo* or Tuna Fillet (*katsuo tataki*)

- Bonito (*katsuo*) fillets or alternatively, fresh tuna steaks
- Coarsely cracked black peppercorns

For dipping sauce:

- 1/2 cup peanut oil
- 1 tsp. sesame oil
- 2 Tbs. soy sauce
- 1 tsp. finely grated garlic
- 1 tsp. finely grated ginger
- 1 Tbs. finely minced green shallots
- spice powder (*shichimitôgarashi*)

Mix sauce ingredients and divide into dipping bowls.

Roll fish in cracked black pepper. Heat a cast iron pan without oil until very hot. Char fish on all sides. Alternatively, use a chef's blow torch set to high and char on all sides. Slice into 1/4-inch slices with *very* sharp knife. Serve with a dipping bowl of sauce for each person. Fish should be charred on the outside and uncooked on the inside.

4

Typical Meals

This chapter is divided into three sections. The first section gives a brief picture of the general etiquette of household meals. Obviously this varies with the educational level and prosperity of the household, but the general features are true for most Japanese households. The second section provides a record of the "standard" daily meals of Japanese households. Again, there is a great deal of personal variation, but the general pattern is there. The final section of this chapter deals with the types of meals themselves and explores Japanese meals on a continuum that ranges from simple one-dish meals—some of which, since they do not contain rice, are not even considered a proper meal in Japanese culture—through meals served in a single course, to multicourse elaborate banquets, which are more commonly eaten outside the home. Generally speaking, multicourse meals are to be found in more elaborate circumstances, whether in the household or outside it. They are also more commonly consumed in the evenings, when people—families or groups of friends or associates—are able to come together. Simpler meals are more common particularly in the daytime of the working week, when individuals sometimes see meals as a mere break in the serious activities of the day. Happily enough, there is enough variation that one can have a very elaborate, or very simple, meal at any time of the day, even if this is an uncommon event.

Tray with Rice Bowl, Soup Bowl, Plate of Pickles, and Side Dish (Fuki)

HOME ETIQUETTE

In traditional Japan, the father was a powerful, remote figure, inspiring awe and sometimes fear, whose mealtimes were sacred: many a husband never ate a meal with his wife and family. Paradoxically, in modern Japan this custom is upheld for quite a different reason: long commuting time. Men often work until late, returning home after a commute of an hour or even two. The children are already in bed, and, if the man is lucky, his wife is still up waiting with dinner. In some cases, this problem is worsened for men who are posted either to another city or abroad, leaving their family, often including school-age children, behind.[1]

Japanese apartments tend to be small. The kitchen area is a side of the LDK (living-dining-kitchen) area, and thus food is served directly from the kitchen. Modern dining rooms often have a Western-style small table and chairs for family eating, though if possible, people will keep a traditional low tea table with folding legs in one of the other rooms for festive occasions, or a stack of individual low tables about a foot and a half square, for truly formal events. Eating utensils consist of chopsticks and bowls: rice bowls and variously shaped plates for side dishes, other bowls for dipping sauces and soup. Saké is drunk out of small cups (sakazuki), beer and soft drinks out of glass tumblers. Diners even in simple family meals often are provided with damp towels (shibori) to wipe their hands during the meal.

While the household is together, it is usually the wife who manages the meal. She will set the table, often with the help of the children. Each individual often has her or his own special bowl and set of chopsticks. Small children might have a set brightly decorated with comic book characters. The wife keeps the hot rice container and rice paddle (*shamoji*) by her side to fill the rice bowls. Each individual will have a bowl and one or more plates for side dishes. In summer, many people drink an unsweetened barley tea (*mugi-cha*) or water, or children will drink soda-pop and adults might drink one of the excellent Japanese beers. In winter, most people drink hot green tea. In some houses, the Western habit of having a sweet—fruit or a cooked dessert—has become popular, but in most households, even today, all dishes are served simultaneously.

DAILY MEALS

Daily meals for most Japanese are fairly standardized. Given that most Japanese workers, women and men, work away from home, there is a natural rhythm to the day and the week. Thus even though most workers eat away from home during lunch time, this is in effect a continuation of household meals. Evening meals, by the nature of things, as well as meals on weekends, tend to be more elaborate and complex.

Breakfast

Breakfast in Japanese households comes in two major variations, roughly Western style or Japanese style. Japanese-style breakfasts are more time-consuming, so in the modern world, most households, particularly those with younger couples, and couples with children, eat a Western-style breakfast. Japanese-style breakfasts in the home are more and more confined to weekends and other nonworking days. Hotels and restaurants that serve breakfast often offer a mix of Western and Japanese style, while traditional Japanese inns are still the best places to enjoy a full traditional breakfast.

Western breakfasts in Japanese homes differ in some details from those in the United States, but are roughly the same. Children have cornflakes or some other cereal, milk, and fruit yogurt. Adults tend to have toast and butter, eggs (fried, scrambled, or in an omelet), and slices of vegetables such as tomato or cucumber. There are also usually a slice or two of ham or a few small sausages. The adults drink coffee and store-bought orange juice, the children, milk.

Japanese-style breakfasts are more complex. The normative breakfast is a one-tray variant of the standard meal structure of rice, soup, and side dishes. For breakfast, this consists of steamed white rice, a bowl of *miso-shiru* soup, and pickles, usually either pickled giant radish (*takuan*), pick-led plum (*umeboshi*), or short-pickled cabbage. Sheets of dried laver (*nori*) cut into standard one- by three-inch rectangles are used to wrap rice and awaken the tastebuds. Commonly, a Japanese-style breakfast will also in-clude a slice of salted grilled salmon (or some other fish) and a raw egg, which is beaten in a small bowl and poured on the hot rice. In eastern (but not western) Japan, a popular breakfast dish is fermented soybeans (*natto*), which are mixed with either the soup or the rice. Obviously preparing all the little side dishes is time-consuming, and unsurprisingly, most busy people, who might have to go to work themselves, prefer preparing quicker Western-style breakfasts.

Mid-morning Snack

Most Japanese pause for a mid-morning snack. Here, too, there is a split between Japanese and Western styles. Individuals choose between them as circumstances and preferences dictate. Japanese snacks can consist of a quick bowl of noodles, a piece of peeled and cut fruit, or a cup of tea with a rice cracker or other Japanese confection. These are mostly consumed by older people who prefer traditional ways.

Western-style snacks (the dichotomy is not as sharp as one could ex-pect) are available to whomever wants them. Western cakes and cookies, or Japanese modifications of them (e.g. green-tea flavored cakes) are available everywhere. Many coffee shops serve special tea or coffee "sets"—a pot of beverage and a cake. Children at home often have ice-cream or some other sweet that would be instantly familiar to anyone from a Western country.

School Lunches

The Japanese government provides school lunches for small children. Older children, in middle and high school, must bring their own. Though the school system provides most of the lunch, it is expected that the child's mother will provide the single most culturally important item: cooked rice. Every child is provided with a small rice container. Providing a helping of rice from home ensures two things, according to Japanese ed-ucationalists: the child will be more appreciative of food knowing it is from its mother, and the mother will be better able to keep an eye on the child's heath by inspecting the remains, if any, in the rice box.

Older children usually bring box lunches. The lunch boxes themselves have become items of prestige and are often made of high-tech materials to ensure the food is kept at the right temperature and free of spoilage. They are often decorated with the latest pop idol or comic book (*manga*) character. The lunch box contains special compartments, one for rice, others for side dishes: cooked chicken decorated with a bit of parsley, a small sausage, and small cakes or yogurt drinks. All of the side dishes are available as ready-made foods from supermarkets, and some homemakers do not make their own, but assemble the necessary store-bought ingredients according to the child's tastes and appetite.

Midday Meal

The midday meal in most Japanese households is lighter than the evening meal and occurs in different venues for various family members, because most of them are at work or at school. For the stay-at-homes, it might mean little more than a bowl of noodles, or some other light meal. Midday meals thus fall into three different types. People at home will usually eat a light meal of some sort. People at work will either bring a boxed lunch, similar to the school lunch described above, but in more adult proportions and suited to adult tastes. Alternatively, many office and factory workers eat either at the company canteen, if there is one, or at a nearby restaurant, usually one that caters to working people.

There is a huge variety of box lunches available in Japanese cuisine, and they are dealt with extensively below. One must keep in mind two things: box lunches brought from home tend to be less elaborate than bought ones. On the other hand, many box-lunch ingredients can be bought ready-made from department stores and supermarkets. The simplest of box lunches—*onigiri*—is little more than a ball of vinegared rice surrounding a piece of pickle or dried bonito shavings. It is indeed one of the origins of a far more refined food: *sushi*. Greater elaboration requires more effort and is consequently rarely seen in a daily meal.

At work, workers may leave the office or workshop for a quick half hour. Near or within all major business districts throughout Japan, and many industrial zones, it is possible to find restaurants that cater to people working in the neighborhood. The places are usually small and the pace frantic. In many places catering to hurrying office workers, set lunches can be prepaid at the vending machine placed at the restaurant's entrance. A colored plastic tag identifies each set, and the tag can be handed immediately to the hurrying waiter; the food is usually set on the table within a

minute or two. The sets are usually simple rice-soup-pickle-side dish combinations: salt-grilled fish, fried fish or meat, stir-fried vegetables. Most
diners are in a hurry, and any empty seat is soon filled. Waiters accept the
ticket, and return with the meal, which is usually gobbled in silence with
several glasses of cold water or hot tea for dessert. Rather than a dining experience, these are usually simple pit stops in a busy day.

Evening Meal

The main meal for most Japanese is the evening meal. The composition
of such a meal varies, of course, according to taste, but it almost always
will contain, or conclude with, plain rice. This is also likely to be an event
where etiquette is preserved and where the entire family eats together
(though many commuters arrive home too late to join their family at
meals on weeknights).

These daily meals are rarely elaborate. The major components tend to
be rice, a soup, and side dishes of vegetables, pickles, and fish or meat. Depending on whether an adult has been at home during the day, they may
have a greater or lesser component of ready-made foods from the store. In
some households where the adults are working outside the house and
there is no time to prepare a meal, home-cooked meals are confined to the
weekends; during weekdays, pre-cooked frozen food packs, similar to TV
dinners, have, unfortunately, become very popular. In households where
an adult, usually the wife, stays at home, there is time to prepare a proper
meal of rice, soup, and several side dishes.

TYPES OF MEALS

As this chapter has described, there is a natural rhythm to the ways in
which people consume food in Japanese society. The following section of
the chapter moves away from eating patterns to concentrate on the composition of the meals themselves. In practice, simpler meals occur during
the mornings and midday, elaborate meals in the evenings and weekends.

The One-Dish Meal

One-dish (or more properly, one-bowl) meals are very popular, particularly among people at work. One-dish meals might include rice, or
they may not, but they almost always include some form of pickle on the
side.

Perhaps the most popular one-dish meals are noodles. These come, as we have noted in a previous chapter, in a bewildering number of varieties. Not only are the toppings different, but the variety of noodles itself allows the diner a range of choice to suit the mood, time, weather, and of course, the purse.

The cheapest and quickest way to dine in any of the large Japanese cities is a stand-up noodle shop. Thousands of workers eat at such shops every weekday lunchtime. There are no stools nor chairs; a counter with a ledge provides the eating surface. The menu is limited to two or three types of noodle topping at most. Once the order is given and paid for, the person behind the counter quickly ladles some soup into the bowl, slips in some hot noodles and whatever topping was ordered, and passes it over. Disposable chopsticks in a container, a water or tea dispenser with a stack of glasses or cups, and a jar of pickles complete the offerings. People help themselves and gobble down the noodles. The quickest of quick meals: you can be out and back at your desk in under 10 minutes.

At a slightly more relaxed pace are shops that provide other types of one-dish meals, many of which are also popular with families. Noodles in soup—Chinese noodles, buckwheat noodles, Sapporo noodles, thick wheat noodles—are most common. But one can also eat rice bowl (*donburi*) one-dish meals, in which a topping is layered over rice: chicken meat or a pork cutlet fried with leeks, then simmered briefly in stock, soy sauce, and an omelet, which is then poured on rice, or stir-fried onions and beef strips known in the United States as a beef bowl. These particular dishes are closer to the traditional *ichijûsansai*, because they are most often served with a small dish of pickles and bowl of *misoshiru* soup on the side.

One particular favorite in the summer are grilled eel fillets simmered, dipped in sauce, and broiled several times to an unctuous smoothness. These are placed on square lacquered containers filled with rice. The eel is considered a particularly strengthening food, and specialist grilled eel restaurants do a roaring business in midsummer. Another favorite, particularly in Hokkaido where it was invented, is a bowl of freshly cooked rice topped with the glistening ruby pearls of fresh salmon eggs.

The ease of making one-dish meals makes them very attractive for busy homemakers. There are two perennial children's favorites, though many adults carry an appetite for these dishes into later life. Curry-rice entered Japan with British merchants who set up shop in Yokohama in the second half of the nineteenth century. This Anglo-Indian dish (its cousin can still be found in Britain today) is classically served in a boat-shaped porcelain bowl or in a Western soup plate and eaten with a spoon. A serving of rice in the plate is accompanied by a thick stew redolent of cinnamon, turmeric, and fenugreek. The stew is made of chunks of vegetables—potatoes, carrots, peas—and meat or fish, accompanied by a dab of red gourd pickle in lieu of Indian chutney. Another popular one-dish meal is a rice-omelet, which, like curry-rice, is of European origin. Cooked rice is quickly fried, a plain omelet is layered on top, and this is garnished with a squirt of tomato ketchup—simple, easy to prepare, and very satisfying for hungry young stomachs.

Standard Soup and Three Side Dishes

The main meal—any main meal—is structured around three separate elements: rice, soup, and side dishes. Dating from traditional times, Japanese have considered this structure, called *ichijûsansai* ("one soup, three dishes": the presence of rice is automatically assumed), the "natural" structure of a meal. If one of these elements is missing, particularly rice, the eater is likely to consider the meal incomplete, possibly a mere snack before the actual main meal. All of these three elements are served together. With the exception of the rice, in most cases these elements provide a field for variety. The three traditional dishes in *ichijûsansai* structure were one of raw fish (*sashimi*), a food cooked in a sauce (*nimono*), and a grilled or roasted dish (*yakimono*). Individual variations were the result of many factors. Economic ability, seasonality, the cook's ability, personal and family preferences, and the significance of the meal are major considerations. Japanese meals can be conceived of as variations on this theme. Like the "standard" meal in other cultures—think of steak, potatoes, and a salad, or a burger and fries—there is a normative framework that allows for huge variation. This structure is, of course, very flexible. The one soup and three dishes can be served simultaneously, or in courses. The soup is, of course, either a clear soup or, more commonly in modern Japan, a cloudy *misoshiru*. All "proper" meals include, of course, two other components, rice and pickles, which, in larger multicourse meals are served at the end, after the other dishes have been consumed.

Many Japanese people having a quick meal at home or a restaurant will have a set meal of soup, rice, pickles, and a single side dish such as fresh or grilled fish, served together on a tray. Combinations of one soup and one dish or one soup and two dishes are also acceptable, though they fall short of the modern ideal. Many more side dishes than the traditional three are also possible, but then the event falls into the category of banquet or feast.

Of course, the idea of *ichijûsansai* is a cultural norm: something that aesthetic philosophers have dreamed up. There are, in practice, many types

Stew-pot (*nabeyaki*) dinner. Courtesy of the authors.

of meals, depending on location, cook, and preferences. Yet we should always remember, at the back of our minds, that the model educated Japanese have of the proper or almost perfect meal consists of a bowl of rice, a bowl of soup made of *dashi*, and three side dishes of fish and vegetables.

Tray and Box Lunches

Weekday lunch times tend to be busy for most Japanese people, whether at home or at work. This has led to the emergence of "set" meals that are widely available in most restaurants, and, like TV dinners in the United States, have become staples of the busy home as well. These set meals, usually served on a single tray, have a related meal—the box lunch (*obentô*)—which is one of the delights of Japanese cuisine. A set meal (*teishoku*) is a fixed replication of the *ichijûsansai* concept for the modern world. Order it in a cheaper restaurant, and you will get an inevitable bowl of *misoshiru* soup, white rice, a dish of pickles, and a side dish of your choice. The choice depends on the type of restaurant: freshly cut *sashimi*, the slices of fish glistening pinkly and lying neatly on a bed of thread-cut radish; a perfectly grilled fish, the salt on its fins causing it to curl as it might have in life; a deep-fried pork cutlet resting on a bed of shredded cabbage and decorated with a trickle of sauce. In a more expensive restaurant, set lunches can be much more varied, though they are almost always

Compartmented Lunch Box

served in a single course, with all the dishes arranged on a tray in individual plates and bowls.

Box lunches, in effect a variation on the set/tray meal, appear in four different ways. During New Year, multi-tiered, elaborately packed boxes containing special New Year's food (see chapter 6) are shown and offered to guests. Children bring packed box lunches to school, and an entire industry has sprung up around the boxes themselves, and the foods inside, with cookbooks and magazine issues devoted to the subject. The stations of interurban trains usually sell a third type of box lunch. Station box meals *(ekiben)* are hugely varied and can be found throughout Japan. Finally, specialist box-meal restaurants *(bentôya)* allow one to indulge in mock travel through the medium of a lunch in a compartmented tray.

Station box meals come in flat boxes divided into small compartments. The largest holds the rice. Others hold whatever the local specialty is: pickles (of course!), fish, noodles, bits of meat or chicken, or perhaps crab or prawns. The trick is just to try it and enjoy. Most box meals look like a box of exquisite pirate treasures, with surprising flavor and textures, and many Japanese admit they are addicted to them.

Some station box meals come in odd shapes. One of the favorites is "cooking-pot rice" *(kamameshi)*, which comes in a small ceramic bowl formed like a wide-lipped traditional pot. The rice in the pot is covered with a layer of cooked fish and vegetables, with bits of pickled ginger mixed in.

NOTE

1. Japanese mothers are responsible for their children's education. Given the competitiveness of the Japanese educational system, parents are very reluctant to disrupt a child's schooling, preferring to send the husband off on his own.

5

Eating Out

Japanese sociologists argue that the Japanese eat out a great deal because Japanese houses are small and not suited for entertaining. This may well be the case, but the deeper truth may be that Japanese like to eat out because the choice is great and there is a lot of fun to be had.

There are as many ways and choices in eating out as there are groups of Japanese with shared tastes. This chapter discusses some of the major ways in which people eat out and why they do so. The places one can eat out in vary from traditional Japanese-style restaurants (with or without *geisha* entertainment), through snack bars of various descriptions, to restaurants that combine foreign ideas with Japanese tastes.

STREET FOODS

Urban streets are full of small vans selling various street foods, most of which (according to taste and personal preference) are worth trying. These barrows or vans are particularly common around train stations, where there are many potential customers. And, of course, street foods are a feature of the Japanese festivals covered in chapter 6.

There is neither much etiquette nor much order to the consumption of street foods. Most of them are highly appetizing, and though Japanese etiquette frowns on walking about while eating, many people consume the street food "on the premises" as it were: under the awning or near the barrow that supplied them.

Yatai—Street Food Stall

Any street food vendor is also a performer. To this day the haunting cry of the sweet-potato man, who makes his rounds in the cold winter nights through the streets, can evoke a bout of nostalgia:

> *Yakiiiii-imo, Yakiiii-imo, yakitate*
> *Oishiiii yakiiiiiiii-mo.*

> (Baked potatoes, baked potatoes, fresh baked
> Delicious baked potatoes.)

The *"yaki-imo"* (roast potatoes) sound, so drawn out, and then the quick syncopation of the *"yakitate"* (well roasted) spell out much of what street foods on a wintry night are like: the contrast between the cold outside and the potato in your hands.

Octopus Puffs, Fish Waffles, and Stuffed Buns

Decorated with red or blue bunting depicting a cheerful octopus, his head tied with a towel *(hachimaki)*, the octopus puff vendor *(takoyaki-san)* advertises his wares with a loudspeaker-enhanced song, calling people to taste his wares. Large drops of batter filled with chopped octopus meat and vegetables, the octopus puffs *(takoyaki)* are sold on little styrofoam plates and doused with a thick, sweetish, spicy sauce *(sôsu)*.

Fish waffles (*taiyaki*) are just as much fun. They are filled waffles in the shape of a fish (hence the name: *tai* is a sea-bream). The filling is crunchy purple sweet bean paste (*an*). The warm fish-shaped waffles are delicious in cold winters. The bunting that advertises the van often has pictures of a fish and of a round-faced monk. Here the Japanese indulge in a favorite pastime of punning. As noted elsewhere in this book, the *tai* (sea bream) is loved not only because of its wonderful flavor, but also because the name can be read as a homonym for *medetai* (congratulations). Another pun is in order as well. Buddhist chanting in monasteries and temples is often accompanied by ringing a wooden bell, which, because of its shape, is known sometimes as a fish. This, and the supposed invention of the dish as a vegetarian treat at a monastery (where meat and fish are not permitted) has led to the association of *taiyaki* with the image of a monk. The dish itself is a perfect marriage. A loose waffle batter is poured into a hot fish-shaped waffled iron. When cooked on one side, one adds a spoonful of *an* (sweet bean paste) and another dollop of batter. The iron is then closed, flipped, and the other side allowed to cook. From there to eagerly waiting hands it goes in seconds.

Other street foods characterize the winter as well. Chinese steamed buns (*manju*), stuffed with a meat, bamboo-shoot, and leek mixture or with sweet beans come hot from steamers in neighborhood grocery stores. Though these are generally commercially made, they provide a spot of warmth during cold winter days for anyone who needs them.

All of these street foods are most visible during *matsuri*, the frenetic and colorful festivals that most Japanese neighborhoods throw once a year in honor of their guardian shrine, and of course, of themselves. Grilled corn-on-the-cob and corndogs slathered with sweetish, ketchuplike *sôsu*; cotton candy; candied apples would be familiar to any reader. But there are also the street foods unique to festivals and to Japan: grilled squid glazed with soy-sauce; plates of rice cooked with beans; plates of stir-fried noodles with ribbons of red ginger pickle (*okonomiyaki soba*). And of course the pounding of the *mochi*-making mortar is usually there to remind everyone that a festival is on.

Stew

Another perennial favorite to be found near virtually every commuter train station is hodge-podge stew (*oden*). When night falls, and commuters head for home in the late evenings, the best stew barrows open for business. Often consisting of nothing more than a hand-pulled barrow

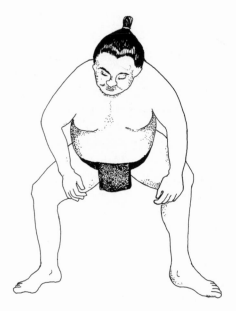

Sumo Wrestler

and a bench, one can recover somewhat from the rigors of an evening's drinking with one's officemates.

A pot of strong stock is set simmering. In it go brown tubes of fish paste (*chikuwa*), sweet potato and white potato slices, bundles of shiny-green tied kelp (*konbu*), glistening peeled boiled eggs, and white and pink half-moon slices of fish paste (*kamaboko*). Little brown fish-meal balls are well flavored by the immersion, as are pieces of jelly-like devil's foot root (*konnyaku*), rolls of parchmentlike *tofu* neatly tied with bow knots of dried gourd, or chunks of small gray taro. For about 150 yen, you can choose whichever of these you want. And with a dab of mustard and some beer or fiery sweet potato *shochu* liquor to quench your thirst, you can regain your strength. Of course it is possible to get *oden* at fancy specialist places, but they are far less entertaining, and far less flavorful, than at the humble barrow.

EATING AT A COUNTER

Unlike the United States, where counter foods are generally foods of the cheaper and quick-food variety, Japanese take their counter foods very seriously indeed. There are, of course, food counters where you get the Japanese equivalent of a hamburger and shake. But for some of the best

Japanese foods, one must belly up to the counter. The three most important types of high-class counter foods are all relatively well known outside Japan. Interestingly enough, the first Japanese food style that became popular in North America—hot plate *(teppanyaki)*—is far less common in Japan. Instead, the three top favorite counter foods in Japan are *sushi*, *tempura*, and deep-fried pork cutlet *(tonkatsu)*. All three of these eating styles have two things in common: the less the distance between the cook's hands and the diner's mouth, the better they taste (thus the counter), and they are often not worth making at home: eaten out is usually best.

Sushi

Freshness is, above all, the central point of *sushi*. The freshness completely exemplifies the nature of the relationship between people and food: a direct, unmediated relationship to nature. *Sushi* comes in a number of different shapes, depending on the fish involved. Open sandwich type, with a slice of fish on top *(nigirizushi)*, roll *(maki)*, and cone *(temaki)* are the most common ones. The shapes are determined by the type of filling. Fish and seafood that can be made into a largish slice are made into the open sandwich. Vegetables and pickles, and some kinds of seafood that need to be well contained, are made into rolls. Long stalks such as fresh radish sprouts and massed foods such as roe often go into cones.

Native Tokyoites will usually start with something slightly pickled—perhaps pickled herring *(kohada)*—then go on to the wide variety of fresh raw fish and seafood, and end (since Tokyoites have a sweet tooth) with

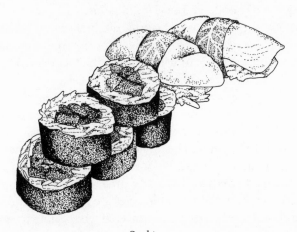

Sushi

one or more sweet morsels: raw sweet shrimp (*amaebi*) or sweet omelet wrapped in laver (*tamago*). The progression is sour or light pieces, such as *kohada*, followed by something slightly fatty (tuna belly [*torô*], squid [*ika*], or some white-fleshed fish), then something lighter to end the meal. These are merely general outlines based on a regional preference, but years of experience have shown most countermen how this particular progression enhances the dining experience. And a true *sushi* aficionado will never drink alcohol, particularly not rice-based *saké*, with *sushi* because the rice wine will spoil the flavor of the cooked rice.

Besides the freshness, the most important part of eating *sushi* is interacting with the counterman. It is the counterman, observant and knowledgeable, who makes the *sushi* experience what it is. The competent counterman—and inevitably it is a man, because Japanese believe that women's basal temperature is higher than men's and that this will affect the flavor of the product—will assess the customer and suggest, to the veteran and novice alike, what is appropriate. Quite often, an observant counterman will design the series of *sushi* for a customer, choosing and balancing to fit the customer's taste and perceived preferences.

A *sushi* meal does not fit neatly into the structure described in chapter 4 of soup and three side dishes (*ichijûsansai*) with rice. *Sushi* is both a snack and a meal: a snack, because the experience is much more loosely structured than the *ichijûsansai* model, and a meal, because, after all, *sushi* is based upon rice, which in the Japanese scheme of things defines a meal in contrast to a snack.

A *sushi* meal is a progression of tastes shaped by three main factors: the season, the counterman's expertise in judging his customer, and the customer's taste and mood. The season, of course, dictates the kinds of fish that are at their best. In the real world, the best season (*shun*) of particular fish is often disregarded. Nonetheless, for the true aficionado, it would be strange to consume eels in winter, *tai* in the fall, or bonito in the summer.

Modern restaurant developments such as rotating *sushi* (*kaiten zushi*) in which the plates circulate on an endless chain and the customer chooses plates without consulting the counterman are, unsurprisingly, the cheapest form of *sushi*. This should be obvious: rather than the personal service that is expected in a Japanese restaurant, the service is impersonal, even mechanical. To add to that, there is no order in the presentation: any dish can succeed any other. When addressing a counterman directly one also has a wide choice, and a first-class *sushi* chef will be able to subtly steer his customer in order to enhance the dining experience.

Tempura

Perfectly fresh morsels—fish, seafood, wild mountain vegetables such as young fiddlehead ferns, sweet potato, squash—are rapidly dipped into a light batter, then placed delicately in a wok of hot oil. Watched anxiously by the chef, who is watched by the discerning customer, the food metamorphoses into golden crunchy edibles, which are placed onto a straw plate lined with a sheet of white paper. The cooking is often so perfectly timed that the paper does not get greasy. The morsels may be dipped into flavored salt, or, more commonly, into a mixture of soy sauce, stock, grated ginger, and grated giant radish (*daikon*) to enhance the flavor. A few quick bites and it is gone, and, if the counterman is up to snuff, another tidbit is there for you to pick up.

The batter ensures that the flavors of the food are perfectly preserved. The good cook knows precisely when the particular foodstuff is cooked through, but before the fat penetrates. The control is so perfect that some tempura chefs will make a *tempura* ice cream. A ball of green tea–flavored ice cream is wrapped in a layer of sponge cake, then frozen. Dipped in batter and quickly fried until the batter is crisp, the ice cream is still frozen: a perfect dessert for a *tempura* dinner.

The two principles—freshness and personal service—that go into *sushi* are also what make the perfect *tempura*. The difference is of course in the product. Where *sushi* is barely cooked, tempura is all about heat and temperature, and what determines the experience is the ability of the cook to control the temperature to perfection.

Deep-Fried Pork Cutlets

The final counter food discussed here was originally, like *tempura*, a Western import. The name tells it all: *ton* (pork) *katsu* (cutlet). *Tonkatsu* come in different varieties depending on the cut. The three most common are a roast-cut, the more expensive fillet, and chunks on a wooden skewer (*kushiyaki*).

The pork cutlet is coated with flour, egg, and bread crumbs, then slipped gently into a deep wok of hot oil. When sufficiently cooked it is roughly chopped into bite-sized chunks and placed on a flat plate on a bed of shredded cabbage. It is eaten with purple pickled aubergine, hot, full-flavored pork broth thickened with *miso* paste, and filled with bits of onions and chunks of radish and Chinese cabbage (*tonjiru*) and glistening, steaming fresh rice. Fiery Chinese mustard and a thick, sweetened sauce based on Worcestershire (*sôsu*) sauce add contrast.

TRADITIONAL JAPANESE RESTAURANTS

Traditional Japanese restaurants, some of them very expensive, are called *ryôtei*. Unlike restaurants in the West, these are not solely for eating a meal. They are places for leisurely dinners, for banquets and drinking parties, for important events, and even for assignations.

The approach and internal fittings of these places are designed to be as elegant as possible. All are furnished Japanese style. As one enters, one is drawn into the world of Japan of yesteryear. Many *ryôtei* do little if anything to advertise their presence, which might not be marked at all, or merely feature a modest sign. The entrance, even in large cities, may be little more than a door set into a blank wall, through which one can glimpse a small dwarf tree on a stand, perhaps a miniature garden. After entering this small space and removing their shoes, guests are ushered into a world of elegance and exquisite sensibility. The waiters and hosts wear traditional Japanese clothing. Guests are led along polished wooden-floored corridors. These are often bordered by tiny gardens that appear to meander off into the lush vegetation of bamboo and bushes, and where one would, it seems, wander forever, but which in reality are little more than a few feet to a side. Sliding doors let the guests into the room which is surfaced with *tatami* mats. Against one wall there is always a niche containing flowers appropriate to the season, arranged by a master arranger. Seated on flat cushions, guests await the food, which is usually served on footed trays, sometimes on low tables.

The choice of food in a *ryôtei* is often the privilege of the chef or owner. He will select the foods and dishes appropriate for the season and the occasion. The customer specifies the price per guest, or the total sum, and the cook does the rest. In a proper *ryôtei* there is no itemized bill: merely a final sum written on a slip of Japanese paper in good brush calligraphy. The order of foods follows one another in succession, building upon the principles we have discussed above. As the dinner stretches on, the guests have an opportunity to move about, and if the party is large, circulate among guests they have not talked to before. The sliding doors to the gardens outside might be opened to allow the natural season to enhance the festivities.

At the end of the meal, rice is served (if there has been heavy drinking, this might be in the form of a rice and tea soup), and the guests are escorted out, to the bows and thank yous of the staff.

Ryôtei are venues for special occasions—for events that need to be celebrated or marked in some way. Few Japanese would think of going to a *ryôtei* for a night out. Nonetheless, *ryôtei* are very important in the culinary scheme of things. It is here that the most refined foods and the tradi-tional art of Japanese dining is practiced. *Ryôtei* are thus the setting both for specialist schools of cooking and for that most refined of Japanese cooking styles, *kaiseki*, which is discussed in Chapter 6.

Restaurant Etiquette

The strength and depth of emotion expressed by the serving staff as one enters a Japanese food establishment are the key to its quality. The enthu-siasm of the staff and their desire to please their customers are evident from the greeting "*Irashaimase*" (Welcome) one hears upon entry. Arriving at a Japanese restaurant, one is sometimes offered the choice of sitting at the counter or at a table. Sitting at the counter makes it is possible to see the show as the cook prepares dishes, and one can also judge the quality of the food, as the cook's hands go through well-practiced motions smoothly and without hesitation (good) or jerkily and without confidence (bad).

In summer, a cold hand towel and in winter, a warm one is provided to wipe one's hands and face. The cost of a restaurant can be judged by the utensils: well-cut bamboo or wooden disposable chopsticks in individually printed slips for expensive places, a container of machine-cut chopsticks for cheaper establishments.

Whether at a counter or on the table, the food arrives in a variety of at-tractive plates, some small, some large. The owner or manager may well have chosen them him- or herself to complement the decor or simply be-cause they were found to be attractive. Many establishments will display pieces of art, whether it is the owner's collection of craft pottery pieces, ink paintings, or, in one Tokyo bar, the owner's collection of swords and sword furniture—sword guards, sheaths, and so on—from the owner's other occupation as a fencing teacher. Even restaurants that do not have art for art's sake will often have sheets of paper with calligraphic notices on the day's menu.

A word is appropriate about menus. Most reasonably priced restaurants in Japan will have, in addition to a menu (printed in Japanese, and occa-sionally in very broken English), a display window outside the shop. In it are either photographs, or, more common by far, wax replicas of the foods sold in the shop, labelled with price and dish name. The replicas are in-credibly realistic, often mouth watering, and they are made to order in the Kappabashi area of Tokyo where hundreds of workshops cater to the restaurant industry. These replicas can be very useful for the foreign visi-tor, who can simply lead one of the waiters outside to the display and point at the most attractive dish.

TRADITIONAL BARS

If *ryôtei* exemplify the most refined style of Japanese dining out, Japanese-style bars *(izakaya)* represent the more informal Japanese style. There are thousands of bars in Japan, many of them Western-style, with a Western atmosphere and drinks. But others are Japanese-style drinking places where the food is as important or more so than the drinks. In fact, most *izakaya* have a very small selection of drinks, limited to *saké* of many different brands, beer, whiskey, and soft-drinks. It is, rather, in the variety of foods offered that Japanese bars excel. In most bars, one can order specialties that the barkeep enjoys. These might range from floury baked potatoes from northern Iwate Prefecture to pickled octopus or sea cucumber. Some *izakaya* specialize in skewers of grilled chicken bits *(yakitori)*, others serve fish grilled on charcoal fires, small elegant dishes of tofu or boiled green soy beans in their pods, or any of the literally myriad little dishes that make up Japanese cooking.

As in many traditional eating establishments, the most important (and sometimes most enjoyable) part of the proceedings is interacting with the person behind the counter. And though many *izakaya* have tables where individuals, couples, or parties might entertain themselves with drink and food, taking part in the counter's unofficial debating society contributes greatly to the fun.

Izakaya come in a great variety of guises, ranging from small hole-in-the-wall shops with five stools near the counter, serving workers on their way home, to multistoried halls serving elaborate dishes. They rarely serve rice: they are, after all, drinking places, and rice inhibits drink. But they provide an enormous range of little (and not so little) tidbits that must all be washed down by copious amounts of beer or *saké* (and now, more often than not, whiskey and water, or wine).

Grill Bars

Charcoal cooking comes into the Japanese kitchen in several guises. Fish and other foods can be consumed in specialist fireside grills *(robatayaki-ya)*, where diners sit around sand pits filled with glowing charcoal. Grilled bird *(yakitori)* specialize in providing chicken bits on skewers, somewhat like shish kebab of the Middle East. *Robata-yaki* provide different grilled foods, as the taste and expertise of the cook and the demands of the customers dictate. These two types of traditional grill bars are convivial places, filled with smoke and the mingled odors of grilling fish and charcoal. *Yakitoriya* are more frequently seen, perhaps because the investment is smaller: a narrow charcoal grill, just wide enough for standard bamboo skewers, some cuts of chicken, and a refrigerator full of chilled beer, and voilà: *yakitori*.

Of course, like any other form of dining, grill bars come in a wide variety of styles to fit any purse. Smaller shops have a more limited choice of tidbits but the small size offers an opportunity to talk with the owner as the food grills. Larger places have much wider menus, and new types of grilled meats and other food are added all the time. For vegetarians, there is a wide array of vegetables: *shiitake* mushrooms, asparagus, leeks, as well as other nonmeat dishes. One popular dish is cubes of tofu topped with a spread of thick tea- or *miso*-flavored paste, then grilled *(dengaku)*. A local specialty from northern Japan is glutinous rice grilled on a thick skewer *(kiritampo)*. For the carnivore, there is heaven, whether for the fish-lover or the pure carnivore, as almost every part of the chicken and every kind of fish is to be found. Often the greatest dilemma is whether to season the food with the special sauce of the house *(tare)* or with plain salt.

COOK YOUR OWN

Though one of the major distinguishing characteristics of Japanese food is the service that accompanies it, sometimes one needs or wants to direct one's own cooking. The solution for that is one of the many styles of "cook-your-own" dishes. These range from a dish that is favored by students for its cheapness, to expensive yet convivial party dishes. Specialty restaurants have emerged for each of these types of dish.

Griddle Cooking

A *teppan* is a large iron griddle that, before the advent of electricity, was heated over coals, and nowadays over gas or electricity. Cooking is simple: the griddle is oiled with a piece of beef fat or some vegetable oil. Finely sliced vegetables, usually starting with onions, then carrots, Chinese cabbage *(hakusai)*, leeks, and then more delicate vegetables such as chrysanthemum leaves and bean sprouts, are added. Each diner has plate of dipping sauce made of soy sauce and the juice of the Japanese lime. At the end of the meal, the inevitable bowl of rice awaits. A variant on the flat griddle is a domed fluted griddle called, from its similarity to a Mongol warrior's helmet, a *jingizkan* (in honor of Mongol conqueror Genghis Khan). The cooking method remains the same: pieces of fish, vegetables, shellfish, and meat are placed on the hot griddle and each diner helps himself.

There are numerous other variants of *teppan-yaki*. Korean barbecues emphasize beef flavored in the Korean style: hot chilies, sesame oil, and finely minced shallots. In Hokkaido, a popular version offers simply sliced onions and thinly sliced mutton or beef. At many marine resorts, a *teppan-yaki* consists of a mound of shellfish with a dipping sauce of Japanese lime, soy-sauce, and butter. The possibilities for home entertaining are of course there as well, and many Japanese families have an electric *teppan* for just this purpose. A more flexible alternative is a flat, bottle-fed gas burner on which one can place a *teppan*, a *jingizkan*, or a bowl for pot stews (*shabu-shabu* or *sukiyaki*).

"As You Like It" Pancake

At the cheap end of the scale is a students' favorite. In the neighborhood of most universities one can find one or more "as-you-like-it" (*okonomiyaki*) restaurants. Students gather after hours, pooling their money when funds are low, and order these giant stuffed pancakes. A large "mug" or smallish bowl is filled with a loose batter of egg and flour and whatever bits the customer desires: fish, octopus, chicken, chrysanthemum leaf, Japanese scallions. The whole is mixed with a raw egg and noodles. The diners pour the batter onto a hot griddle, making a giant pancake, which, when cooked on both sides, is cut up and shared among the hungry participants after being liberally doused with a sweet sauce (*sôsu*). The shared pancake and the smell of it cooking is enough to bring tears to the eyes of adults as they remember their student days.

The sauce used on *okonomiyaki* has made the fortunes of at least one commercial company. Evolved from the British Worcestershire sauce, it is a thick brown substance, somewhat between ketchup and thick soy sauce in consistency, and somewhat like the British HP sauce or Philadelphia relish in taste. The company that has been making it since the nineteenth century (and has a virtual lock on the market) is constantly seeking new recipes for *okonomiyaki* and *tonkatsu*.

"As-You-Like-It" Pancake
- One large true yam (available at Asian and Caribbean markets)
- 5 oz. flour
- 1 medium Chinese cabbage, sliced medium fine
- 1 spring onion, chopped
- 1/2 cup small peeled veinless or dried shrimp (or other seafood if preferred)

- 6 eggs
- 1 Tbs. instant stock (*dashi*) granules
- 6 oz. chopped fatty pork, Chinese sausage, mushrooms, or whatever preferred for topping
- mayonnaise
- Worcestershire sauce or, preferably, Japanese *sôsu* (can be found at some Asian groceries)
- mustard
- soy sauce

Grate the yam, keeping the liquid. It should be a rather sticky, frothy liquid. Make a loose batter of flour and beaten eggs, then add yam. The quantity of yam added should be greater than the flour, and a fairly loose batter is desirable. Season with instant *dashi*. If yam is unavailable, the batter can be made with water in the same proportions as yam.

Add the cabbage to the batter. The cabbage should be greater in volume than the batter. Add the spring onion and stir in, then the shrimp (dried shrimp for those who prefer a crunchy texture).

Heat and oil a flat griddle (a very large iron frying pan will work, provided the omelet is smaller than the pan), preferably on a tabletop gas burner (or use an electric griddle). Spread the batter on the hot griddle. The batter should be about 1/3-inch thick. Move thinner edges inward, since the yam tends to cause the batter to separate. Put topping on top (much like a pizza). Cook one side to crisp brown. Using two spatulas, flip over quickly (a trick that needs practice); do not attempt to do it slowly, or the omelet will separate. Press mixture gently to ensure even cooking. When bottom is done, flip over again onto plate, topping side up. The interior should be soft and melting, the exterior crisp.

Dress with mayonnaise, Worcestershire sauce (or *sôsu*), soy sauce, and mustard and eat warm.

Shared Pot Stews

Eating things from a shared pot probably antedates the concept of cuisine. A range of shared-pot restaurants serve these dishes, the partaking of which is notable for its conviviality. Even the most formal and stiff people would be likely to get into the spirit of the thing. Ceramic pots and cast iron pots are deep-bellied, covered pots used for cooking soupy stews, of which the most common version is *shabu-shabu* (which translates roughly as "swish swish"). A quantity of stock is heated, then placed in the pot over a tabletop burner. When the liquid is smiling (just below simmer-

Stewpot on Tabletop Gas Range

ing), fish and meat are added. Each diner takes out tidbits to dip in a sauce—Japanese limes and soy sauce (*ponzu*) is very common—before eating. As the stock absorbs the meaty flavor, vegetables—Chinese cabbage, *shiitake* mushrooms, *enoki* mushrooms, sliced leeks, carrots, chrysanthemum leaves, bean sprouts—any vegetable that will cook quickly in liquid—are added and consumed. Finally, once the soup is fully flavored, thick udon noodles, which absorb flavor better than most noodles, are added and consumed as well. Obviously the communal work (as well as the inevitable misses and splashes) ensure that everyone must interact with everyone else: a desirable objective in the Japanese scheme of things.

Shabu-shabu Pot Stew

- 1 lb. *very* thinly sliced good beef, preferably good marbled beef
- 8 to 10 *shiitake* mushrooms
- 1/2 lb. *enoki* mushrooms
- 1/2 lb. *shimeji* mushrooms
- 1/2 lb. thin devil's foot root jelly noodles (*shirataki*)
- 1 lb. Chinese cabbage
- 2 carrots thinly sliced on the diagonal
- 1/2 lb. chrysanthemum leaves (a few leaves from a home garden will work, provided plants are not treated with pesticides)

- 1 to 2 blocks tofu, cut in 1-inch cubes
- 2 to 4 leeks, sliced on the diagonal
- 1 pack Japanese wheat noodles (*udon*) or bean thread noodles (*harusame*) per person (use less if appetites are small or there are larger quantities of meat and vegetables)

For dipping sauce:

- juice of 1 lemon, lime, or preferably Japanese lime (*yuzu*)
- 2 Tbs. soy sauce

Mix citrus juice and soy sauce to taste. Divide into a dipping bowl for each person.

Make a kelp (*konbu*) stock either on the kitchen range or on the tabletop range by heating 1 1/2 to 2 quarts water in a large pot. Using scissors, cut off 4 to 5 inches of dried *Konbu* (kelp) and immerse in water while it is warming, until boiling gently. Remove kelp before the water boils, and allow stock to boil very gently.

When the water is bubbling, each diner takes a slice of meat and swishes it in the liquid until cooked, then eats it after dipping it in sauce. When the liquid is flavorful, repeat with vegetables and tofu. Toward the end, add noodles. Diners help themselves from the pot and dip the noodles in the sauce.

Alternatively, one person simply adds ingredients to the pot (in the order meat-vegetables-noodles) and the diners help themselves.

Sukiyaki is said to have originated as a quick cooking method for farmers or soldiers out in the field. Taking a hoe (*suki*), the men would place some thinly sliced boar, duck, or venison, perhaps with a slice of Japanese lime on the blade, and cook it quickly over charcoal. The *sukiyaki* served today is an altogether more complex variant of that humble meal. Using a special cast-iron, flat-bottomed pot, thin strips of beef are cooked in a sweet rice liquor (*mirin*), lime juice, and soy sauce and eaten dipped in beaten raw egg. The sauce is thinned with *saké*, and then vegetables and bean thread noodles (*harusame*), whose translucent delicacy evokes the Japanese spring rains, are added.

TRAY-MEAL RESTAURANTS

While the station box meals (*ekiben*) described in Chapter 4 are at the lower end of the price scale of box or tray meals, there are also restaurants (*bentôya*) that specialize in preparing box meals (*bentô*) either for consumption on the premises or for taking out. In fact, very luxurious restaurants will pack a lunch in a traditional three- or four-tier set of lacquered boxes, which must be returned. Truly wealthy traditional-minded households might have their own elaborate set of nested boxes, which they send to a favorite restaurant for filling before embarking on a flower-viewing picnic.

Inside-the-curtain box-lunches (*makunouchi bentô*; like "above-the-salt" in English, the term means "the elite" in Japan) are a specialty of Kyoto, the ancient capital of Japan. Known for refined elegance, Kyoto cooking is unlike the robust food of business-oriented Tokyo or Osaka. Tray meals come served on a large black lacquered tray. Like its country cousin, the *ekiben*, the tray is divided into cells of various sizes, each containing a morsel of food. The morsels are generally exquisite concoctions, as delicate to the eye as they are to the tongue: tiny jewel-like tidbits, each one exquisitely molded. Even the rice is often shaped into intricate shapes, including rolls, simulated mountains, or five-petaled cherry blossoms in the appropriate season. The food, reflecting its origins as a travel food, is usually not hot, but in many places it is accompanied by hot soup. Trays generally allow the cook to display mastery of the different ways of preparing Japanese food. A good tray meal will normally have representative foods from all the cooking forms: vinegared food, raw, grilled, and stewed, each in its own compartment, and the whole designed to please the eye as well as the palate.

COFFEE, TEA, OR SWEET BEANS

The ambition, it is said, of every retired bit actress in Japan is to open a coffee shop. There are as many variations on the coffee shop theme as one could expect, including modern types that specialize in coffee (*koheeshoppu*) and traditional tea houses that serve green tea with a Japanese sweet (*kisaten*). Other shops offer German-style, French-style, or American-style confectioneries with elegant tables and coffee service. Everyone has his or her favorite.

Coffee shops do not only serve tea and coffee. They are generally places for a quick snack. And most of them serve at least two of the three most popular standards: toast, Japanese-style pilaf (*pirafu*), and curry-rice. *Pirafu*, as its name implies, is the Japanese version of pilaf, a Persian dish in which finely chopped vegetables, ham, and egg are cooked in rice. Most people outside Japan would probably identify it as Chinese fried rice, and indeed, in Chinese restaurants, the same pilaf would appear as fried rice (*chahan*).

Toast deserves a special mention. "Tea and toast" was one of the many culinary ideas introduced into Japan by the English. The Japanese took over the idea with gusto. However, being without prejudice in the item of toast, they conceived of the food as a kind of confection (since not all Japanese confections are sweet), and as a consequence, buttered toast became an entrée item in its own right. Thus, many *kisaten* will display in their windows or have on their menu a one- or two-inch thick slice of white bread crowned by a pat of semimelted butter. The bread is sliced to perfection and toasted a beautiful golden brown. The butter is precisely calculated to cover the entire surface, without leaving a greasy pool.

6

Special Occasions: Holidays, Celebrations, and Religious Rituals

The Japanese enjoy numerous festivals and holidays and observe a variety of religious rituals. To understand the relationship of these occasions to Japanese food, it is necessary to introduce the concept of *matsuri*. Usually translated as "celebration," *matsuru* (the verb form of the word) has wide implications that connect humans to the deities. In native Japanese theological thinking, the deities and humans are related in the form of an extended family. And what often holds families together is shared meals. Buddhism, which was introduced to Japan in the sixth century from Korea, opted into this family-religion system as well, and it coexists today with Shintô, the original religion of the Japanese, in a reasonably comfortable manner. Buddhism, as noted earlier, limited Japanese cuisine's use of meat and introduced aesthetic and other refinements. But when it came to celebration, it seemed to have borrowed more than it gave, celebrating the relationship with the Buddhist deities with food as well as prayer.

At the basis of every festive day in Japan, therefore, there are two elements. One is food and drink, often in the form of a full feast, but at the minimum, a sharing of rice or even a bite of seaweed, and wine. The other element is festivity: the joyous (often *saké*-fueled) celebration of the relationship between people, and between people and their deities. As a consequence, few Japanese festivals fail to include food, whether formally presented at a shrine or temple ritual; eaten at home in a solemn meal with family, friends, and perhaps a visiting deity; or consumed from one or more of the street stalls that populate every festival.

Another aspect of Japanese culture is that the Japanese enjoy festivities for their own sake. Many festivals in modern secular Japan are nonreligious. To add to that, there is no central authority—a pope or chief priest—who regulates all of Japanese religion. Shrines (Shintô) and temples (Buddhist), some belonging to one or another sect of Buddhism, Shintô, or other religions, others completely autonomous, celebrate different festivals at different times and in different ways. What is constant, however, is the sharing of food and the sense of joyous participation.

In describing Japanese special occasions, therefore, we have to differentiate between national festivals, which, according to the separation of religion and state, are rarely defined as religious, and local special days, festivals, and events, many of which are defined as religious. In truth, of course, most people simply ignore those niceties, throwing themselves into the spirit of the event.

PARTY ETIQUETTE

The Japanese love formal drinking parties, and they are an important location for social exchanges. Banquets and parties rarely take place at a home. Commonly a group of people will reserve a space at one of the many traditional Japanese restaurants, or have the food catered either as a picnic or in a public hall. This is true of special events such as weddings, as well as of other ritual and ceremonial events.

Most group activities—club activities, business projects, and even annual meetings of friends, an important event, or the celebration of some accomplishment by the group—end with a drinking party (konpa). The rules for such parties are similar, and the pattern is familiar to all Japanese. In formal konpa, the participants sit around a table arrangement that is either a hollow square or some variation on that pattern. Each participant has a sitting cushion and utensils: chopsticks, saké cup, beer glass. The senior person—a teacher, a manager, an important guest, or merely the oldest person present—is usually seated with his or her back to an alcove decorated with a flower arrangement and scroll.

Drinking parties start with a brief speech by someone appointed master of ceremonies, and perhaps a speech by the senior participant. During this stage, which is usually very formal, most of the diners are seated on their knees, their feet tucked under them, which can be exceedingly painful, even on sitting cushions, when one is not used to it. Once the speeches are over, there is always a toast. Peculiarly, in modern Japan, even when saké is available, the toast is drunk in beer, perhaps because beer is a better thirst-quencher than saké.

Once the toast has been drunk, the guests are free to sit more comfortably. Food is served individually, the number of plates or dishes depending on what is being consumed. It is improper for any participant to fill her or his own glass: this act is the responsibility of one's neighbors, which inevitably leads to everyone drinking more than they might perhaps drink otherwise. As the party warms up, people start moving about from one person to another, so that there is a constant circulation of people in the room, frequently driven by junior members trying to ensure that they have an opportunity to talk to, and drink with, every senior person present.

The end of the drinking phase of the party is usually signaled by the entrance of rice. Quite often, if a great deal has been drunk, the final dish will be cooked rice in a bowl with tea and soup (*ochazuke*), its surface scattered with toasted sesame seeds, a remedy to combat overindulgence in alcohol. Once the soupy rice has been consumed, the participants, whatever their stage of inebriation, manage to straighten up, bid one another formal farewell, and leave. To continue the revelry, smaller groups may go elsewhere.

THE ANNUAL CYCLE AND ITS FOODS

Virtually all of the main national holidays are marked by special foods. Of them all, the most sumptuous are the special foods of the New Year. Other holidays are also celebrated with colorful and unusual foods, each of which has its own symbolic meaning.

The national calendar of events starts with the celebration of the New Year (*oshôgatsu*: December 31–January 3), which is both a national and religious holiday, the most important of the year. Most businesses stop for a few days. On the eve of the New Year (December 31), shrines and temples hold special services, and many people dressed in kimono visit a favorite shrine and temple, particularly at midnight, when the temple bells toll out 108 times, representing the 108 Buddhist sins. The New Year is the time to consume special foods (*oseichi*), to decorate the entrances of homes with cut green bamboo poles wrapped in straw rope and decorated with pine branches and oranges (*kado matsu*), and to visit friends and family. The green of the pines and bamboo represents the family's hopes for renewal; the straw rope, similar to the one that encircles sacred precincts, circumscribes the end of the year; and the many seeds of the Japanese orange (*daidai*) represent growth and fertility as does the name *daidai*, a pun on "many generations." Performers present their art at special "first performance" events at shrines and temples.

A variety of civil holidays, including Adults Day (when young people are formally accepted as adults); National Foundation Day; Constitution Day; Respect for the Aged Day; and Sports Day follow as the year unfolds. These are all more or less newly established holidays that serve the needs of the state and rarely have any special foods attached to them. Far more important popularly (and gastronomically) are the traditional special days that follow the seasonal progression. The second day of the second lunar month (often moved to February 2) marks the traditional end of winter. This is *Setsubun*, when people expel evil from houses and call for good fortune by pelting invisible demons with roasted beans. The third day of the third month is Peach Blossom or the Doll Festival *(Hinamatsuri)*. The peach flower is the harbinger of spring, as the plum blossom signifies the end of winter. April 8 is the Buddha's birthday, celebrating the birth of Gautama Buddha, Buddhism's founder. It is celebrated in most temples with sweet tea, which is poured over a statue of the founder, and with the erection of flower-bedecked pavilions and in some temples by the consumption of sweet foods. This is also a time when many temples prepare the tea ceremony to offer visitors. The fifth of May is Boys' Day, now known as Children's Day *(kodomo-no-hi)*. *Tanabata*, the Star Festival, is celebrated with outdoor picnics in many places around July 7. It celebrates lovers overcoming obstacles to their love. *Bon*, the Day of the Dead, is celebrated in mid-July. Graves and houses are cleaned for the visit of the family's departed. In the evening, there are bonfires, fireworks displays, and street dancing in many communities. The foods that a departed member of the household was particularly fond of may be served or offered at the family altar or the grave. The tenth day of the tenth lunar month (shifted often for convenience's sake to October 10) celebrates mid-Autumn *(Higan)* and the flowering of the chrysanthemum. *Shichigosan*, observed on November 15, is a day on which children of three years of age, boys of five, and girls of seven are brought to the local shrine to ensure their growth and health. Eating *mochi* on the boar day[1] of the tenth month *(Inoko)* was believed to ward off diseases, a belief imported into Japan from China during the Heian period (794–1185). In western Japan, *Inoko* is celebrated for children who go from house to house singing songs and receiving *mochi*.

In addition to the formal "national" days, every local shrine and temple (there are at least 100,000 of them throughout Japan) has its own festival. Popular festivals such as the Asakusa Kannon temple in Tokyo, the Gion parade in Kyoto, and the Edoro *matsuri* in Akita attract millions of visitors each year. Smaller local festivals may attract only the residents of a neighborhood or town or a sprinkling of tourists. What they all have in common from our point of view is an association with food.

The New Year Feast

The days leading up to the New Year (*oshôgatsu*) are as solemn and as important to Japanese, children and adults alike, as those before the Christmas season are in North America and Europe. On December 31, stores close and people come home from work early. After a warming bath, many dress in traditional clothes—thick, many-layered kimono, worn with formal overcoats elaborated with family crest badges. Toward midnight, people start streaming toward their favorite local shrine or temple. At precisely midnight, the temple bells start tolling 108 rolls, the list of Buddhist sins. People may pray briefly, or simply wander among the booths and stalls, which sell everything from lucky charms to draughts of sweet *amazake*. Many people also go to shrines, where they buy blunt arrows, symbolic of good fortune; pray or make offerings of money or uncooked rice; and receive a sip of *saké* to start the new year. Then it is home to a feast that has been prepared beforehand. The tock-tock sound of the traditional wooden sandals people wear with their kimono lasts until dawn, as people wander from one temple or shrine to another.

New Year is also the season for visiting. On the first day, many go to visit family members. On January 2, friends visit one another, and the following day is allocated to more distant acquaintances. And of course, each stop requires some refreshment. With the exception of a strengthening soup prepared specifically for the day (*ozoñi*), most New Year food is

Kadumatsu (Pine, Bamboo, Orange Bundles) New Year's Decoration

cold, having been prepared well in advance. Foods colored red, white, or gold are preferred: succulent *tai* fish, mounds of red-and-white rice cakes, and golden gingko nuts, sometimes strung on pine needles. And diners use the best dishes: expensive china, red lacquer bowls and cups, decorated baskets.

Another custom is observed in many households: the consumption of the seven herbs. The dwarf deity Sukunabikona was one of those responsible for the creation of the land. When he had finished his work, and before he departed to his homeland in Tokoyo over the sea, he was appointed the deity of wizardry and one of the deities of medicine. As part of his duties, he taught people to consume seven herbs for their health: chickweed (*Stellaria media*, in Japanese, *hakobe*), aster or starwort (*Aster yomena: yomena*), wild rocambole (*Allium japonicum: nobiru*), hawk's beard (*koonidabirako*), cottonweed or cudweed (*hahakogusa* or *gogyô*), shepherd's purse (*nazuna*), and wild parsley (*seri*). These herbs are eaten in a rice gruel for the new year to ensure strength and health throughout the year. All of these are elements in many modern herbal remedies.

New Year food is traditionally packed in special three-tiered square lacquered box trays (*jûbako*) decorated with an indication of the season: pine needles or branches, plum blossoms, and bamboo leaves, all indicating the approach of spring and the turn of the year. The foods themselves refer to the season as well, whether through a well-placed pun on the name (*konbu* [kelp] = *yorokobu* [felicitations]) or by their color or shape. Red, green, white, and gold colors predominate. For example, red and white fish paste (*kamaboko*) slices might be alternated in a checkerboard pattern. Pink cooked whole prawns might be placed next to erect, hollowed out spears of cucumber filled with brilliant reddish orange fresh salmon roe. Mandarin oranges, whose plentiful seeds[2] hint at fecundity, might be filled with brilliant, gold-colored jelly. Lotus root, chicken breast fillets, taro bulbs or burdock roots are fried a golden color or glazed with golden sauce and added to the trays. The variations are endless, depending only on the household's budget. The arrangements of these box trays are so delicate and pleasing to the eye, that many households keep the traditional three- or sometimes four-tiered box trays for display only, bringing in piled plates for actual consumption.

Traditionally, the topmost tray holds particularly appropriate seasonal foods. Black beans, a symbol of health, are boiled in syrup (symbolizing a sweet, thus easy, year). Herring roe (*kazunoko*) symbolizes fecundity and plenty and the word is a pun on "winning-child" (*kazu* = victorious; *ko* = child). A pickle made with small sardines expresses hopes for a plentiful harvest. Sweet chestnut and sweet potato mash boiled in a sweet sauce are present as well wishing for a sweet year.

The second tray traditionally contains seafood and wild vegetables (*sansai*). Marinated octopus and squid and grilled shrimp or prawns are particularly common. These are accompanied by vinegared vegetables as a contrast, particularly some form of wild vegetable salad.

The third tray contains vegetables seasoned with sugar, stock, and soy sauce, repeating the sweetness theme. Devil's foot root jelly dyed in the appropriate colors, cooked giant radish and various forms of root vegetables—yams, taro, and potatoes, both sweet and white, are common, often cooked in syrup or syrup and soy sauce.

The fourth tray (if present) contains simmered vegetables: carrot, burdock root, lotus root, and other vegetables that have been simmered in stock. Their blandness contrasts with the slight sweetness and richness of the top trays.

Many of the individual foods are extremely time-consuming to make. Threading boiled golden gingko nuts individually on a pine needle or cutting carrot slices into the shape of a plum blossom requires a great deal of time and skill. So, in modern Japan, one can purchase either an entire tray or the more finicky of the prepared items from the many supermarkets and particularly from the elite department stores.

Perhaps the single most important food of the New Year is the soup called *ozōni*. This soup is based on the finest first stock (*ichibandashi*), often flavored with a strip of decoratively cut Japanese lime, the intense aroma of which fills the bowl. Besides the stock, the single most common ingredient in *ozōni* is pounded and roasted rice cake. Beyond those basics, *ozōni* varies from one household and area to another: hexagonally marked fish or chicken slices (evoking tortoiseshell, the symbol of longevity), chrysanthemum flowers and leaves (evoking both spring and majesty), taro, fish roe, particularly brilliant colored salmon roe, various mushrooms, sliced carrots. The variations are endless. A bowl of *ozōni* is traditionally offered immediately after the New Year's toast made with spiced warm *saké*. The spices themselves, which are generally bought in a sachet for the purpose, are less a flavoring agent than a medicinal compound to ensure health during the transition from one year to another: a hazardous period in all cultures.

In modern Japan, some of the old foods have been supplemented by imports. Cold roast beef is a popular addition, as are canapés and Chinese dim sum. This means that many households mix and match to fit their own taste, purse, and the palates of their expected guests.

Most Japanese households will eat "year-end noodles" at the stroke of midnight on New Year's eve. The elongated shape of the noodles has obvious symbolic connotations: a wish for a long life. There is, however, also a charming apocryphal story about the origin of this custom, dating from some time in the Edo period (1600–1868). The goldsmiths of Edo, as was the general custom, would close all accounts before the New Year and have a general stock-taking. As part of the process, they would clean their workshops. To ensure that no gold dust was lost, they would wipe all surfaces with balls of sticky buckwheat dough. Gradually, the more affluent among them started eating the gold-speckled dumplings, rather than burning them to extract the gold, and a new custom was born. Since most people prefer buckwheat noodles to buckwheat dumplings, the custom spread in modified form. The gold is optional.

Special Days of the Year

Though many of the national holidays are the result of modern practice, there are several days throughout the year that are recognized as special by most Japanese, even though they are not in any sense formal or recognized (by the state) as holidays. Schools and businesses operate as usual, but the populace continues to celebrate them nonetheless. And most of these special days are marked by food consumption.

Doll Festival

The Doll Festival (Hinamatsuri) is celebrated on the third day of the third month in the traditional calendar, although most households now celebrate it on March 3. During the festival, parents of girls set out the court dolls (hina-ningyo), which portray an ancient imperial court, complete with emperor and empress, ladies-in-waiting, ministers, and musicians. Interspersed among the miniature implements and dolls are hexagonal, multilayered rice cakes. Young girls entertain one another with a sweet slightly fermented drink made of rice gruel (amazake), colored rice cakes, and red rice cooked with beans. Another special food is also offered: Myth says that Sukunabikona, the dwarf god of medicine and wizardry, who was one of a pair who brought forth the dry land, distributed a grass called okera (Atractylodes japonica) to humankind. Eaten with dumplings at the start of spring, this grass ensures health and is still eaten today at Hinamatsuri.

Boys' Festival

Two months after *Hinamatsuri* is the boys' turn with the celebration of the Boys' Day *(Tangonosekku)*. Miniature helmets, armor, or swords on special stands are set out on a household altar, which also sports lanterns (for vigilance); fans (indicating command and leadership); and an image of Shôki Demon-queller, a figure from myth who is to teach children to fear nothing; and figures of famous heroes. Boys take a bath with iris leaves, which resemble sword blades, and drink a cup of *saké* in which the leaves have been steeped. Around this date, most households and public places sport one or sometimes three carp-shaped windsocks, which swim against the wind, indicating strength and fortitude to encourage children to reach great age, and to strive against the odds. The most common food of the holiday is *chimaki dango* of special rich rice. These dumplings are wrapped in a bamboo leaf into the shape of a demon's horn, then steamed. Pounded-rice cakes wrapped in oak leaves called *kashiwa mochi* are eaten because oak leaves symbolize authority and governance.

Hanami: The Season in a Box

Many Japanese observe at least one of the precepts of seasonality: the picnic. Eating in the great outdoors, as a cultured activity, has had a lengthy history in Japan. Emperors and their consorts and concubines, famous warlords, and saints and priests have all enjoyed formal or less for-

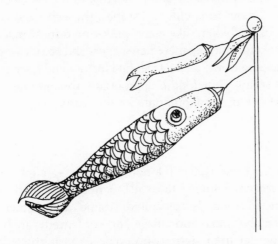

Carp Windsock

Cherry Blossoms

mal meals in the outdoors, at some site famous for its blooms, its mountain air, or some historical anecdote.

For the average Japanese person, the most appropriate time for a picnic is during blossom viewing (*hanami*), which, in the general sense of the word, often means the flowering of the cherry blossoms. There are a great many famous cherry blossom sites, ranging from the ancient site of Yoshino, made famous in poems and stories, through local groves of the trees, which look, in bloom, like giant, pink-tinted snow mounds. So important is this event, that Japanese newspapers and broadcast media chart the "cherry-blossom front" as the trees bud further and further north with the coming of spring. Any food is appropriate, though many restaurants will supply take-out meals appropriate for the season.

The Day of the Dead

The Day of the Dead (*Obon* [Honored lantern—a euphemism for the dead] or *bon matsuri* [lantern festival]), a festival of both Shintô and Buddhist-Chinese origin, is celebrated around midsummer, usually in mid-July. In neighborhoods and villages, fires or lanterns are hung to light the way for the departed spirits who come to visit their descendants.

While they wait, people dance in the streets. In many places, the dancers wear masks or veil their faces in some way, so that the ancestors, if they wish, can join the festivities without being recognized. Many families pay a preliminary visit to their family graves (city people who have migrated from the countryside will often come back to their ancestral villages). The graves are cleaned, and food offerings are made at the grave of rice, pickles, and other vegetarian items, as well as flowers. Chopsticks are thrust upright into the rice bowl. This relates the offering to the upright wooden slats which commemorate the dead in most graveyards. As a consequence, Japanese children are warned early in life not to stick their chopsticks upright into their rice bowls, as it is a symbol of death.

Shichigosan

On November 15, three-year-old children, five-year-old boys, and seven-year-old girls visit their neighborhood shrines, dressed in their finest traditional clothes. After a brief blessing by the Shintô priest to ensure their health, well-being, and continued growth, they receive bags of gifts, including ten-thousand-year candy: sweet, but hard and durable as the children are expected to be.

THE LIFE CYCLE AND ITS FOODS

People all over the world pass through similar stages in their life, and these stages are marked, in virtually every society, by ritual activities that anthropologists call "rites-of-passage." Soon after birth, infants are inducted into the world. Their passage into greater maturity is marked as well, as is their passage into adulthood. The next major stage is that of marriage, when an individual starts a family of his or her own. Retirement from active social activities may also be marked, as is, of course, death itself.

In Japan, as in many other societies, these stages are clearly marked with rituals. Birth, adulthood, marriage, maturity, retirement, and death were marked ritually, and each ritual accompanied by something of a celebration. Some of these rituals, such as maturity, are no longer celebrated universally, though many places still perform local rites. The major food associations of these rituals are discussed below. It must be borne in mind, however, that many households have other rituals of their own, handed down from the misty past, or newly created, which they practice in private, and almost all of these involve food.

Birth

Immediately after a child is born, birth rice—white rice, highly mounded on a bowl, and decorated with a small stone from the shrine of the god of birthing, which represents the god—is offered to as many people as possible in the family and neighborhood. This offering celebrates the safe delivery as well as publicly announcing the new birth. For a girl infant, the mound of rice is depressed with two "dimples" in the hope of imparting them to the baby's cheeks. For a boy infant, the rice is flavored with salt, so that he will mature into a person who has a strong and unspoiled disposition.

About a month after the birth, the infant, dressed in decorated clothes, is taken to the local neighborhood shrine and introduced to the deity. The parents might receive some uncooked rice and a drink of *saké*. The rice is to be made into the baby's first food, the *saké* is considered a drink shared with the deity.

One hundred days after birth, once the infant is deemed ready for solid food, its first meal is celebrated. The festive meal consists of rice (the rice received from the shrine) cooked with *azuki* beans and a grilled fish with head and tail intact. Fish with a very hard, solid head is chosen in the hope that the infant's new teeth will be firm and strong. This is also the time when the child's first set of eating implements is bought: rice bowl, chopsticks, and a footed tray. Even if the infant is unable to eat solids (and it obviously will be unable to eat on its own yet), the mother will dab some of the food on the child's lips.

Weddings

Weddings are celebrated with a great deal of pomp in modern Japan. This was not always the case. Marriage was considered a private family affair, marked only by the families concerned. In the nineteenth century, Shintô authorities popularized weddings—called *sansankudô* ("three-three-nine times," since each of the three cups is sipped from thrice [3 × 3 = 9])—at Shintô shrines in emulation of Christian weddings and to increase shrine incomes. The bride and groom, in the presence of their families and their go-between, all wearing formal Japanese dress, shared three

Bride's Headgear

sips of three cups of *saké*. Elaborate lacquered red *saké* cups were used, as well as special utensils for storing and pouring the drink.

Because a wedding according to traditional Japanese thought (traces of which still exist) is an arrangement between two families, there are today of course traditional gifts in the form of a dowry. These include food items. Prominent among them are *katsuobushi* (a homonym for "'victorious warrior"), whose phallic shape is unmistakable; kelp *(konbu)* packs (again referring to the similarity with the word *yorokobu,* meaning joy); and herring *(kazunoko)* or some other roe meaning a wish for many progeny.

In modern Japan, there are often three wedding rituals: *sansankudô* at a shrine; a "white wedding," with the bride in Western bridal dress and the husband in a tuxedo; and finally, the all-important civil registration at the city office. Guests are expected to bring envelopes bordered in celebratory red and gold and stamped with a picture of a packet of dried abalone to help defray the costs of the wedding. They also bring along a large purple shawl. They are usually offered a box-lunch to take away with them and share with their families. The lunch may include a variety of celebratory foods (and sometimes expensive gifts). Sea bream, kelp, and decorated sugar candy symbolizing a sweet future are always included. Various clams are also considered wedding food, since the two shells cling together like a married couple. Conversely, abalone is never served, because its single shell signifies unrequited love. Aside from the obligatory *saké* and the food gifts given the guests, there are no nationwide customs for wedding feasts. Certain areas may have their particular customs, but couples are free to observe them or not.

Soon after their marriage, a couple usually sets up their own household. In modern Japan, this of course often happens earlier. They may also move several times during their lives. Recognition of social obligations by newcomers is particularly important in Japan. Thus when they move to a new neighborhood, most families will offer their neighbors—the three houses opposite, and one on either side (*"mukai sangen, ryodonari"*) as the Japanese saying has it—packets of noodles (or tickets for a free meal at the neighboring noodle shop). *Soba* means both noodles and "neighbors," and by offering the gift they are asking to become members of the local community.

CELEBRATIONS

Central to Japanese religious practice is a social process uniting deities and humans. Generally titled *matsuri*, it can be translated as "celebration," though this hardly does justice to the word. Every Shintô shrine, many Buddhist temples, and even some churches have a *matsuri* where social relations are renewed and a communion with the deity is sought. In practice, this generally means that somewhere in Japan, at any given day of the year, someone will be celebrating. Most such *matsuri* are small, local affairs, though some—the *Sanya matsuri* in Tokyo, the *Gion matsuri* in Kyoto, *Tanabata* in Sendai—are world-famous. Exciting, sometimes wildly popular events, they also have a calm center, a religious ritual where the deities and worshippers are invited to participate in a communal meal.

Food in Shintô

Food is central to the Shintô religion. One of the most prominent features of any busy shrine is the alter laden with offerings of food before the *honden* (the hall where an item representing the deity is stored). These offerings must follow two criteria. Only the freshest and purest of items are allowed, and there should be something representing the different realms where food is found: the mountains (*yama no sachi*), paddy fields (*ta no sachi*), sea (*umi no sachi*), forests (*mori no sachi*), and fields (*hatake no sachi*). Because the deities abhor death, live fish are offered on a tray for a brief time, then returned, in many cases, to their ponds (in other cases, when purchased whole from a fishmonger, they are of course eaten: religion, as always, has plenty of room for individual interpretation). Rice appears both as uncooked rice (since humans may not be pure enough to cook the deities' food) and as *mochi* (since round flat cakes of *mochi* represent the mirror, which is both emblematic of deities and of the soul). Fresh vegetables, preferably local (though imported pineapples and mangoes can also be seen) are laid on the altar as well. After the ritual, they will be consumed by those who have managed and supported the ritual. The managers will also distribute parts of the banquet—*mochi* cakes, handfuls of rice, bits of fruit—to the members of the community, sometimes going house-to-house if necessary so that all the parishioners can share in the god's bounty.

Common celebratory foods at Shintô and other festivals are white rice in assorted forms. Uncooked rice constitutes one of the altar offerings to the god or gods in whose shrine the celebration takes place. A mound of choice, unbroken white rice grains is placed on a square footed tray made of fresh cedar, the pale wood pristine and untouched by lacquer or other finish. Another rice-based offering is *saké*, arranged at the altar in pairs of 1.8 quart bottles, also in their own cedar trays. Completing the rice offerings, in similar trays, are mounds of freshly made pounded glutinous rice cakes, arranged in sets of three plain white or alternating white and pink layers, and red glutinous rice cooked with *azuki* beans.

In Shintô myth, human food came from the dying throes of the food goddess, just as the food we eat is the result of decomposition of dead plants and animals into the earth. Thus Shintô recognizes and even celebrates the truth of the natural cycle. So important is food in the Shintô scheme of things that one-half of Ise-jingû, the central shrine of Shintô, is dedicated to Ukemochi-no-kami, goddess of food. Ukemochi-no-kami is not the only deity concerned with food. Inari, deity of prosperity, whose red-painted, fox-guarded shrines are the most common in Japan, is also the deity of rice, and his name means "Rice seedling." And each locale in Japan, and many paddy fields, are overseen by Ta-no-kami, deity of the rice paddy.

Food in Buddhism

From its origins in India in the sixth century B.C.E., one major Buddhist principle has been the preservation of life. Accordingly, most Buddhist sects in Japan (there are six major ones divided into many schools) do not allow the flesh of living things—beasts, birds, fish—into the diet. Offerings at Buddhist temples, as sumptuous as at Shintô shrines, therefore include largely fruit, flowers, and confectionery. Perhaps because of the association with the foreign, certainly because flowers and fruit are very prominent in Buddhist symbology, many foods offered at Buddhist altars are sweet or sweetened. Sweet tea is poured over statues of the Buddha on his April 8 birthday. Sweets such as *mochi* cakes stuffed with sweet bean jam *(manju)* and piles of dried persimmons are almost always offered at temples. Significantly, Buddhism is also credited with the elaboration of tofu cuisine in Japan, since monasteries forbade eating meat or fish, and the need for protein to sustain the monks' hard lives was paramount.

Many foods are directly or indirectly associated with Buddhism. Primary among them is lotus root *(renkon)*. The lotus plant grows in water and is not anchored to the ground. It reproduces vegetatively and brings forth a perfect blue or white flower with intense perfume. It is thus a major symbol for the Buddhist Law. The eating of lotus root in Buddhist tem-

Statue of Buddha

ples, aside from its aesthetic appearance, is thus an act of piety as well. Diametrically opposite is the pomegranate. A ferocious man-eating demon named Dakini had a thousand children whom she supplied with human meat. The Buddha trapped one of her offspring under his begging bowl. To secure the infant's release, Dakini promised to refrain from eating human flesh, and to serve as protectress of children. She is usually depicted carrying a pomegranate, symbol of her thousand infants and of fecundity in general. However, as a consequence, many Japanese refuse to eat pomegranate, claiming that the seeds taste like human flesh.

BANQUETS AND *KAISEKI*

As seen earlier, Japanese attach a great deal of importance to the sociable consumption of foods. Obviously, feasts or banquets punctuate and are part of most social life. The standard meal, consisting of rice, soup, and side dishes, can also be expanded into a full banquet or feast in which the entire corpus of cooking styles available to the Japanese cook are brought into play. Obviously such banquets are only indulged in on special occasions, and they are very rarely undertaken at home.

A banquet starts with an appetizer of small delicate tidbits (*zensai*), followed by a clear soup (*suimono*) intended to awaken the appetite, and possibly some *sashimi*: the delicate flavor of fresh raw fish is best appreciated when one is not completely hungry, but before the taste of other foods dulls the palate.

The central dishes of a banquet come in a fixed order. A grilled dish, which today might also be baked (*yakimono*) starts the process. This is followed by a soft steamed dish (*mushimono*), which contrasts with the stronger flavors of the grilled food, and then a dish of vegetables or fish simmered in stock (*nimono*). Softer foods are followed with a crisp, fried item (*agemono*), and the oil is subsequently cut and the mouth freshened by vegetables or fish dressed in vinegar sauce (*sunomono*). The banquet then concludes with a rice dish (*gohanmono*), usually plain steamed white rice, sometimes rice that includes beans, chestnuts, or flavoring, which is accompanied by a heavier soup, usually *misoshiru*, and pickles (*tsukemono*). Finally, most modern banquets conclude with a sweet (*okashi*) and green tea. Note that the "side dish" element of the *ichijûsansai* concept—the normative meal of rice/soup/three side dishes—has been expanded to include numerous dishes, while the rice/soup/pickle element remains almost constant.

There are, of course, many regional variants of cooking and serving. The order described here is based on one of the most popular cooking styles, that of the Kyoto-Osaka area, but other styles and orders of preference can be found as well. In all banquets, three guiding principles are observed. The first is time. Banquets are to be savored slowly, over a period of some hours.

The second principle is attention to detail. There are rarely (or at least there should not be) unintended elements in a Japanese banquet. Placement, color, choice of plates and utensils, the dining space, and of course, the foods chosen—their colors, shapes, textures, and flavors—are all chosen with exquisite care to match and contrast with one another. All the elements must harmonize to enhance the appreciation and harmony of the moment. The harmony may not be easily noticed by an outsider. More often than not, the Japanese cook will give way to the Japanese preference for puns, whether visual, olfactory, or verbal.

The third important principle is the need to keep the diner interested. To explain this, we need to turn to some of the general principles of Japanese aesthetics, which can be seen not only in food, but in gardens, paintings and other items. Japanese art places a great deal of emphasis on the relationship of the artistic endeavor to nature. Zeami, one of the major codifiers of the Noh theater form, claimed that an actor's art lies in his ability to project the natural features of the person he plays without injecting any of his own personality or mannerisms. This idea of emulating nature to perfection is prevalent in Japanese art. Moreover, this emulation is done as subtly as possible: the stance in acting, a brush stroke to represent the feel of a leaf in the wind in painting, or a simple pebblelike item on a box-meal tray to indicate a river bed. A second general principle of Japanese art is to allow the observer to use her or his own imagination. That is, Japanese art is predicated on suggesting rather than stating. Empty spaces—called *ma*—are prevalent in painting, for example, because it is up to the viewer to supply the missing parts based on the artist's suggestions. It can also be supplied by hiding part of the image from the viewer. Thus in Japanese gardens, flower arranging, or food, the viewer should never be able to see the entire garden, arrangement, or dish. It must always be positioned so that there is something else to discover. A rock may be partly hidden by bushes, a path turns away from the viewer, flowers in an arrangement are hidden by leaves.

The same artistic principle holds true for food. For example, there are many different ways of arranging food on a plate. What they have in common is the desire in Japan to ensure that all the food, even if served together, be not visible immediately. Thus items may be placed in mounds resembling mountain folds, or piled into log piles, if they are cylindrical. Single objects will be obscured by a garnish. Banquets allow a chef to utilize all of these preferences, playing them against one another to create a thematic whole: winter, summer, or a particular event.

The most refined form of dining is that brought about by the tea ceremony. The practice of ritually drinking tea was originally imported from China, where it is still practiced today. But the Japanese, partly under the influence of Buddhism, made this ritual their own. And, in line with the third principle described above, they soon realized the need to vary the drinking of tea with food. Thus was born the full tea ceremony, and its child, *kaiseki* cooking.

The Tea Ceremony and *Kaiseki* Cooking

Kaiseki cooking, under the influence of Buddhism, eschewed meat to a large degree and encouraged the use of delicate morsels of food that would complement the bitter-blandness of tea, as well as the refined atmosphere of the tea ritual itself. Thus, above everything else, the *kaiseki* cook must be responsive to the seasons and to the event. Only the freshest of ingredients, only small portions, and only the most perfectly arranged utensils and foods can complement the staid ritualization of drinking frothy, jade-green tea. *Kaiseki* cooking has become a cuisine in its own right, and can be enjoyed without the tea ritual that is its parent. Nonetheless, the same principles of simplicity, compactness, and austerity still hold true.

A *kaiseki* banquet is formal in every sense of the word. While the tea-drinking element is described in greater detail in chapter 3, an outline of the food consumption process helps here. One ought to keep in mind that this description is the bare bones of a *very* formal and proper event. Users do modify this according to time, circumstances, and pocket.

The entire tea ceremony takes place in a specially built room or hut dedicated to this event. In addition to the host, there may be one to three guests. All the participants wear formal kimono, with black loose coats. The guests sit in a row, the most senior closest to the flower arrangement in the *tokonoma* alcove. The host brings in one tray of the first course, bows, places it on the mat before the most senior guest, rotates it so it faces the guest properly (soup and rice bowl away from the diner, other foods closer). He then brings the next tray for the second diner, and so on. Other foods are passed, if necessary, from senior to junior. The guests use both hands at all times to handle utensils. Bowls raised to the mouth are never to obscure the face. After one course, the host will offer a light tea to each guest, together with a morsel of sweet confection. Then, once the utensils have been cleared away, again, in strict order, there might be another service of tea, and, after a while, another course. Every motion must be as deliberate and neat as possible.

Paradoxically for something so formal, the tea ceremony as a whole is imbued with a sense of the natural. Natural materials are favored for the construction of the tea room, the water is heated on a charcoal brazier, the tea room is expected to overlook a garden that reflects nature, and, like the Noh performances mentioned previously, the artificiality of actions is expected to be so controlled that it contains the essence of naturalness. Odd as it may seem to an outsider (and difficult though it is to describe in words on paper), the very rigidity of, for example, wiping a bowl with a napkin seems to exude the very essence of cleaning.

Unsurprisingly, therefore, *kaiseki* dishes are expected to reflect and express the flavor of natural things. Nature enters into the *kaiseki* by minute attention to the types of plates used as well as the types of foods, which are to fit each season. Brightly colored plates and bowls are used in summer, more somber colors in winter. In the fall, there are various evocations of the season, such as decorations of red maple leaves, flying geese, or chrysanthemums, which flower in October. Spring utensils feature plum blossoms or some fresh greenery. There are even differences in the shape of utensils: summer bowls and dishes tend to be airy, open-mouthed, and often flat, while winter plates are more solid, with thick vertical walls and often lids

Following are some examples of the kind of dishes one might come across in a tea-ceremony banquet. Of course, they can be found in other types of banquets and even in simple meals in a household or restaurant, but it is at the tea ceremony that the greatest attention will be paid to proper presentation, and the proper utensil.

Spring

Sea bream and vegetables simmered in *saké:* small slices of bream with the skin on, simmered in stock together with fresh *shiitake* mushrooms, chrysanthemum leaves, and a small sheet of kelp *(konbu)* served without the liquid in mounded *(moritsuke)* style on a light open-mouthed bowl.

Slices of rough tofu spread like an open-faced sandwich with a green paste of chopped young buds of the mountain ash *(kinome)*, egg, and sweet rice liquor *(mirin)* skewered on green bamboo, then quickly grilled over charcoal. They might be served on an open plate, or a bamboo basket.

Grilled-eel omelet, flavored with stock, and served with spears of pickled ginger sprouts and grated raw giant radish. Served in a plate on top of a fresh ginger leaf.

Summer

Cold thin wheat noodles in stock garnished with a slice of grilled fish, some snow peas, and trefoil leaves. This might be served in a lacquered soup bowl or even in glass.

Grilled sweetfish *(ayu)*, the tail and fins heavily salted, which causes the fish to curl as if swimming. Served in a flat brightly decorated plate, the fish is partly obscured by a couple of spears of pickled ginger whose green-white-pink colors emphasize the season.

Simmered slices of young bamboo shoot served with the liquid, bits of kelp *(konbu)* from the stock, and garnished with mountain ash buds *(kinome)*. This would be served in a white china or pale blue celadon bowl.

A single cake of sesame-tofu (made by simmering sesame paste with kudzu gelatin), garnished with grated horseradish.

Fall

Mackerel fillet lightly fried then simmered with grated radish in a stock enriched with *mirin*, *saké*, and soy sauce. Garnished with trefoil, it is served in a deep-sided heavy dish.

Grilled eggplant (aubergine) in a sesame paste sauce garnished with grated dried bonito fillet *(katsuobushi)*.

Dry-cooked, pencil-shaved burdock root flavored with soy, *mirin*, white sesame seeds, and a touch of chilies. This might be mounded in a deep light-colored bowl to show off the glistening brown of the burdock.

Winter

Steamed silken tofu with a sauce of warm soy-flavored stock, garnished with finely cut chives (*Allium ledebourianum*, in Japanese, *asatsuki*), shaved *katsuobushi*, and finely chopped spring onions.

Steamed chunks of octopus and soy beans stewed in a sauce of *saké, mirin,* soy sauce, and a touch of sugar.

A slice of yellowtail *(buri)* marinated in ginger, sesame, soy-sauce, and egg yolk, then quickly grilled. Served on a flat thick plate with a garnish of pickled ginger-sprout spear and a small mound of roughly shredded radish.

As one can see, a full *kaiseki* banquet is complex for both guest and host. Only three dishes per person are listed here, but a full *kaiseki* banquet is likely to have one or more dishes for each of the categories of Japanese cooking. Unsurprisingly, a full tea ceremony and banquet can take up an entire day. Few individuals experience this type of meal frequently, and many Japanese have never tried it at all. Nonetheless, *kaiseki* is very important in Japanese food culture. It is here that the standards of excellence in food preparation and presentation are maintained. Each tea master is a member of a formal school, and the school licenses practitioners and supervises the quality of their work. Moreover, because the tea ceremony is so formal, the utensils used, the type of foods, the room architecture and decor are expected to be of the highest quality, fitting the ideals of Japanese aesthetics. As a consequence, these become the standards for all other types of banquets, and ultimately, standards by which all Japanese food culture is measured, either directly or at a remove.

NOTES

1. Using a calendar system adapted from a Chinese origin, Japanese astrologers devised a way of classifying good and bad days and years according to several independent cycles. These are still used today, and many Japanese will only reluctantly go against these astrological signs.

The cycles are the twelve zodiacal animals, ten Buddhist principles, five traditional elements, and two Daoist dualities. The first day of the system (the starting date is a mythical event, and different for each astrologer) is "1" in each cycle. The third day is "3" in each cycle except the Daoist, where the cycle restarts and it becomes "1" again. The sixth day of the system is "6" in the zodiac and Buddhist cycle, "1" in the element cycle (which has started again), and "2" in the Daoist cycle, which is on its third iteration.

The system allows each day and each year to be identified exactly by its place on each cycle. More importantly, it is a fundamental element in Japanese astrology and fortune-telling. Certain combinations are good or bad, depending on their juxtaposition. The classic example is women born in a year juxtaposing "fire" (one of the elements) and "horse" (in the zodiac) who are bound to lose their husband, except if they were born on a Buddhist-cycle *tomobiki* ("bring-a-friend") day. In such a case, they would not be widowed, but would die together with their spouse. Unsurprisingly, women born in the year of the fire-horse find it extremely difficult to marry. "Bring-a-friend" day is, under other circumstances, a good day to hold a party, and a very bad day to hold a funeral (since the dead person will drag someone else down to death as well).

2. Modern eating mandarin oranges are of course seedless, but the traditional Japanese *mikan* or *daidai* was full of seeds.

7

Diet and Health

Japanese culture has drawn heavily on its dominant neighbor, China, for many things. One of the most prominent is attitudes to the body and to health. Most Japanese recognize that the key to healthy life can be found in two things: exercise and diet. Many Japanese make an effort to engage in some physical exercise, whether calisthenics at work (some factories and offices have special calisthenics teachers who will come by for mass exercises), a round of golf (or, considering the high greens fees, a visit to the driving range), or some other pursuit.

Related to this is the emphasis on healthy eating. White-collar workers who feel they suffer from tiredness and stress (and very likely do: their day can start at 5:00 A.M. when they prepare for the daily commute and end at 10:00 P.M. when they finally get back home) consume health supplements, many sold from vending machines at train stations. And certain foods at certain seasons—grilled eel in midsummer, fiddlehead ferns in autumn, the seven wild herbs in midwinter, *mochi* at any time—are considered particularly health-giving.

The Japanese diet as a whole is (with a few exceptions) extremely healthy. Scientific evidence is emerging that certain foods—kelp, laver, tea, *shiitake* mushrooms—have health benefits above and beyond the basic nutrients they supply. Japanese actuarial tables offer possible evidence of these benefits, especially over the long term. Notwithstanding the stresses of living in modern Japan, the Japanese consistently come at the head of the average life-expectancy tables, hovering around 80 years for women and slightly less for men. There is no clear, unambiguous evidence that this is the result of the Japanese diet. Nonetheless, certain qualities of the Japanese diet are significant in inducing good life-expectancy.

There is, of course, another side to the coin. Unlike in the United States, where the greatest killer is heart disease, in Japan the major cause of death is cancer, particularly what has become known as the east Asian syndrome: cancers of the bowels, spleen, and liver. There has been some argument that this is due to elements in the east Asian diet, notably the high consumption of salt from soy-sauce and pickles, but as yet these findings are still too ambiguous for anyone to state the cause with any certainty. The pros and cons of Japanese food are explored below.

PROS: LOW FAT, LOW PROTEIN, HIGH HDL, DIETARY VARIETY

The traditional Japanese diet (leaving aside the modern addiction to sugar and saturated fats that has crept in) is a healthy one, on the whole. Some of these points are contentious, but it is well to note them.

High Proportion of Vegetables in the Diet

Traditional side dishes were largely based on cooked vegetables, because meat, for both ecological and religious reasons, was kept at a minimum. Moreover, these vegetables are treated with a very light hand: blanching, light steaming, and quick cooking in preference to heavy frying or long stewing. Thus both caloric value and vitamins are maintained, and more roughage persists in the diet.

Low Fat

Though fats have been used in the traditional Japanese diet to produce foods such as fried tofu, on the whole Japanese prefer to simmer or grill foods. Deep frying, though available, was only one of a range of food preparation methods, and far from the most sought-after. Most fat intake was from vegetable and fish fats, which are generally high in high-density lipoprotein (HDL)—higher levels of which have been correlated with reduced coronary risk—and Omega-6 fatty acids. Thus, even the consumption of fat in the Japanese diet is generally of the more beneficent types of fats.

High Fish Consumption

Japanese have traditionally consumed fatty fish leading to an increase in HDL and a decrease in low-density lipoproteins (LDL), high levels of which have long been linked to coronary disease. Moreover, there is evidence that some of the chemistry of other seafood has beneficial effects as well. This includes the various seaweeds—lavers, kelps, and true seaweed—without which no Japanese meal is complete.

Freshness

The Japanese insistence, on the whole, on consuming fresh food, or at least food that has come as quickly as possible from the producer to the consumer (problems of hygiene and modern mass-production aside), probably has beneficial aspects as well.

Small Quantities

Finally, and perhaps most importantly, the Japanese diet has always been a "meager" diet, in the traditional, Middle Ages sense of the word. Quantity has always been eschewed in favor of quality. Moreover, the small, and lengthy, service of desirable meals has meant that the diner has the time, the emotional resources, and the leisure, to savor each morsel and to digest properly. Rather than the giant cuts of meat and potatoes that sometimes define quality in the West, a Japanese meal, consisting as it does of many small portions, ensures that the digestive process is not being put under stress. This is not to say that Japanese do not gobble their food, or that the office worker, struggling to eat in the half-hour he has allotted himself before getting back to his desk, does not damage his digestive system. It does, however, mean that there is a different model that people can aspire to and sometimes achieve. In the modern era, where in some societies people eat to excess (and suffer for it) while in others some struggle to feed themselves, the ability of the Japanese cook to prepare nourishing, tasty, low budget and nutritionally balanced dishes is something to emulate.

Health-Promoting Foods

There are several ingredients of Japanese diet that actively promote health. Many such ingredients are being studied, and quite often claims of their efficacy can be exaggerated. However, there seems to be substantial evidence of active health-promotion by foods as diverse as tea, kelp (*konbu*), and *shiitake* mushrooms, among others.

Tea has been regarded as a palliative for most diseases almost since it was discovered in China in prehistory. Teas contain a variety of phenols such as tannin, which help the body dispose of free radicals and assist in the breakdown of triglycerides (another form of fat found in the blood and one linked with coronary risk). Argument is still raging about the relative efficacy of the three kinds of tea consumed: green (unfermented), oolong (semifermented and smoked), and black (fermented). Some experimental evidence exists to show that oolong tea, for example, can help in control of obesity, since the phenols contained in it from nature and from the production process speed up the breakdown of triglycerides.

There are also strong claims by Japanese and other scientists that consumption of kelp (*konbu*), several kinds of which the Japanese consume in both cooked and fresh form, may help in suppressing absorption of cancer-inducing chemicals. The claims that consuming kelp actually suppresses cancer development need to be investigated fully. Nonetheless, there is evidence that Okinawa Prefecture, where much kelp is consumed raw in salads, has a lower incidence of stomach cancer than other areas of Japan where the kelp is consumed cooked (destroying some of the chemical properties).

Recent research has suggested still another healthy component in the Japanese diet. Bonito fillet (*katsuobushi*) flakes have the property of reducing blood pressure, and some studies have shown that the flakes themselves contain amino acids that act to suppress high blood pressure. One of the problems with these findings is the troubling fact that most of the solid matter of the bonito flake is discarded after the material has been steeped to make stock. Nonetheless, further research may well show that the low average blood pressure of many Japanese, and their ability to control their blood pressure notwithstanding the stress of modern living, may owe much to the prevalence of processed bonito flakes in the diet.

CONS: HIGH SALT, GROWING CONSUMPTION OF FAT AND REFINED FOODS

Not all is good in the Japanese diet. Though on balance Japanese cuisine is healthy and worth emulating, there are negative elements in Japanese cuisine today that must be kept in mind. Cancer is still the greatest killer in Japan, where people have the longest life expectancy in the world. And these cancers show a pattern, affecting liver, spleen, and other internal organs more than they do in the West.

Salt

Some evidence has been produced to show that high rates of bowel cancer may be caused by the large quantity of heavily salted pickles that are a mainstay of the diet. The Japanese government has taken those findings seriously and run several campaigns to reduce salt consumption. Nonetheless, the pattern of cancer deaths continues, which may be a feature of genetic makeup, or may be due to some as-yet unknown factor in the environment or in food consumption.

Industrial Food

Perhaps one of the greatest threats to health in Japan is the prevalence of factory-processed food. Over the decades since the end of the war, the Japanese populace has been affected by a series of problems such as outbreaks of e-coli, contaminated milk, and overconsumption of sugar that have been traced to industrial processes in food manufacturing.

The average Japanese consumer is moving further and further away from the traditional cuisine ideal: the consumption of food fresh from the producer and the environment. So pervasive is this trend that many Japanese foods are not "natural" at all. Lettuce and other green vegetables are produced in giant hothouses, sometimes in hydroponics farms where the leaves never even see the sun. The famed Matsuzaka and Kobe beef (which some cite as the best-tasting beef in the world) come from cows that, though pampered and protected, do not generally live in pastures, but in byres. The dearth of many fish due to overfishing has brought about a massive rise in sea farming: a beneficial change ecologically speaking, but one that yields fish of slightly inferior nutritional quality. An indication of the pervasiveness of factory-processed food is the authorization by the Japanese government, in the past decades, of purely synthetic food bars. Made by biochemists from chemicals and fermentation, they yield full nutritional value (with very little taste).

Even many of Japan's traditional foods—soy sauce, fermented soybean paste (miso), pickles, fish paste (kamaboko)—are no longer made by hand, or by artisans who know their product and love their jobs. They are made (as in all industrialized cultures) in giant factories, often overseas, with a marked decline in quality. In fact, so marked is this decline, that many a middle-aged Japanese person complains of the inability of younger Japanese to discriminate between good and bad foods or between the produce of one part of Japan (which may be famous for a particular food) and the inferior produce of another area. It has to be noted, of course, that this is an almost inevitable change: the ease of modern communications and transportation, the growing affluence of every part of society, and better education mean that there is a growing demand for foods that until the twentieth century were the province of only the rich and the powerful.

Refined Foods

Related to the issue of industrial food is a feature of Japanese cuisine that has been present for centuries. As in most complex societies (societies divided into stratified classes), Japanese elites have always distanced themselves from the common people. They have done so by cultivating an aura of refinement and elegance. One primary example is the consumption of rice. Until well into the modern era, few Japanese families had rice as a staple. Rice was a desirable commodity, not necessarily an item of daily consumption. And the rice that was desirable was the softest, moistest, most glistening rice: white milled rice grains, where every vestige of discoloration was removed. Of course, the discoloration is, nutritionally speaking, the most important part: the husk and the germ together provide vitamins and protein, whereas the white part is merely a simple starch. As result of this cultural preference, even in the mid-1970s, it was possible to see elderly Japanese with the bent legs and spine of rickets: a deficiency disease brought about by consumption of large quantities of rice with little supplementary food. This over-refinement still continues today, with refined breads being consumed in preference to heartier loafs, white rice commonly available for every meal, and foods such as fish paste (kamaboko) from which much of the vitamins have been removed eaten very frequently.

Sugar

Of all the problems that can be traced to the growing power of Europe in the colonial and imperial era between 1500 and 1900, few have been as pernicious and as destructive as the addiction to sugar. At its worst it brought about the destruction of entire societies and millions of lives as Central and South American natives were decimated and Africans forced as slaves to work the sugar plantations of Jamaica and Brazil. At its least, it causes manifold health problems. The Japanese as well have become addicted to the substance, and the consumption of sweets in Japan, in myriad forms, has increased in many ways. High consumption of the many sweet foods and candies available to Japanese children has contributed to poor dentition among Japanese as they become adults and has also encouraged obesity, which is currently becoming a problem among Japanese children.

LEARNING FROM THE JAPANESE WAY OF EATING

After a slow start, Japanese food has managed to travel very well all over the world. Few major urban centers outside Japan do not have a Japanese restaurant or two. Yet, aside from *sushi* and noodles, Japanese food is barely known. There are several reasons both for its attraction and for difficulties in translation into the food cultures of other countries.

The jewel-like visual quality of many Japanese dishes and the insistence in Japanese cuisine on ensuring the freshness of ingredients are perhaps the most attractive to outsiders. Though Japanese food may seem bland to those who are accustomed to more robust cuisines, the delicate flavoring and subtle interplay of color, flavor, and texture soon become apparent to multitudes worldwide. Added to that is the vast array of dishes, not just variations on the same theme, but completely different ways of preparing similar ingredients.

One of the major difficulties with exporting Japanese food abroad has to do with the ingredients. Many common ingredients can rarely be found outside Japan. This problem is being overcome with large numbers of Japanese expatriates abroad and a growing demand for Japanese foodstuffs elsewhere. Small stores, branches of Japanese supermarkets, and above all, mail order and the World Wide Web have contributed much to changing this balance, as have growing contributions to understanding the basis of Japanese cooking in the many cookbooks that abound.

The foundation of Japanese food can be found in scarcity and simplicity. Japan has few material resources besides access to the sea and its climate. Poverty was a major issue until the middle of the twentieth century. Even the court cooks of the Heian court and the Sengoku period barons had to restrict themselves in terms of quantity. Thus, Japanese cooks learned from early on to focus on the quality of the foods they served. Throughout history, Japanese religions and philosophy have insisted on the virtues of naturalness and simplicity. These principles have passed into the domain of food as well, in terms of freshness and as light a hand as possible.

In the twenty-first century, many people in the world, notwithstanding widespread malnutrition in many countries, are enjoying a greater access to food than at almost any previous time in world history. This tends to

create an imbalance in food consumption. Americans and Europeans consume far more calories than they ought, a fact evident in the many life-
style diseases to which people in technological societies are prone:
obesity, heart disease, diabetes. Others consume far less than they need
and are hungry, or consume the wrong balance of foods and are malnour-
ished.

The single most important lesson of Japanese food is the recognition
that good eating, even excellent eating, does not require the consumption
of large quantities nor of elaborate preparations. Westerners often com-
plain about the small size of Japanese servings. This is to the credit of Japanese food culture. Small servings, each one exquisitely fashioned within
a harmonious whole, are far more satisfying to the palate than a large mass
of the same foodstuff. Most people would rather eat three or four different
things, than, say, a pound of mashed potatoes. And Japanese meals, it is
clear, provide the necessary amount of calories for any individual. By their
composition and their ingredients, these meals also discourage overeating
and, because the attitude toward fat in Japan is quite negative, tend to
promote health indirectly. This is not to say that Japanese foods must be
adopted helter-skelter, but rather that the *principles* of simplicity, naturalness, elegance, and balanced quantities provide solutions to both personal
and worldwide food problems.

Contemporary technological developments have brought about a wider
awareness of Japanese culture, traditional and modern, all over the world,
and once again, Japanese design has influenced the West. In the same way
that exposure to woodblock prints (*ukiyoe*) resulted in the Impressionists'
breaking out of the mold of orthodox Western painting, exposure to the
restraint of the Japanese tea ceremony food arrangement resulted in Western chefs' creation of nouvelle cuisine. Ongoing exposure to Japanese
food has resulted in a more profound exchange. Nowadays, it is not only
the superficial, external element of display that has been borrowed from
Japan. At a deeper level, the intrinsic characteristics of Japanese seasoning—with soy sauce, rice wine (*saké*), cooking liquor (*mirin*), horseradish
or pickled plum—and cooking methods—or rather more appropriately,
noncooking of fish and seafood—have been ingeniously incorporated in a
true international integration of Japanese sensibilities with other styles of
food.

Glossary

abura age   Fried tofu in rectangular flat cakes.

aemono   Cooked vegetables in thick dressing.

agedofu   Fried tofu.

agemono   Fried foods. General term.

an   Sweet bean paste.

ayu   Sweetfish. *Plecoglossus altivelis*. A small delicious river fish.

azuki   A bean used, among other things, for making *an*.

bentô   Box lunch.

chanko-nabe   A rich stew. The daily fare of sumo wrestlers in training.

chawan   Literally, "tea bowl." A small bowl used to eat rice from. Also used to cook steamed savory custard (*chawan mushi*).

chawan-mushi   A soupy, savory, steamed custard.

chirashi-zushi   A simple form of *sushi* made from vinegared rice with bits of vegetables and fish mixed in.

chûka-soba   Chinese noodles, usually served in soup.

daikon   Giant radish.

dashi   Stock.

donburi   Rice bowl topped with some meat or fish topping.

ebisen   Rice crackers flavored with shrimp. Many varieties have an actual small shrimp pressed into them.

eda mame   Unripe soybeans cooked in the pod. Eaten as a snack or drinking food.

edokko   A native of Tokyo. Specifically someone whose family members are registered as parishioners of Sanya Jinja shrine in the Asakusa working-class district of Tokyo.

edozushi   Form of *sushi* most commonly known in the West: a ball of vinegared rice with a slice of fish on top.

ekiben   Packed lunch from an intercity train station.

fugu   Puffer fish. One of about 15 edible species of the family *Tetraodontidae*. Delicious but highly poisonous fish if not prepared by a professional chef.

furofuki daikon   Slices of daikon cooked in a broth of *dashi*, soy sauce, and *mirin*.

gohan   Cooked rice. By extension, a full meal.

gohanmono   Rice course of a formal meal.

gurume   Gourmet. A japanized foreign word that came to be used in the 1980s.

gyûdon   *Donburi* with a stir-fried beef and leek topping.

hakusai   White (Chinese) cabbage.

hatchô-miso   *Miso* made for dipping.

hinomaru bentô   "Rising Sun" *bentô* (box lunch) of white rice with a single pickled plum (*umeboshi*) in the center, replicating the Japanese Rising Sun flag.

hôchô   Kitchen knife.

ichibandashi   First class stock (*dashi*) made by steeping fresh bonito flakes (*katsuobushi*) and kelp (*konbu*) in simmering water. Used as a base for other dishes or drunk on its own.

ichijûissai   One soup, one side dish. Basic Japanese meal until the Edo period (1600–1868).

ichijûsansai   One soup, three side dishes. Basic Japanese meal since the middle of the Edo period (1600–1868).

iemoto   School of training in a traditional Japanese art, including cooking.

ikuradon   *Donburi* with a salmon roe topping. A specialty of Hokkaido.

Inari   Deity of prosperity and rice.

inarizushi *Sushi* made by wrapping a ball of sweetened rice in a sheet of thin fried tofu.

itamae Literally, "before the counter": chef.

izakaya Drinking place (bar), but generally refers to a Japanese-style establishment rather than a Western-style one (*bâ*).

jûbako Three- or four-tiered deep trays or boxes holding New Year foods.

kadomatsu A New Year decoration placed at the entrance to most houses, composed of cut green bamboo, pine branches, and oranges bound in straw rope.

kaiseki-ryôri The elaborate and refined cuisine of the Japanese kitchen. Equivalent to *haute cuisine* in France.

kaiten zushi Cheap *sushi* restaurant where ready-made *sushi* plates circulate before diners on an assembly-line sort of arrangement.

kamaboko Fish paste.

kamado Traditional charcoal-fed Japanese stove.

kansai West of the Barrier: the Kyoto-Osaka-Kobe area.

kanten Gelatin made from agar agar (a seaweed).

Kantô East of the Barrier. The Tokyo area.

kappa-maki A sushi roll (*makizushi*) with cucumber filling.

kara-age Deep frying, Chinese-style, with a cornstarch and ginger batter.

kareraisu Rice with a thick, curry-flavored sauce.

kasutera A sponge cake, the specialty of Nagasaki.

katsudon Deep-fried pork cutlet.

katsuo Bonito. *Katsuwonis japonicus*.

katsuobushi Dried and preserved *katsuo* fillet used as basis for *dashi*. Homonymous with "victorious warrior."

katsuo-tataki Charred, rare *katsuo* fillet.

kazunoko Herring roe. Homonymous with "victorious child."

kibidango Dumplings flavored with parched ground *kibi* millet.

kimuchi Pickled Chinese cabbage (from the Korean *kimchi*).

kinome Dried, ground buds of the Japanese mountain ash tree.

kisaten Tea shop.

koheeshoppu   Coffee shop.

koku   About 180 quarts. Traditional measure of rice sufficient to feed one man for one year.

konbu   Kelp. Various species of *Laminaria*. Used principally to make stock.

konnyaku   Devil's foot root jelly. A completely calorie-free food loved for its texture and for its ability to take on any flavor.

konpa   Drinking party.

konrô   Gas range in modern houses.

kuroshio   Black Current. Important ocean current which flows near the eastern coast of Japan, bringing migrating fish.

kuzu   Kudzu vine. *Pueraria lobata*. A form of gelatin is made from the roots.

makizushi   Various forms of rolled *sushi*.

makunouchi   "Inside the curtain." Box lunches that originated from meals patrons took to theater performances.

manju   Steamed buns filled with sweet bean paste *(an)*.

matcha   Powdered green tea used in the tea ceremony.

matsuri   Festival.

matsutake   Pine mushroom. *Tricholoma matsutake*.

Matsuzaka   Area in central Japan where famous *wagyû* cattle are bred for meat, said by many to be the best in the world.

meibutsu   Famous product of an area.

menrui   Generic term for noodles.

mikan   Japanese mandarin orange.

mirin   Sweet rice liquor used for cooking.

miso   Fermented bean paste.

misoshiru   Soup of *dashi* with *miso* paste.

misozuke   Vegetables pickled in *miso*.

mitsuba   Japanese trefoil. *Cryptoaenia japonica*.

mochi   Pounded glutinous rice cake.

momotarô   Peach Boy. Character from legend associated with *kibidangô*.

moroheya   Young jute leaves, a favorite green of the Middle East adopted into Japanese cooking.

mushimono   Steamed foods. A course in a formal Japanese meal.

myôga   A form of ginger whose buds are eaten in soup or as garnish. *Zingiber myoga*.

nabemono   Foods cooked in a pot with a sauce or stock. A sort of stew. A course in a formal Japanese meal.

namban   Southern barbarian. A style of preparation in which strips of meat are cooked with leeks.

nameko   A small, slightly slimy mushroom.

nanakusa   Seven herbs eaten ritually for health during the New Year season.

natto   Soy beans fermented in straw wrapping. A breakfast delicacy from Kantô.

nibandashi   Secondary *dashi* made by reboiling *katsuobushi* and *konbu* after *ichibandashi*, made by steeping these ingredients, is drawn off.

niboshi   Small dried sardines used to enhance the flavor of *dashi*.

nigirizushi   "Squeezed" *sushi*. The various forms of *sushi* based on a ball of vinegared rice with a topping of fish.

nihon-shû   Japanese liquor. *Saké*.

nimono   Foods simmered in a sauce.

noh   An ancient, highly ritualized form of traditional theater.

nomiya   A drinking place: *bâ* or *izakaya*.

nori   Laver. Various forms of marine algae of the *Porphyra* species. Dried and pressed into sheets, it is used to wrap *sushi* and garnish various dishes.

nukazuke   Vegetables pickled in rice bran.

obon   Day of the Dead in midsummer, when the ancestors return to visit the living.

ochazuke   Cooked rice mixed in a bowl with tea and soup. A popular hangover cure.

oden   A light stew of vegetables and *kamaboko* often served from a barrow late at night.

okashi   Confectionery, both Japanese and Western style.

okazu   Side dishes in a meal, excluding the soup.

okonomiyaki   "As-you-like-it": a large self-made omelette or savory pancake.

okusan   Homemaker.

omakase   Chef's selection.

omeraisu   Fried rice covered with plain egg omelette and a dab of ketchup. A favorite of Japanese children.

omiotsuke   A respectful and poetic name for *misoshiru*.

omiyage   Gift brought by a traveler for those left at home. Often a gift of some famous local delicacy.

onigiri   Rice ball. Often surrounding some traditional garnish such as pickled plum *(umeboshi)*, or herring roe *(kazunuko)*.

oolong   A semifermented tea from Fujian, China, with reputed health-giving properties.

osechiryôri   New Year's cooking.

oshiruko   A sweet bean soup with *mochi* cakes. A winter *wagashi*.

oshôgatsu   New Year.

osôzai   Side dishes.

otsumami   Small snacks to go with alcohol.

oyatsu   Snack between meals.

ozoñi   New Year's soup with herbs.

pirafu   Pilaf. Rice steamed with bits of vegetables and meat (from the Middle East).

ponzu   Lime juice mixed with soy sauce used as a dip.

râmen   Chinese-style noodles.

ryôtei   Japanese-style restaurant.

sansai   Mountain or wild greens.

sansankudô   "Three-three nine times." A Japanese-style wedding at a Shintô shrine.

sashimi   A dish of thinly sliced raw fish.

satoimo   Taro. *Colocasia esculenta.*

satsumaimo   Sweet potato. *Ipomoea batata.*

sekihan   Rice cooked with azuki beans from which it acquires a red tint.

senbei   Rice crackers, usually savory.

setsubun   Ritual during the first day of spring to exorcise demons.

shabu-shabu   Literally, something like "swish-swish." One-pot shared stewlike dish.

shamoji   Paddle used to serve rice from container to individual bowls.

shibori   Small towel used in cooking, serving, and to wipe diners' hands.

shiitake   Brown, dense-fleshed mushroom. *Lentinus edodes*. Cultivated on logs of a type of oak.

shimeji   Small delicate straw mushrooms. *Lyophillum* species.

shincha   New tea. Made only from the first three leaf buds of spring on each plant.

shiozuke   Salt pickle, also a short-pickling method.

shirumono   Soup dishes.

shisô   Perilla. Beefsteak plant. *Perilla frutescens*.

shôchu   A refined liquor made from sweet potatoes with high alcohol content (about 80 proof).

shôgatsu   New Year.

shôjin   Vegetarian foods based on Buddhist principles.

shoyu   Soy sauce.

shun   The best season to consume a particular food, usually fish or vegetables.

soba   Noodles in general. In particular, Japanese buckwheat noodles.

sobaya   Noodle restaurant.

sôsu   A thick, sweetish condiment sauce tasting a little like Worcestershire sauce, after which it is named.

suimono   Foods cooked in a water base.

sukiyaki   Meat strips and vegetables quickly braised in an iron pan.

sunomono   Vinegared foods. Equivalent to salads in Western cooking but more extensive.

surimi   Mock crab and crustaceans made by shredding, then compressing and dyeing, *kamaboko* fish paste.

surume   Dried squid eaten usually as *otsumami* (drinking snack).

sushi   Food made of vinegared rice and pieces of fish and vegetables, usually compressed into one of several shapes.

suzuke   Vinegar pickle. Usually made at home using a quick-pickling method.

ta   Rice paddy.

taiyaki   Fish-shaped waffle filled with sweet bean paste *(an)*.

takuan   Pickled giant radish. One of the most common long-pickles.

tamari   The liquid extrusion from *miso* paste. Use is similar to soy sauce.

ta-no-kami   Rice paddy deity.

tatami   Grass mats packed with straw used to floor most traditional Japanese houses.

teishoku   Set meal.

temaki   A type of *sushi* looking like an ice-cream cone of *nori* used for certain kinds of fish and vegetables.

tempura   Deep-fried battered fish and vegetables.

teppanyaki   Cooking on an iron griddle.

tofu   Soybean curd.

Tohoku   Northeastern Honshu Island, renowned for cold climate.

tokkuri   *Saké* flask, usually ceramic.

tonkatsu   Deep-fried, crumbed pork cutlet.

tororo   Sticky, glutinous sauce made from mountain yams (*Dioscorea* species).

tsukemono   Pickles.

udon   Thick Japanese-style wheat noodles.

umeboshi   Salted, dried apricot-plum (*Prunus mume*). Probably the most common and important Japanese pickle.

umeshû   Sweet liqueur made by immersing *ume* apricot-plums in sugar and alcohol.

uoshoyu   Fermented fish sauce. Historically in use the same way as soy sauce, which replaced it in the eighteenth century.

ûsta-sôsu   Japanese pronunciation of Worcestershire sauce. (see *sôsu*).

wagashi   Japanese confectionery.

wakame   Seaweed of various species eaten as salads or in soups.

wasabi   Japanese horseradish. *Wasabia japonica*.

yakimono   Grilled or roasted foods.

yakisoba   Stir-fried Chinese-style noodles.

yakitori   Skewered and charcoal-grilled bits of chicken and vegetables.

yamaimo   True yams. *Dioscorea* species.

yôkan   Stiff jellied bean jam *(an)*.

yuba   Thin sheets of tofu.

yuzu   Japanese lime or citron. *Citrus junos*.

zarusoba   Buckwheat noodles served drained on a flat bamboo colander *(zaru)*. Eaten with a dipping sauce.

Resource Guide

BOOKS

Ashkenazi, Michael, and Jeanne Jacob. *The Essence of Japanese Cuisine: An Essay on Food and Culture*. Richmond: Curzon Press, 2000.

First full-length scholarly treatment in English of the relationship between Japanese culture and food.

Ekuan, Kenji. *The Aesthetics of the Japanese Lunchbox*. Edited by David B. Stewar. Cambridge, Mass.: MIT Press, 1998.

Illustrated discussion of Japanese lunchboxes.

Frederic, Louis. *Japan Encyclopedia*. Cambridge: Harvard University Press, 2002.

Compact sourcebook on things Japanese, including some entries relating to food.

Harper, Philip. *The Insider's Guide to Sake*. Tokyo and New York: Kodansha, 1998.

Entertaining book on varieties of *saké*, rules of consumption, and the drink's history.

Hendry, Joy. *Understanding Japanese Society*. London: Croom Helm, 1987.

Complete introduction to all aspects of Japanese culture and society from an anthropological point of view.

Herrigel, Gustie L. *Zen in the Art of Flower Arranging*. London: Kegan Paul International, 1958.

Reprint of classic showing relationship of Japanese aesthetics to Zen Buddhism.

Hume, N.G., ed. *Japanese Aesthetics and Culture: A Reader*. Albany: State University of New York Press, 1995.

Collected scholarly papers on various aspects of Japanese aesthetics and its bases.

Ishige, Naomichi. *The History and Culture of Japanese Food*. London: Kegan Paul, 2001.

Translated scholarly work on Japanese food culture by an eminent Japanese scholar.

Jansen, Marius B. *Making of Modern Japan*. Cambridge: Harvard University Press, 2002.

History of modern Japan and the background to much discussed in this book.

Kamachi, Noriko. *Culture and Customs of Japan*. Westport, CT: Greenwood Press, 2001.

A popular treatment of various aspects of Japanese society.

Kawasumi, Ken. *The Encyclopedia of Sushi Rolls*. Japan Publications Trading Co., 2002.

Collection of how-tos and basic information about the making of *sushi* rolls.

Krouse, Carolyn R. *A Guide to Food Buying in Japan*. (Tut Books) Tokyo and Vermont: Tuttle Publishing, 1995.

Popular book intended for foreign expatriates in Japan, but giving a glimpse into the daily shopping possibilities for food.

Ohnuki-Tierney, Emiko. *Rice as Self: Japanese Identities Through Time*. Princeton: Princeton University Press, 1993.

Major scholarly work on the part played by rice in Japanese culture and consciousness.

Okakura, Kakuzo. *The Book of Tea*. Rutland, Vt., and Tokyo: Charles Tuttle, 1956.

A classic manual of the preparation and etiquette of the tea ceremony.

Reischauer, Edwin O. *The Japanese*. Cambridge: Belknap Press, 1977.

General popular introduction to the history and society of Japan written by a former ambassador and eminent scholar.

Sansom, George B. *Japan: A Short Cultural History*. Stanford, CA: Stanford University Press, 1986.

Excellent history of Japanese art against the background of its political and social history. A classic.

Satterwhite, Bob, Rob Satterwhite, and Robb Satterwhite. *What's What in Japanese Restaurants: A Guide to Ordering, Eating and Enjoying.* Tokyo and New York: Kodansha International, 1988.

Somewhat out-of-date but nevertheless entertaining guidebook to ordering food in Japan.

Varley, Paul. *Japanese Culture.* Honolulu: University of Hawaii Press, 2000.

Comprehensive college textbook useful for in-depth introductory study of Japan. Read with Hendry and Sansom for a well-rounded picture.

COOKBOOKS

Beatty, Theresa M. *Food and Recipes of Japan.* (Kids in the Kitchen Series) New York: PowerKids Press, 1999.

Recipes for children and some background cultural information.

Belleme, John, and Jan Belleme, *Culinary Treasures of Japan: The Art of Making and Using Traditional Japanese Foods.* Garden City, NY: Avery Publishing Group, 1993.

A good introductory cookbook.

Booth, Shirley. *Food of Japan.* Grub Street Publishing, 1999.

General survey of various Japanese foods with recipes.

Detrick, Mia, and Kathryn Kleinman. *Sushi.* San Francisco, CA: Chronicle Books, 1983.

One of the earliest guides to making *sushi*, and still a classic.

Emi, Kazuko. *The Japanese Kitchen: A Cook's Guide to Japanese Ingredients.* New York: Southwater, 2003.

Cookbook written by professional chef.

Kijima, Naomi. *Bento Boxes: Japanese Meals on the Go.* San Francisco, CA: Japan Publications Trading Co., 2001.

Simple guide to making attractive and tasty box lunches. Well illustrated.

Kosaki, Takayuki, et al., eds. *The Food of Japan: Authentic Recipes from the Land of the Rising Sun.* Hong Kong: Periplus World Cookbooks, 1998.

Basic recipes grouped by meal element. Good Glossary.

Ogawa, Seiko. *Easy Japanese Pickling in Five Minutes to One Day.* Japan Publications Trading Co., 2003.

Next to rice and soup, the third most important Japanese food. Domestic cooking at its best.

Omae, Kinjiro. *The Book of Sushi.* Tokyo and New York: Kodansha, 1981.

Classic of *sushi* preparation by master *sushi* chef.

Shurtleff, William, and Akiko Aoyagi. *The Book of Miso*. Hayama-shi, Japan: Autumn Press, 1976.

Detailed history and description of the varieties of *miso*. Work of love.

Tsuji, Kaichi. *Kaiseki: Zen Tastes in Japanese Cooking*. Foreword by Yasunari Kawabata. Introductions by Sôshitsu Sen [and] Seizô Hayashiya. Photos by Muneori Kuzunishi [and] Yoshihiro Matsuda. Adapted by Akiko Sugawara, Kyoto: Tankôsha/Tokyo, Palo Alto: Kodansha International, 1972.

Elaborate recipes and presentation of tea ceremony cuisine.

Tsuji, Shizuo. *Japanese Cooking: A Simple Art*. Tokyo and New York: Kodansha International Ltd., 1980.

Excellent primer on Japanese cooking by a master from the Tsuji school of cooking.

Udesky, James. *The Book of Soba*. Tokyo and New York: Kodansha, 1995.

Easy-to-follow recipes evincing a real love of the subject.

Yoneda, Soei. *Good Food From a Japanese Temple*. Tokyo and New York: Kodansha International, 1982.

Book on classical Japanese vegetarian cooking from the abbess of a Zen monastery famous for its kitchen.

VIDEO/FILM

Cooking a Japanese Meal with Joanne Hush and Ayako Jedlacka. AHVL, Inc., 1981. Videocassette.

Early film in a homemaker series providing some background and basic steps to preparing a Japanese meal.

Tampopo. Directed by Juzô Itami. Tohei Japan, 1985. Videocassette.

A wonderful film that presents an excellent overview of the Japanese attitudes to food through the adventures of a woman trying to make a success of her noodle shop.

WEB SITES

Asia Recipe Site, http://asiarecipe.com/japan.html

Recipes, articles, and links.

Bulldog Co., http://www.bulldog.co.jp/oisii/p_index.html

Website of the Bulldog company, manufacturers of *sôsu*.

Japan Guide, http://www.japan-guide.com/e/e620.html

Excellent site providing pictures, descriptions, and food customs.

The Kamaboko Museum (in Japanese), http://www.kamaboko.com/

Copiously illustrated with different varieties and uses of *kamaboko* (fish paste).

Stanford Japan Guide: Food and Drink, http://jguide.stanford.edu/directory/cat_listing_level_3_category_94_L1_11_L2_0_L3_0_L4_0_L5_0_L6_0.lasso

Gateway to several useful links of food and recipes.

Tokyo Food Guide, http://www.bento.com/tokyofood.html

Includes restaurants, specialty foods, recipes, and menus.

Travel Japan: Food & Drink, http://www.geocities.com/traveljapaneasily/jpfd.html

Excellent site full of detailed and clear photos. Lots of links.

University of Redlands annotated Directory of Internet resources: Asia: Japan: Food & Drink, http://newton.uor.edu/Departments&Programs/AsianStudiesDept/japan-food.html

Comprehensive gateway to everything you need, really.

The World of Food Science, http://www.worldfoodscience.org/vol3_2/focus-tables.html

Tables of food consumption comparing Japan, the US, and other countries.

Effects of Urbanization on Global Food Demand, http://216.239.57.100/search?q=cache:1jhBkx0duNEC:www.ers.usda.gov/publications/wrs011/wrs011e.pdf+%22Japanese+food+consumption%22&hl=en&ie=UTF-8

Statistical tables about Japanese food consumption from the Japanese government.

Konnichiusa Japan: Japanese Food, http://www.scu.edu.au/schools/edu/student_pages/2001/csato/FOOD.htm

Site on Japanese culture including an extensive set of pages on Japanese food for school kids, including activities, photos, a quiz to test your knowledge.

Bibliography

CHAPTER 1

Ashkenazi, Michael. "Japanization, Internationalization and Aesthetics in the Japanese Meal." In *Rethinking Japan*, edited by Adriana Boscaro, et al. London: Paul Norbury, 1989.

Bartlett, Christopher A. *Kentucky Fried Chicken (Japan) Limited*. Cambridge, Mass.: Harvard Business School Case Studies, 1986.

Cwiertka, Katrzynka. "To What Extent Is Foreign Food Adoption Culturally Determined—An Example of Japan in Comparison with Europe." *Appetite* 24 (1995): 272–74.

Ishige, Naomichi. "Développement des Restaurants Japonais pendant la périod Edo (1603–1867)." In *La Gastronomie ou l'homme des champs a table*, edited by Joseph Berchoux, 79–82. Grenoble: Editions Glénat, 1990.

Judson, D.H., and Raymond A. Jussame Jr. "Household Composition and the Consumption of Fruits and Vegetables in the U.S. and Japan." *Journal of International Consumer Marketing* 3 (1991): 73–97.

Kanai, M., et al. "Changing Patterns of Food-Consumption in Japan." *American Journal of Agricultural Economics* 75 (1993): 1293–99.

Ohnuki-Tierney, Emiko. "McDonald's in Japan: Changing Manners and Etiquette." In *Golden Arches East: McDonalds' in East Asia*, edited by James L. Watson, 161–82. Stanford: Stanford University Press, 1997.

Terasaki, Gwen. "Hunger in the Mountains." In *The Japan Reader*, edited by J. Livingston, Joe Moore, and Felicia Oldfather, 465–75. Middlesex, England: Penguin Books, 1976.

Tokoyama, H., and F. Egaitsu. "Major Categories of Changes in Food Consumption Patterns in Japan 1963–91." *Oxford Agrarian Studies* 22 (1994): 191–202.

Varley, H. Paul, and George Elison. "The Culture of Tea: From Its Origins to Sen no Rikyu." In *Warlords, Artists and Commoners: Japan in the Sixteenth Century*, edited by George Elison and Bardwell Smith, 187–222. Honolulu: University of Hawaii Press, 1981.

Varley, Paul, and Isao Kumakura, eds. *Tea in Japan—Essays on the History of Chanoyu*. Honolulu: University of Hawaii Press, 1989.

Yasunaga, Takemi. "Patterns of Living in a Changing Society." *Developing Economies* 10 (1972): 431–50.

CHAPTER 2

Ashkenazi, Michael. "The Can-nonization of Nature in Japanese Culture: Machinery of the Natural in Food Modernization." In *Japanese Images of Nature—Cultural Perspectives*, edited by Arne Kalland and Pamela Asquith, 202–21. Richmond: Curzon Press, 1997.

Bell, Graham, Fan Ng, Janice Waring, and Melissa Vereker. *Exporting to Japan: A Guide to the Food Market and Distribution System*. North Ryde (NSW): CSIRO Japan Project, 1992.

Berque, Augustin. "The Rice Fields of Hokkaido; Les Rizieres de Hokkaido." *Sociologia Ruralis* 19 (1979): 148–59.

Creighton, Millie R. "The Depaato: Merchandising the West While Selling Japaneseness." In *Re-Made in Japan: Everyday Life and Consumer Taste in a Changing Society*, edited by Joseph J. Tobin. New Haven, Conn.: Yale University Press, 1992.

Hirai, Michiko. "An Appetite for Homegrown Food." *Look Japan* 43 (1997): 14–15.

Ishige, Naomichi. "Meshi...The Staple." *AjiCommunications on Japan's Dietary Culture* 1 (1979).

Koyama, S. "A Quantitative Study of Wild Food Resources: An Example from Hida." In *Affluent Foragers: Pacific Coasts East and West*, edited by S. Koyama and D.H. Thomas, 91–115. *Senri Ethnological Studies* 9 (1981). Osaka: National Museum of Ethnology.

Loveday, L., and S. Chiba. "Partaking with the Divine and Symbolizing the Societal: The Semiotics of Japanese Food and Drink." *Semiotica* 56 (1985): 115–31.

Matsuyama, T. "Nut-Gathering and Processing Methods in Traditional Japanese Villages." In *Affluent Foragers: Pacific Coasts East and West*, edited by S. Koyama and D.H. Thomas, 117–39. *Senri Ethnological Studies* 9 (1981). Osaka: National Museum of Ethnology.

Ohnuki-Tierney, Emiko. *Rice as Self: Japanese Identities through Time*. Princeton: Princeton University Press, 1993.

Riethmuller, Paul. "Where Do Japanese Consumers Buy Their Food?" *Agribusiness* 10 (1994): 131–43.

Shimizu, Kay. *Tsukemono: Japanese Pickled Vegetables*. Tokyo: Shufunotomo, 1993.

Shurtleff, William, and Akiko Aoyagi. *The Book of Miso*. Hayama-shi, Japan: Autumn Press, 1976.

CHAPTER 3

Cardozo, Sidney, and Masaaki Hirano. *Uncommon Clay: The Life and Pottery of Rosanjin*. Tokyo: Kodansha International, 1998.

Ishige, Naomichi. "Moritsuke...A Japanese Garden on the Table." *AjiCommunications on Japan's Dietary Culture* 8 (1981).

CHAPTER 4

Allison, Anne. "Japanese Mothers and Obentos: The Lunch Box as Ideological State Apparatus." *Anthropological Quarterly* 64 (1991): 195–208.

Hendry, Joy. "Food as Social Nutrition: The Japanese Case." In *Food for Humanity: Cross-Disciplinary Readings*, edited by M. Chapman and H. Macbeth, 21–37. Oxford: Oxford Polytechnic: Centre for the Sciences of Food and Nutrition, 1991.

Ishige, Naomichi. "Sashimi...A Gorgeous Way of Tasting Seafood." *AjiCommunications on Japan's Dietary Culture* 4 (1980).

———. "Sukiyaki...A New Tradition at the Table." *AjiCommunications on Japan's Dietary Culture* 2 (1980).

———. "(Table) Manners Makyth the Man." *The Unesco Courier* (May 1987), 18–21.

Miyatsuka, Toshio. "Yakiniku—Savory Dish with Simple Origins." *Japan Quarterly* 46 (1999): 31–42.

Noguchi, Paul H. "Savor Slowly: Ekiben—The Fast Food of High-Speed Japan." *Ethnology* 33 (1994): 317–30.

CHAPTER 5

Ishige, Naomichi. "Sushi...Now It's Instant." *AjiCommunications on Japan's Dietary Culture* 5 (1980).

———."Tempura...Another Usage of Lamp Oil." *AjiCommunications on Japan's Dietary Culture* 3 (1980).

CHAPTER 6

Anderson, Jennifer L. *Introduction to Japanese Tea Ritual*. Albany: State University of New York Press, 1991.

Cobbi, Jane. "Sonaemono: Ritual Gifts to the Deities." In *Ceremony and Ritual in Japan: Religious Practices in an Industrialized Society*, edited by J. Van Bremen and D. Martinez, 201–9. London & New York: Routledge, 1995.

Goldstein-Gidoni, Ofra. 1996 *Packaged Japaneseness: Weddings, Business and Brides*. London: Curzon.

Sen, Soshitsu. *The Japanese Way of Tea: From Its Origins in China to Sen Rikyu*. Honolulu: University of Hawaii Press, 1998.

Tanaka, Sen'ô. *The Tea Ceremony*. Tokyo: Kodansha International, 1973.

CHAPTER 7

Hori, Takeaki. *Tuna and the Japanese: In Search of a Sustainable Ecosystem*. Tokyo: Jetro, 1996.

Jussaume, Raymond A., Jr. "The Growing Importance of Food Safety to Japanese Consumers and Its Implications for United States Farmers." *American Journal of Alternative Agriculture* 6 (1991): 29–33.

Index

About the Authors

MICHAEL ASHKENAZI is a scholar specializing in Japanese food and culture. He is the co-author, with his wife, Jeanne Jacob, of *The Essence of Japanese Cuisine: An Essay on Food and Culture* (2000).

JEANNE JACOB has worked in the business world, in marketing to Japan and serving as a liaison. She also has extensive publishing experience, and after having lived in Japan for a number of years, she co-authored with husband, Michael Ashkenazi, *The Essence of Japanese Cuisine: An Essay on Food and Culture* (2000).